NATIONS WITHOUT A STATE

Ethnic Minorities in Western Europe

Edited by
Charles R. Foster

PRAEGER

PRAEGER SPECIAL STUDIES • PRAEGER SCIENTIFIC

Library of Congress Cataloging in Publication Data

Main entry under title:

Nations without a State.

    1. Minorities--Europe. 2. Europe--Ethnic
relations. 3. Nationalism--Europe. I. Foster,
Charles Robert, 1927-
D1056.N37   323.1'4   80-20900
ISBN 0-03-056807-2

Published in 1980 by Praeger Publishers
CBS Educational and Professional Publishing
A Division of CBS, Inc.
521 Fifth Avenue, New York, New York 10017 U.S.A.

© 1980 by Praeger Publishers

0123456789 145 987654321

Printed in the United States of America

CONTENTS

LIST OF TABLES AND FIGURE

PREFACE

I first became interested in the rise (and fall) of ethnic movements in Europe during a visit to Scotland in 1976. Scotland, at that time, seemed to be moving rapidly toward a new constitutional and political structure—"devolution"—which would have provided it with a high degree of autonomy including its own legislative assembly.

In writing an article on the Scottish National Party, I noted certain ties between the SNP and other minorities in Europe. In examining the literature on these other minorities there were almost no studies which focused on the causes and effects of political mobilization using a "political culture" approach.

Out of approximately 50 linguistic territorial regions which could be defined as nations without states, I have chosen nine which exemplify effective political mobilization. Two of these regions, the South Tyrol and Jura, are in states in which the central government has made accommodations for their political and economic self-determination. The others are in various stages of revolt.

The essays in this book are by different authors located in various parts of America and Western Europe. My tasks as an editor were eased at an early stage by the encouragement and advice offered by Erik Allardt of the University of Helsinki while he was a fellow at the Woodrow Wilson International Center for Scholars in Washington. He made me aware of the complexity of the problem as well as the usefulness of a comparative approach.

Editorial assistance was provided by Jack Spilsbury (Johns Hopkins), John Packman (Princeton) and Patricia Rosenmeyer. Expert secretarial and typing assistance was provided by Philomena D'Souza. My thanks go also to the contributors for their willing response in furnishing their manuscripts in a very short time.

1

THE UNREPRESENTED NATIONS

Charles R. Foster

The major thrust of the postwar European Movement was to create a political system to contain the nationalisms that had provoked two world wars. In that climate, the lesser known subnational or regional proposals of many European federalists were virtually ignored. Thirty years later, these subnational ethnic regions challenge the nation-state.

The 1975 founding statement of the Bureau of Unrepresented European Nations, an organization of various ethnic groups located in Brussels, Belgium, states, "The new Europe ought to be based not only on national states, but also on the natural realities of our continent. It is essential that Europe represents the diversity and the rights of all its citizens and its peoples (small and large)."[1] Public attention also focused on this increasingly strong call for political and economic decentralization due to the spectacular electoral gains of the Scottish Nationalist Party (SNP) in October 1974 as well as to the increasing use of violence by the Basque Nationalists.[2]

At the same time, scholars of international affairs wrote of the rise of a New Nationalism[3]—a term used to designate government reorientation toward national welfare policies rather than internationalism. The New Nationalism tended to be introspective and to defend its own cultural values. While national governments are attempting to adopt more self-serving approaches to international politics through sophisticated coordination of domestic and foreign economic policies, ethnic group movements for more independence have emerged to impede these processes.

Numerous analysts, both politically left and right, have written about the prospect of a "crisis of democracy."[4] External pressures on the industrial state, such as the rising cost of energy, have increased the "overload" on government and have given rise to questions about the "governability" of the modern state. Tax revolts, environmental actions, the call for increasing citizen participation, and the reduction of bureaucratization have all affected the substance of political debate. It is clear that, for an increasing percentage of the population in industrialized societies, economic needs and interests are no longer the sole or, in some cases, even the primary motivation for political behavior.

The greatest subnational challenge to the European nation-state is presented by the revival of ethnic identity in the unitary states of Great Britain, France, Spain, and Belgium. At the same time that the outlines of a United States of Europe, along federal or nonfederal lines, seemed clearly discernable, a political awakening appeared in Europe's "submerged" and "unrepresented" ethnic groups. Fueled by a radical political climate, attempts to gain varying degrees of economic, social, and cultural autonomy have taken place. The expression of political, cultural, and economic powerlessness at the grassroots level in Europe is creating a resurgence of Europe's ethnic minorities. Scholars have tended to overemphasize socioeconomic causes of this resurgence, underestimating political concerns and virtually ignoring cultural factors. While this book analyzes all three aspects—socioeconomic, political or administrative, and cultural-linguistic—its major emphasis is on political and cultural issues. The existence of ethnic activists reveals a major shortcoming of the modern nation-state its ability to inspire among its citizens supracultural loyalty and a general sense of belonging to one state.

Direct elections to the European Parliament and expansion of the European Community have encouraged greater contact among ethnic minorities, resulting in the 1975 establishment of the Bureau of Unrepresented European Nations. This bureau was founded by ethnic political parties in Brittany, Wales, Alsace, and the Basque areas, and, from time to time, it issues policy statements on the rights of minorities.

Moves are underway in the new Parliament to establish a European Cultural Bill of Rights to guarantee the preservation of regional languages and cultures. Should the European Parliament acquire new powers, it could provide the framework for establishing working political relationships between ethnic regions and nation-states as well as among the regions of Europe.[5]

An ethnic minority is defined as a group of people that possesses common ancestry, language, and cultural traditions and that is in a process of self-categorization.[6] There are about 50 linguistic minorities in western Europe (see list in Appendix) described in standard works by Stephens,

Straka, and Haarmann.[7] The minority groups on which this book focuses have been chosen on the basis of six objective criteria.

Each has a common language, different from that of the rest of the nation.

All are comprised of a population of at least 100,000 people who share a common ancestry, resulting in feelings of cultural and political identification and solidarity.

Each is located in a particular region. (This criterion is necessary if the groups are to be studied as potentially viable nations and if they are to be defined objectively.)

All are located in western Europe (so that the study would not be complicated by involving comparisons with very different economic systems).

There is adequate data available on each of them.

All have a high degree of political solidarity and influence.

A main focus of this book is the political activism of the various groups, which links traditional ethnic group cultural identity to the broader society of the state. In many cases, this combination of political and cultural elements gives the group all the characteristics of a nation including a definable territory, its own political institutions, distinct traditions, and a strongly held national identity. These regionally based ethnic minorities are on their way to becoming substates. The influence of this substate system on transnational policies will affect not only the substance of such policies, but also the methods used in setting and adopting them. This influence will have serious implications for the future of European politics. The combination of the resurgence of ethnic politics and the direct election of the European Parliament may simultaneously lead to transnational integration and regional independence.

The chapters of this book deal with the resurgence of ethnic identity in Europe. Some of the hypotheses set forth for this phenomenon follow.

The rise in ethnic activism is attributable to a new type of politically astute university graduate.

When the central government has shown responsiveness to the demands of the ethnic minorities and has proposed autonomy or devolution, there has been a tendency to lessen the conflict.

Ethnic nationalism frequently has clear ties to left-wing politics and rhetoric.

Ethnicity provides integrative social and psychological bonds.

The relationship between class and ethnicity is declining.[8]

Minorities tend to fight for recognition as nation-states and to fight against discrimination.

In Chapter 2, Riccardo Petrella provides the framework for a comparative analysis of the various case studies that follow.[9] A vital distinction is drawn between regional territorial tensions over the management and distribution of resources within the existing state and nationalist demands that threaten the very legitimacy of the state by pressing for rights to autonomy and even to "sovereignty/independence." Although the center-periphery model applies to both phenomena, regional territorial tensions are related to administrative and distribution questions.[10] But Petrella makes clear that only the coincidence of "structural" grievances with cultural, linguistic, and historical identities can fully explain the nationalist movements under study.

Petrella also examines "systemic variables as imposed by the established state and societal system." These variables include the stage in nation-state development, degree of centralization/uniformity, and responsiveness of the central authorities to the national group. And he explores the effect of more abstract intervening factors anchored in the political culture, such as public opinion and patterns of behavior, agents of cultural and political mobilization, the role of national political parties and class-based organizations, and outstanding socioeconomic issues that interact with nationalist demands.

Petrella's chapter concludes with an examination of some implications resulting from the coincidence of nationalist demands with the ongoing process of European state integration. This series of complex variables helps to explain the main features, significance, and political/cultural mobilization strength of the nationalist groups examined in this book.

The first case study, in Chapter 3 by Jack Brand, deals with the rise of Scottish nationalism and its vehicle—the SNP. Brand's assessment of Scottish nationalism emphasizes the combination of historically distinct political and cultural identities. Although the party seems in decline, the wish for some form of devolution is still felt by a majority of Scots, and, if the conservative government neglects this issue, the SNP could quickly revive.

In contrast to Scotland's distinct political consciousness, the key to Welsh nationalism lies in its dual identity as both Welsh and British, John Osmond argues in Chapter 4. The activation of Welsh nationalist demands is linked to a confidence crisis in the ability of an overly centralized British economy to respond to Welsh economic problems. This is not, Osmond contends, a matter of simple "internal colonialism" with a causal link to cultural differences, but is, rather, a failure for British state capitalism. Welsh nationalism, like that of other nations, cuts across linguistic, religious, and political preferences by appealing to a "common national heritage and seeking autonomy for the nation as a whole." This chapter reflects the English penetration of the Welsh economy and media and the historical weakness of Welsh institutions in comparion with those of Scotland.

The Basque and Catalan regions of northern Spain present another case of movement toward regional autonomy. Basque and Catalan nationalism, as portrayed by Robert Clark and Oriol Pi-Sunyer in Chapters 5 and 6 respectively, share some common features. Both had distinct political identities before absorption into the expanding Castilian monarchy. Both arose politically in response to the ruthless centralization of all political and economic control by the Spanish state. For both, language became the measure and symbol of ethnic identity and, hence, of their struggle for recognition. Likewise, common cultural life and tradition are seen as central to identification as Basque or Catalan. Finally, both experienced the extremely brutal Francoist repression of regional identity.

Yet, as both Clark and Pi-Sunyer make clear, Basque and Catalan nationalism are distinct phenomena. They emerged from unique social developments and took different forms. Moreover, both have features that run counter to popular theories of ethnic revival. The Basque and Catalan provinces are among the richest in Spain, not economically underdeveloped. Clark contends that the key element is the role they played in Spanish economic development. Both wealthy regions have felt victimized by the inequitably distributed tax burden and revenues as well as by the discriminatory economic policies pursued by an overcentralized Spanish bureaucracy.

In the Basque case particularly, economic grievances are fueled by class grievances against an entrepreneurial class tied to Madrid. Moreover, as both authors point out, neither region is as economically secure as it might seem to be. Increased competition from outside as well as the acute effects of the industrialization process—urban decay, growing pollution, and rootlessness—have added to regional insecurity. In both cases, the large-scale immigration that came with economic prosperity contributes a divisive element, which is particularly threatening to the survival of regional languages. Regional mobilization reacts to these threats.

It remains to be seen how much the new institutionalization of Euzkadi and Catalonia, represented by the regional parliaments elected in March 1980, can counter these threats and contribute to a confident and nonviolent assertion of regional autonomy.

The revival of nationalism in Corsica and Brittany has occurred in the European state with the strongest centralist tradition. In both cases, regional identity was maintained despite the Jacobin legacy of modern France. In Chapter 7, Peter Savigear points to Corsica's insularity in explaining the island's separate identity. But, as David Fortier makes clear, in Chapter 8, the social and economic development of Brittany left it separate as well. Thus, both Savigear and Fortier concentrate on center-periphery tensions aggravated by the overcentralization of political and economic authority in Paris. The resulting economic underdevelopment lends credence to Michael Hechter's model of "internal colonialism" as applied to the "Celtic Fringe" in Great Britain.[11]

The cases of the Jura and the South Tyrol are indicative of increasing efforts to manage conflict by central government. In the case of the Jura, as Kurt Mayer shows in Chapter 10, religious and linguistic conflict led to the establishment of a new canton. There continues to be, however, an agitation to enlarge it.

Flavia Pristinger, emphasizing the political culture of the South Tyrol (based on a declining economy and a rigid social strucutre), shows how the new autonomy has ameliorated the ethnic conflict based on irredentism. By means of her interdisciplinary approach, Chapter 9 offers hope for a courageous search for new ways of developing ethnic identity tied to a larger Europe.

The study of ethnic conflict in the world provides a rich field for research. Despite a large academic interest in the subject and the availability of a large body of empirical data on ethnic attitudes, we do not yet have a theory of ethnicity. Is ethnic conflict in Europe a local manifestation or a global trend? Does the study of ethnicity lead us to neglect economic factors in the resurgence of regional nationalism? What is the appropriate unit of analysis? What are the relevant subgroups of ethnic policies?

These are all questions that the following chapters touch upon but for which they do not provide final answers. The directly elected European Parliament, in providing a new and fertile arena for European ethnic representatives, may be a forum that will provide some of the answers to questions about the compatibility of ethnic ferment with a more integrated Europe. Ultimately, it will be European public opinion in response to increased ethnic militancy that will provide solutions to the problems of these nations within states.

NOTES

1. Founding statement, Bureau of Unrepresented Nations (Brussels, Belgium: June 1975).

2. For an analysis of the SNP, see Charles R. Foster, "The Case of Scotland," in *The New Nationalism*, ed. Werner Link and Werner Feld (New York: Pergamon Press, 1979), p. 119. See also Nick Baxter-Moore, "The Rise and Fall of the Scottish National Party: Revisited," unpublished paper, (Carleton University, 1979), pp. 1–56. For the rise of Basque nationalism, see Stanley Payne, *Basque Nationalism* (Reno: Nevada Press, 1975).

3. Lin and Feld, *The New Nationalism*, pp. 1–25.

4. For example, Richard Rose, *Studies in British Politics*, 3rd ed. (London: Macmillan, 1972). Also, Inergen Habermas, *Legitimation Process* (Boston: Beacon Press, 1973).

5. For a study that attempts to establish that European integration and subnationalism are compatible and even complementary phenomena, see Mary Jane Adams, "Ethnic

Subnationalism, Regional Devolution, and European Integration," M.A. thesis, (Carleton University, 1979).

6. There are numerous definitions of the term *ethnicity*. One can define ethnicity using the variables of culture, territory, and class, which may vary in each case. Or one can define ethnicity in broader terms, and then specify which type one is discussing. See Cynthia Enlow in *Ethnic Conflict and Political Development* (Boston: Little, Brown and Co., 1973) pp. 23–26. See also Anthony Smith "Theories and Types of Nationalism," *European Journal of Sociology*, vol. 10 #1, 1969, pp. 119–132. Also E.K. Francis, "The Nature of the Ethnic Group," *American Journal of Sociology*, vol. 52 #1, Sept. 1967, pp. 338–346. As Daniel Bell states, "The common designation *ethnic* for a culturally defined communal group is too pervasive to escape" in "Ethnicity and Social Change," in Nathan Glazer and Daniel Patrick Moynihan, *Ethnicity: Theory and Experience* (Cambridge: Harvard University Press, 1975), pp. 1–26.

7. Probably the best attempt at categorization is that by Erik Allardt in his excellent monograph, *Implications of the Ethnic Revival in Modern Industrialized Society* (Helsinki: Societas Scientiarum Fennica Press, 1979). He used correlation and factor analysis on resources and ethnicity. The list in the Appendix is largely based on Allardt's. See also Meic Stephens, *Linguistic Minorities in Western Europe* (Llandysul, Dyfed, Wales: Gomer Press, 1976); Harald Haarmann, *Soziologie und Politik der Sprachen Europas* (München: Deutscher Taschenbuch Verlag, 1975); and Manfred Straka (ed.), *Handbuch der europäischen Volksgruppen* (Wien-Stuttgart: Wilhelm Braumüller, Universitäts-Verlagsbuchhandlung, 1970).

8. See Allardt, *Ethnic Revival*, p. 66.

9. The Petrella chapter is a revised version of a paper presented at the March 1980 Quebec meeting on ethnic regionalism of the Committee on Atlantic Studies and Relations.

10. Sidney Tarro, Peter J. Katzenstein, and Luigi Graziano (eds.), *Territorial Politics in Industrial Nations* (New York: Praeger, 1978).

11. Michael Hechter, *Internal Colonialism, The Celtic Fringe in British National Development 1536–1966* (London: Routledge & Kegan Paul, 1975).

2

NATIONALIST AND REGIONALIST MOVEMENTS IN WESTERN EUROPE

Riccardo Petrella

The territorial tensions that emerge in any societal system are the result of conflicts between social groups with varying interests that are unequally situated in the power structure, whether it be political economic, cultural, or religious. Any system that wishes to ensure its stability and continuity must anticipate and evaluate these tensions and bring them under control. Sometimes they lead to the breakdown of the system. More frequently, they give rise to operational crises in a specific subsystem; they act as sources of partial or latent instability.

Territorial tensions are not necessarily a result of the differentiation and heterogeneity of social phenomena. Territorial diversification only leads to tensions when it results in unequal structural relations among social groups, giving rise to domination over peripheral groups and regions by the groups that control the available strategic resources. Whenever the effects of domination threaten the very existence of minority and/or "minorized" groups, territorial tensions are inevitable, especially when the groups become aware of the critical nature of their situation and when an active segment of their population manages to mobilize a sufficiently large part of the social strata of the peripheral areas around watchwords such as "survival," "resistance," and "freedom." Tensions may exist at all levels: within a commune or town, between towns, between town and country, within a region, between regions, and between states.

The author is presently working at the Commission of the European Communities in Bruxelles. He is entirely and uniquely responsible for the opinions here expressed.

Whatever the level, such tensions express the differences in perception, conception, and strategy of the various social groups regarding the goals of the production of desirable goods and services. In this sense, they reflect the imbalances that exist among the social forces in the appropriation and management of available resources, and they have a bearing on the mechanisms for their use, valorization, and meaning.

The opposition of the small winegrowers of Larzac, France, to the appropriation of their area for military purposes by groups representing other interests (the high command of the French army and central government); the resistance of the inhabitants of the Breton commune of Plogoff to the installation on their territory of a nuclear power station wanted by a bureaucratic central body; the fight by the inhabitants of a district of Schaerbeek in Brussels against the construction of a shopping center in their area by a group with interests opposed to theirs (a Belgian subsidiary of a Swiss distribution company); the search by communes for means of lessening financial dependence on central powers; the Basques' struggle for independence; and the tensions among Walloons, Flemings, and the inhabitants of Brussels are all different forms of the same phenomenon: the yearning by individuals, groups, and areas for the right to exist, to be different, and to have an autonomous vision of their future in the face of the trends and choices expressed by the dominant groups.

The existence of these territorial tensions would not in itself be new and would not give rise to serious problems were it not for the fact that in certain countries, certain specific forms of tension have reached a critical threshhold of credibility and mobilization (political and/or cultural), calling into question the existing nation-states as stable and definitive social formations—the predominant development model of European societies.

ETHNONATIONALIST AND REGIONALIST DEMANDS

By *nationalist territorial tensions*, I mean those that originate in the action of certain groups that, being the bearers or being aware of a specific territorial identity (sociocultural in particular) and applying the logic on which the legitimacy of the state to which they belong is based, demand for their nation or people the right of autonomy or even of sovereignty or independence.[1]

So that this definition will not give rise to any misunderstanding, in my opinion *nationalist demands* are to be seen most clearly at the present time in the Basque country, the Canary Islands, Catalonia, Corsica, Scotland, and Greenland. They are apparent in a more subtle and less precise way in Brittany, Occitania, Sardinia, Galicia, Andalusia, and Wales.

They take on a special form in Northern Ireland, and they are evolving in Wallonia. They have been successful in the recent past in Ireland, Iceland, Malta, the Jura, and Flanders.[2]

The characteristic of ethnic nationalist demands is the termination of existing political, economic, and cultural relations and the creation in their stead of a new political entity (state) outside the existing state.

By *regionalist territorial tensions*, I mean those brought about by certain groups that, being the bearers or being aware of a specific territorial identity (sociocultural or economic) and anxious to ensure that their community or region has its collective social needs satisfied and participates in the management of the available resources, demand a change in the political, economic, and cultural relations between regions and central powers within the framework of the existing state. The change demanded may be greater legislative, executive, and financial autonomy for the region or reorganization of the mechanism of public administration in the economic (regional plans), social (decentralization of the educational system), cultural (regional cultural charters), or other fields. The distinction drawn between nationalist and regionalist territorial tensions is accurate and justified as it applies to situations that are historically observable at the present time. It must not, however, be interpreted in a rigid and exclusive manner. As with any other dynamic and complex phenomenon, nationalist and regionalist demands coexist, overlap, are superimposed on each other, and are opposed to each other, cutting across the same social groups within a single area. Furthermore, if nationalist demands are by definition and in fact more radical than regionalist demands, it would be a mistake to adopt a linear approach and consider that nationalist demands are at the end of a continuum proceeding from their absence to their presence by way of regionalist demands. Regionalist demands do not necessarily lead to nationalist demands. In certain cases, regionalist demands have no possible basis for expression. On the other hand, regionalist demands can sometimes turn into nationalist demands.

Beyond their differences, current nationalist and regionalist demands in western Europe are also characterized by common cultural sources (ideological in the widest sense of the word) and common political content ("mean" objectives). The two kinds of demands:

> call into question the nation-state as a unitary and centralizing entity,
>
> attack the hegemonic (denying participation) and standardizing (discrediting differences) management of the societal system in acordance with the cultural model of the dominant groups and areas, and
>
> express a demand for a new socioeconomic and cultural development based on the revival of broader territorial democracy, on management of the resources at the service of the individual rather than at the service of ill-defined and misapplied profitability, and on pluralism of creative expression and innovation, including technological innovation.

Thus, ethnic nationalist demands overlap with territorial tensions within the context of the rise of ecological movements (regard for the equilibriums of the ecosystem and promotion of "soft," flexible technologies) and other action groups (urban, feminist, minority rights, and new labor movements).

IN SEARCH OF SOME EXPLANATORY VARIABLES

For the analyst of social movements, every case reflects specific dynamics that should be studied in depth, beyond any real or supposed similarity to analogous cases. At the same time, due to the total nature of history, each case possesses an historical contemporality (where time is not constant) that calls for comparative analysis of analogous cases.

In this chapter, I sketch a highly condensed comparative reflection on the subject. To this end, I shall consider 16 cases: Scotland, the Basque country within Spain, Brittany, Wales, Catalonia within Spain, Occitania, the Canary Islands, Corsica, Galicia, Alsace, Sardinia, Wallonia, Friesland, Friuli, Flanders, and the Jura.

From the questions for research that call for a comparative analysis, I have selected the following.

Why did nationalist territorial tensions not cease to occur within European states after the so-called "national liberation" period in the midnineteenth century?

Why, in western Europe, have nationalist tensions appeared since the 1950s with greater intensity in France, Spain, and the United Kingdom (the first three nation-states of Europe) and in Belgium (the most disputed nation-state since its founding 150 years ago)?

What is the explanation of the changes that have taken place in recent years in the balance (in terms of mobilization) between nationalist and regionalist movements within the same region, sometimes favoring the former, sometimes the latter?

Why have demands for bilingualism been met in Friesland and Wales, for instance, while in other regions serious difficulties remain? Why are these same "winning" regions continuing to fail in their political demands?

Why has the Jura succeeded where Corsica and Brittany still meet with formidable opposition?

Why is Sardinia, which more than 30 years ago obtained an autonomous status from which Brittany, Alsace, Andalusia, Corsica, or Wales would be pleased to benefit, asserting nationalist demands of the same nature as those in the Canary Islands, Catalonia, and the Basque country?

Many studies have supplied interesting answers to one or another of these questions, for such-and-such a region or group of regions, relating to the political, sociocultural, or linguistic aspects of history.[3] In this connection, the most important comparative research study in this field is, to my knowledge, that undertaken in 1977 by the late Stein Rokkan, entitled *Economy, Territory, Identity: The Politics of the European Peripheries*. It should be completed shortly under the direction of Derek Urwin.[4] The reflections that follow are not, therefore, designed to fill a gap, but simply to throw some light on points that I think are important to the understanding of nationalist and regionalist movements.

To this end, I propose to single out three categories of variables. *Endogenous variables* define what might be called the basic structural ingredients necessary to the development of nationalist and regionalist tensions. *Exogenous variables* relate to the nation-state and the encompassing societal system, which are also involved as basic structural ingredients. *Intervening variables* define the states, processes, and mechanisms that help to increase or check territorial tensions.

Endogenous Variables

In this category, I have selected five variables:

> 1. the presence/absence of a cultural identity or set of data that is perceived and experienced as a nation,
> 2. the presence/absence of a specific linguistic character that is represented by a more-or-less standardized language that still has some sort of social function (communication) or the threatened disappearance of which is seen as a serious blow to individual and collective identity,
> 3. the politicoinstitutional status of the region that is a source of territorial tensions, prior to and after its integration into the nation-state,
> 4. the relative level of economic development and potential, and
> 5. the autonomous or heteronomous nature of the economic development.

The presence/absence of a cultural identity or set of data perceived and experienced as a nation is difficult to pin down, despite its apparent obviousness, but it is of fundamental importance. It is not a question of defining what a nation is, but of determining to what extent the nation is the subject of a symbolic representation/significance/identification, perceived and experienced as such by the people living in the 16 regions in question as well as by outsiders.

According to what is perceived and experienced by the peoples directly concerned, there is no doubt that there is territorial identification as a nation in Scotland, Wales, the Basque country, Catalonia, and Flanders. It is developing in Wallonia and in the Canary Islands. Similarly, the term "people" easily carries the day in the Jura and in Friuli. Territorial identification is a reality for an active minority in Galicia,

Brittany, Corsica, and Sardinia. It disappeared long ago in Friesland. It has never existed in Alsace; here, the words "Alsatia people" have always reflected and expressed more accurately the sense of belonging and of territorial identification. It has appeared among an infinitesimal percentage of the local population in Occitania only in recent years. (See Table 2.1.)

Regarding the perception of those outside and within particular dominant social groups of the nation-state or groups culturally identified with it, Scotland, Wales, the Basque country, and Catalonia have widely been considered nations. This recognition has never been questioned as far as Scotland is concerned. It has been uncertain and alternating in Wales. It has even been denied until recently, notably under Franco's dictatorship, to the Basque country and Catalonia. Flanders won such recognition in the 1950s and 1960s in particular. It is denied to Brittany, Corsica, and Sardinia, not to mention Occitania. As no claim has been made, it has not been considered for Alsace. This is also the case for Friesland and Friuli. In the case of the Jura, recognition of a people has not given rise to any problem in principle.

Closely connected with the first variable is the second variable of the presence/absence of a specific linguistic character. With the exception of Scotland, this character exists to varying degrees in all the areas in question. It has always played an important strategic role in the Basque country, Catalonia, Flanders, the Jura, Wales, Alsace, and Friesland. It has sparked nationalist and/or regionalist mobilization over the last quarter century in Brittany, Corsica, Galicia, and Occitania. It has recently assumed great importance in Sardinia. It is one of the strong points of the demands in Friuli.

Language is one of the most important expressions of the specific identity of a human group. It is not, of course, the only one, but it is the most obvious and the most diffuse expression of specificity. It immediately and physically differentiates "us" from "them." It constitutes a barrier externally, but it is an instrument of recognition and integration internally. Its acquisition by children is the most direct means of existing as part of the collective whole and for acculturation. The acquisition of the standard code of the language of the group of origin is one of the necessary and essential conditions for participating in the "higher" level of communication functions. In this sense, language plays a decisive role in social alienation and differentiation within the group. When the linguistic code of the group of origin is not that recognized as the official language of the state to which the group belongs, problems arise. There is a source of potential conflict at both the individual and collective levels. It is not necessary to indicate the specific linguistic nature of the regions in question. (See Table 2.2.)

TABLE 2.1

**National or Regional Territorial Identification
of Western European Ethnic Minorities**
(by percent)

Consider Themselves	Scotland (Glasgow only)	Wales	Northern Ireland
British	29	15	29
Scottish	67	1	—
Welsh	1	69	—
English	—	13	43
Irish	—	1	28[a]
Other/Don't Know	3	1	

	Catalonia°	Basque Country°	Galicia	Andalusia	Castile	Valencia	Canaries
From Their Region	56.4	32.4	43.8	30.3	17.2	28.9	25.8
Spanish	37.7	41.1	49.6	54.7	67.1	59.0	56.9
European/Citizen of the World	4.2	24.5	4.8	13.8	13.5	11.4	17.3
Nothing/Indifferent/No Reply	1.7	2.0	1.8	1.2	2.2	0.7	—

[a]Including 21 percent Ulster.

°Among the interviewees born in Catalonia and the Basque country, 70.6 percent in Catalonia and 40.7 percent in the Basque country considered themselves to be from their region.

Sources: Glasgow information is from the Strathclyde Monarchy Survey, 1968; Wales information is from the Opinion Research Centre Survey, 1969; Northern Ireland information is from the Strathclyde Northern Ireland Survey, 1969. Spanish regionalist information is from the results of a survey carried out in 1975 on a sample of 1,928 people for Spain as a whole and on additional regional samples of 613 people. S. del Campo, M. Navarro, and J.F. Tezano, *La Cuestion Regional Espanola* (Madrid: Cuaderno para el Dialogo, 1977).

TABLE 2.2

**Specific Linguistic Character
of Western European Ethnic Minorities**

Regions	Local Language(s)	Speakers of the Local Language(s) (principal estimates)
Scotland	English	Almost all of the population
	Scottish Gaelic	Between 81,000 and 89,000
Wales	Welsh	542,000 (1971 census)
Basque Country	Basque	Between 500,000 and 700,000
Catalonia	Catalan	Between 5.5 million and 6.6 million
Brittany	Breton	Between 0.5 million and 1.1 million
Occitania	Occitan	Between 950,000 and several million
Corsica	Corsican	Between 175,000 and 200,000
Alsace	Alsatian	Between 1.3 million and 1.5 million
	German	1.2 million
Sardinia	Sardinian	Between 1.0 million and 1.2 million
Friuli	Friulian	Between 430,000 and 800,000
Friesland	Frisian	About 200,000
Jura	French	About 130,000

Note: Local language means a language other than the standard, literary, and official one of the state.

Source: Riccardo Petrella, *La Renaissance des Cultures Régionales en Europe* (Paris: Editions Entente, 1978).

Language can pose problems and become a source of territorial tensions because it is not merely a subject for private and individual preference, as the perception of identification with a nation or a people can ultimately be. It belongs to the field of public and collective recognition-valorization: official social recognition is conferred upon it. As a customary value, it falls within the scope of individual and private choices. But what makes it historically decisive and significant is that it is primarily and basically the province of collective and public choices.[5]

The presence/absence of identification with a nation and the presence/absence of a specific linguistic character are not occasional or contingent data. They undoubtedly vary not only in time, but also in the course of a lengthy historical process that can be measured in centuries, particularly in regard to language. The subjects of individual and collective valorization-significance, they are closely linked with an awareness of history. (Some people prefer to speak of "collective memory.") In this connection, a third variable assumes considerable importance, namely, the political history of the region and notably its politicoinstitutional status prior to and after its integration into the nation-state.

Using this variable, a heterogeneous distribution of the regions under consideration should be noted:

The region has enjoyed the status of political independence/sovereignty as such.	Scotland Wales Catalonia Brittany
Certain territories in the region have had a tradition of autonomy or independence, but not the area as such.	Basque Country Flanders Wallonia Friuli Friesland Occitania The Jura Alsace
The region has never been independent.°	Canary Islands Corsica Galicia Sardinia

To have enjoyed political independence or autonomy (whether real or relative is of little importance) prior to integration into the nation-state constitutes a potentially favorable factor for nationalist and/or regionalist mobilization. The fact assumes a clear symbolic value. Paradoxically, in regions that have never experienced any form of independence, the same result occurs whenever specific linguistic character and sociocultural factors foster a particular territorial identification. In this case, as in Corsica, Sardinia, and the Canary Islands, the fact that the country has been able to preserve its identity and its specific character despite centuries of foreign domination is highlighted. It is asserted that it is time, therefore, for the country to find means of managing its future in an autonomous fashion.

These three variables, with other exogenous and intervening variables soon to be mentioned, enable an outline reply to be given to the first two questions.

In order to embark upon an analysis of the factors explaining the other questions, the two socioeconomic endogenous variables must be

°Corsica was independent 1735–1760 and 1793–1796. The very short period of independence Sardinia enjoyed in the ninth century cannot invalidate its inclusion in this category.

taken into consideration. These relate to recent historical data—indeed, to current situations.

The impact of the fourth variable, the relative level of economic development and potential, is to be seen particularly in situations of structural underdevelopment and of deteriorating economic conditions. As Smith's "invisible hand" has been incapable of ensuring a harmonious and balanced territiorial development of the productive forces and of the material well-being, the people in the poor and underprivileged regions have lost confidence in the capacity of the central powers and the dominant economic forces to resolve their problems. As a result, they are increasingly rejecting underdevelopment as a natural and inevitable phenomenon. Unequal development appears to them to be the consequences of an economic and politicoinstitutional system that encourages regional imbalances and inequalities in participation in the production and distribution of wealth. The centralist nation-state appears to them to be an inadequate, outdated institution.

In situations of deteriorating economic conditions, the central bodies of the nation-state and the dominant social groups in the central regions inevitably become the target of the grievances of the social forces in regions that are declining or facing serious reconversion problems. Wallonia provides one of the most telling examples. This is also true of Scotland from the 1950s onward and of Wales from the period between the two world wars. The flagging economy is also the reason why certain middle and agrarian classes (lower middle-class rural landowners) have joined the regionalist movement in Occitania, as was the case in the Basque country at the beginning of this century, when the urban lower midde-classes, which had close connections with the rural world, originated the first genuine modern Basque nationalism.

Underdevelopment and decline being signs of unbalanced use and valorization of the resources available, based on unequal appropriation and management of these resources among the social forces of the various regions, the fifth variable of the autonomous or heteronomous nature of the economic development has a preponderant role to play. According to this variable, most of the regions in question are distinguished, to varying degrees, by an accentuation since the 1950s of the dependence of their economies on decisions and investment capacities beyond the control of local forces. (Exceptions are Catalonia, the Basque country, and, since the 1960s, Flanders. Among the economic peripheries, the situation of Alsace, for example, is not comparable to that of Corsica.) See Table 2.3.

Being economic peripheries (in the sense, too, that they are generally at the bottom of the scale of the various economic indicators), their participation in the management of changes, innovations, and the future is limited or, at any rate, subordinate. To be peripheral has also become a

TABLE 2.3

External Control of the Economy of the Peripheral Areas in Three European Countries
(territorial distribution of the head offices of main corporations)

Regions	The 100 most important corporations (1965) Number	As Percent of Turnover
Greater London	67	73.8
West Midlands	7	7.9
Other Regions	26	19.3
Greater Paris	92	93.5
Other Regions	8	6.5
Milano	46	42.1
Torino	8	17.5
Genova	11	15.6
Roma	11	12.7
Other Regions	24	13.1
The 20 or 30 Biggest Banks		
London	21	86.3
Edinburgh	4	4.9
Manchester	3	4.4
Liverpool	1	2.9
Glasgow	1	1.5
Paris	19	87.6
Strasbourg	3	3.6
Lille	2	3.3
Other Regions	6	5.5
Roma	4	33.9
Milano	6	31.8
Napoli	1	8.1
Torino	1	5.6
Other Regions	8	21.6
The Largest Corporations' Percent of Managerial Functions		
Southeast England	62	(1977, industrial only)
Other Regions	38	
Greater Paris	78	(1976, industrial only)
Other Regions	22	
Northern Italy	65	(1975, industrial and nonindustrial)
Southern Italy	35	

Sources: Leif Ahnström, *Styrande och Ledande Verksamhet i Västeuropea* (Stockholm Ekomiska Forskningsinstitutet: Almquist and Wiskell, 1973), pp. 33, 34, 39, 40, 59; *The Mobilization of Indigenous Potential* (Project report draft, Wissenschaftszentrum Berlin, February 1980, p. 34).

perceived, subjective datum. In the past, the emigration of the most dynamic fringe of the working population from peripheral areas was a way of escaping such a situation. Today, demands for direct and autonomous management of its own future and of the available resources to meet local needs constitutes, together with the refusal to emigrate, the new response of the periphery. This is the case in Brittany, Corsica, Sardinia, and Galicia. Here rejection of centralized management of the economy, subordinated to world markets profitability and efficiency imperatives as determined by oligopolistic groups (multinational corporations, state bureaucracies, and financial holdings), seems to be increasingly inspiring nationalist and regionalist demands. This would explain the leftward swing of these movements in recent years. The sociocultural and linguistic components and the economic component come together under the slogan "living and working in one's home region." The rejection of the absolute mobility of the work factor is seen as one of the tools necessary to safeguard the economic potential of the homeland and its existence as a community.

The Importance of Endogenous Variables

In light of these variables, it is possible to give a partial summary analysis of the nationalist and regionalist phenomenon, its causes, and its various modes of expression.

A close relationship is to be noted, first of all, between the presence of the first three variables and the assertion of nationalist demands (see Table 2.4). On the other hand, when one of the three variables, particularly the first, is missing, the regions are solely a source of regionalist territorial tensions. Seemingly of little importance, this correlation in fact highlights the importance of dynamic factors; the perception of identification with and membership of a nation is not a static, absolute datum. It may disappear in time, just as it may assert itself where it has never existed before. Wallonia is an example of this latter possibility. The recent events in Andalusia also show the emergence of a national awareness in this region, a totally new political and cultural phenomenon, the long-term consequences of which could be considerable for Spain as a state.

The linguistic variable plays a decisive role everywhere except Scotland and Wallonia. It is not, however, a variable that discriminates between nationalist and regionalist demands. The relative level of economic development is unquestionably a factor in territorial tensions. Underdevelopment is usually associated with regionalist demands. On the other hand, a relatively high level of development (as in Catalonia and the Basque country) or a previously high level of development that has given way to continuous and steady decline (as in Scotland, Wales, and Wallonia) are associated with nationalist demands. This may mean that the existence of an industrial middle class coupled with great economic and

TABLE 2.4

Classification of Regions by Four Endogenous Variables

Nature of Demands	Presence of a Cultural Datum		Politicoinstitutional Status, Notably Before Integration into Nation-State			Relative Level of Economic Development		
	Perceived and Experienced as a "Nation"	Specific Linguistic Character	Have Had Independent Status	Certain Parts Have Had a Tradition of Autonomy or Independence	Never Independent or Autonomous	Developed	Old Industrialization Structural Deterioration	Semi-Industralized or Under-developed
Total Independence Is Proposed	Scotland Wales Basque country Catalonia Canaries° Flanders Wallonia° Sardinia° Jura	Wales Basque country Catalonia	Scotland Wales	Basque country	Canaries	Basque country Catalonia	Scotland Wales (southeast)	Scotland Wales (northwest) Canaries
More Effective Federalism or Introduction of Federal Structures	Sardinia° Jura	Sardinia Jura Galicia		Flanders Wallonia Jura	Sardinia Galicia	Flanders	Wallonia	Sardinia Jura Galicia
Regional Forms of Autonomy		Brittany Corsica Occitania Alsace Friuli Friesland	Brittany	Occitania Alsace Friuli Friesland	Corsica	Occitania°° Alsace°°		Brittany Corsica Occitania Alsace Friuli Friesland

°"People" is the most common perception in place of "nation," at least for the time being.

°°Relates to certain parts of these areas only.

Source: Compiled by author.

urban potential (past or present) goes hand in hand with the nationalist phenomenon in western Europe.

Should this correlation be interpreted as showing that the nationalist phenomenon is mainly the doing of the local middle class? The first three variables show that such an interpretation would not be entirely justified. On their own, the five endogenous variables could only account for regionalist territorial tensions. They require the first three variables to come into play in conjunction with them to explain nationalist demands.

Exogenous Variables

I have selected three variables in this category: stages in and modalities of the nation-state formation process, notably since the eighteenth and nineteenth centuries; the degree reached and pursued in uniformization and centralization; and the resistance put up by the central powers (the dominant socioeconomic groups in the nation-state) to recognition and official acknowledgment of diversity and decentralization.

The states and modalities of the nation-state formation process, notably from the nineteenth century onward, throw light on the current differences among the United Kingdom, France, Italy, and Spain. In this context, industrialization as an accelerating factor in the formation process of the nation-state occupies an important place. In the United Kingdom and France, the industrial revolution and the middle class that brought it about strengthened the preexistent nation-state structures in the course of the nineteenth century. Capitalism on the one hand and industrial and technological development on the other encouraged the true formation of nation-states in economic terms (domestic market), sociocultural terms (thanks to the press, compulsory schooling, military conscription, dissemination of the system of middle-class urban values, and the national language), political terms (bureaucratic centralization), and ideological terms (inviolable national unity, rise of imperialist nationalisms, and colonial empires). These phenomena proved true much later and, to varying degrees, in Italy and Spain.

The degree of uniformization and centralization reached and pursued is not, in fact, the same in the various countries. While linguistic unification and sociocultural uniformization were the result of a lengthy and profound process in the United Kingdom, they were more rapid and brutal in France, notably since the last quarter of the nineteenth century.[6] They were of short duration in Belgium and recent and weak in Italy. The case of Spain has features specific to both the French and the Italian models.

Regarding the degree of politicoadministrative centralization, all the countries are situated more or less around the same model. Power and sovereignty are indivisible; they belong to the center, which may delegate certain administrative or even legislative duties to other peripheral bodies for reasons of managerial expediency and efficiency. Beyond variations in the details of deconcentration, centralization is the rule, basis, and inspiring principle of the political organization of the nation-state.

For the purposes of comparative analysis, the resistance shown over the last thirty years by the "central" powers to the recognition and official acknowledgement of diversity and decentralization has played a more important discriminatory role than has the degree of politicoadministrative centralization.

The violent oppression under Franco of the specific Basque character, pursued in an even more systematic and brutal way than vis-à-vis the Catalans (for reasons also connected with the last civil war), explains the strength and toughness of Basque nationalist demands. On the other hand, the concessions made to Wales by London since the 1950s have certainly helped to cut the ground from under the nationalist demands. This is also true of Friesland and of Brittany and Corsica.

The policy followed by Paris in recent years has fostered and strengthened autonomist streams of opinion. The refusal to grant autonomous status could even, in the long term, cause the autonomous solution to lose all credibility and give official recognition to a separatist solution.

Intervening Variables

These are variables that have an important role in the strengthening or weakening of nationalist and/or regionalist demands. They intervene in the modes of expression and in the variability of the territorial tensions. They can act now as lubricants, now as brakes.

I have selected four of them:

> perceptions, attitudes, and behaviors of the people in the critical regions vis-à-vis the uniformizing and centralizing ascendancy of the center,
> nature of the agents of cultural (school, press, churches) and political (nationalist and/or regionalist parties or movements) mobilization and forms of mobilization,
> place and support granted to nationalist and/or regionalist demands by the big national parties, the workers' trade unions, and employers' organizations, and
> internal contradictions and weaknesses of the dominant socioeconomic system (ecological disruption, energy crises, and squandering of energy, structural unemployment, disaffection toward work, nongovernability of the state, crisis in representative democracy, bureaucracy, and so on).

Any social movement involving total or partial opposition to the societal system in force—to the established order—does not immediately arouse a general consensus among the people concerned. For many reasons, including alienation, inertia, and compromise, the uniformizing and centralizing ascendancy of the dominant powers is perceived and experienced in a discontinuous manner by the people living in the peripheral areas. The data in Table 2.1 show that sudden awareness of a specific territorial identity does not necessarily result, to the same extent, in attitudes favorable to nationalist demands. On the other hand, regionalist demands that are considered to be more moderate are viewed more favorably. The strength of the nationalist movement in Flanders and the Basque country has always been its popular nature, that is, its basis in all the strata of the population of the region. The weakness of the nationalist and/or regionalist movement in Corsica until the mid-1970s was the absence of popular support. The situation has changed considerably in recent years, and this explains why Corsica is now a source of territorial tensions greater than those in Brittany, where, after a period of popular mobilization between 1965 and 1976, some degree of settling down is apparent, due to a relative decrease in tension and to the espousal of the "Breton" theme by the public at large. (The Amoco Cadiz disaster and recent conflicts between certain Breton municipalities and the central government regarding the setting up of nuclear power stations would seem capable of giving fresh popular impulse to the Breton movement.)

In Wales, the strong "Britishization" of the native population explains the low level of interest in political themes (independence, autonomy, and so on) on the part of the majority. In this aspect, the Welsh movement differs from the Scottish one, the relative success of which from the political viewpoint (despite the ups and downs of the last two years) is due to the receptiveness of the Scots to autonomy and political independence, for both historical and cultural (first and third endogenous variables) and economic (fourth and fifth endogenous variables) reasons. (The impact of the discovery of North Sea oil on the Scottish nationalist revival has been overestimated. Even more important, in my opinion, has been the process of deindustrialization of Scotland and the decline in the standard of living.)

The reticent, almost embarrassed or suspicious attitude of the general public to the emergence of the Occitan phenomenon in the various regions in the south of France accounts for the difficulties experienced by the Occitan movement, for its flights forward (extremist positions), and for its splitting up into various marginal clans indulging in infighting.

Regarding the nature of the agents of cultural and political mobilization, analysis of the successes and failures of the various movements seems to show:

> the importance of the attitude and behavior of the traditional agents of socialization (school, churches, and so on), particularly in conjunction with

cultural and linguistic demands. The creation of a territorial identity requires control of the school system.

the strategic role of the mass media (the written and, above all, the electronic). To the extent that the electronic media do not transmit any symbol or speech stressing the value of the specific character of the peripheral region, the breakthrough of the nationalist or regionalist movements meets with serious obstacles. Such a situation can, however, act as a factor favorable to the nationalist or regionalist movement; the more the central powers pursue a policy of negation of the region's specific character by refusing all access by the minority to the right of expression via the mass media, the more the demands become, or appear to be, legitimate and justified. As for schools, the acquisition of the *droit à la parole* should be accompanied by access to television;

the reconquest of schools and the mass media implies, nevertheless, the existence of one or more organized political forces that can catalyze the available energies around a few concrete goals capable of mobilizing the imagination and sensitivity of the masses.

The Basque nationalist movement owes its success to a unique situation, difficult to find in any of the other areas under consideration—namely, the existence of two agents of political mobilization, one (the Basque Nationalist Party or BNP) representing historical continuity and moderation and the other (Basque Homeland and Freedom or ETA) the revolutionary revolt against Francoist oppression and a liberating desire for a new future. (In addition, forced into exile, the BNP was the symbol of the Basque struggle and the Basque nation's will to survive during the Francoist period.) On the other hand, despite many steps already taken, the Breton movement has so far failed to make a political breakthrough for lack of genuine forces of popular mobilization, among other things.°

The capacity for local, cultural, and/or political mobilization is, in turn, influenced, if not conditioned, by the attitude and behavior of the big national parties and of the big trade union organizations. In general, the big political parties traditionally in power pay only lip service to nationalist demands when they are not openly combating them. This is perfectly understandable due to their positions as managers of the political, economic, and cultural system in force. They may, however, be sensitive to regionalist demands. Cleavages may appear between holders of Jacobinic ideas (unitarist and centralist) and holders of regionalist ideas. The case of Suarez' party in Spain is highly significant in this respect. Contrary to what might be believed, big political parties in the opposition (traditionally left

---

°Cultural and linguistic movements are to be found in profusion in Brittany. This has also been and still is the case of spontaneous action groups connected with one or another social economic conflict. The Breton Democratic Union is the only properly organized regionalist political party in Brittany. Its growing influence is still far too limited, however.

wing) are not markedly different from the former. In general, they too are traditionally defenders of the dominant nation-state.° The favor they grant to regionalist demands is frequently dictated by tactical reasons in their struggle for power. The regionalism of the western European socialist and communist parties has always been basically a strategic objective of secondary importance. (This explains the emergence, from time to time, of regionally based political formations quite separate from socialist or communist parties.) It is true that in recent years a change in attitudes and modes of behavior on both sides has been witnessed. The French Communist Party says it supports the cultural (not political) demands in Occitania. It pledged support for Alsatian cultural demands. In Italy, the Communist Party in 1979 took the step of proposing legislation in favor of the promotion of minority "national" languages and cultures, even though until recently its attitude toward the revival of Sardinian linguistic region-alism has been marked by latent opposition. For its part, the socialist group in the European Parliament took the step in September 1979 of sub-mitting two proposals for a resolution on a European charter for regional languages and cultures.

Regarding the trade unions, the situation is far more complex, due to the close connection at the local level between socioeconomic demands and nationalist demands. The situations vary considerably when the policy of the confederal bodies at the national level or the practice of the local federations are considered. Let us take, for example, the revolt of the small winegrowers in Larzac, France. The trade-union organizations in the region did not hesitate to develop or use Occitan-oriented watchwords (for example, *voleum viure al pais—"don't steal our country"*).

Conversely, the central authorities of the FNSEA (Fédération nationale des syndicats des exploitants agricoles), the CGT (Con-fédération générale du travail), and the CFDT (Confédération française du travail) have never shown any special sympathy for the Occitan phenomenon. Recently, the trade unions have also changed; it was no longer possible to demand greater participation in the management of the country's economy, greater autonomy in the allocation of resources at the company or enterprise level, better working and living conditions, and a pluralist and participatory democracy and then to refuse to meet these same demands for participation and autonomy when they came from regions, minority nations, "minorized" cultures, and so-called "regional" languages.

Among the "push factors" that have contributed to the expansion of the nationalist and regionalist movements in western Europe, an im-

---

°Curiously, the ideological reason referred to has always put forward both the inter-nationalism and the national comradeship of the working class. Yet past and present history shows the weaknesses of both.

portant role has been played since the 1960s by changes in the value system of the European peoples. The emergence of new values preceded the current crisis, the nature of which exceeds the structural dysfunctions of the production system (unemployment, inflation, energy crisis, slowing down in productivity, fall in the propensity to invest, international monetary disorder, accentuation of economic "wars"). The social and the politicoinstitutional structures are also in crisis (loss of credibility of the representative parliamentary democracy, oligopolization of social life, nongovernability, weakening of the regulating role of the traditional socializing institutions such as the family and the church, dissatisfaction toward work).

The new values stress the need for putting down roots, at least as much as the need for mobility; the legitimacy to express a plurality of allegiances to be recognized as much as the need for unity; the quality of life and not only the maximization of the quantity of goods and services available (*being* as much as *having*); more even distribution of material progress as much as its growth; the creativity and autonomy of individuals and groups as much as efficiency, profitability, and integration; and cultural diversity as much as the need for interdependence and interpenetration.

The weaving of these new values into the social fabric and into the practices of the socioeconomic and cultural protagonists "who count" must not be overestimated. What is noticeable is a contemporality between the emergence of these new values and the assertion of the nationalist and regionalist territorial tensions. Without the former, it would not be possible to understand or, indeed, explain the latter.

NATIONALIST AND REGIONALIST DEMANDS AND EUROPEAN INTEGRATION

Many ask whether the reassertion or the discovery of the regional dimension is compatible or in conflict with the process of European unification? Some people stress their complementary natures. Thus they speak on the one hand of the regional vocation of European construction, in the sense that the Europe in formation could only be more mindful of regional differences than the nation-states have been, and on the other of the European vocation for contemporary regionalism, in the sense that it is impossible for regions to submerge themselves in new micronationalisms or old-fashioned provincialisms.

Others draw attention to the conflict between the two dimensions. Among these, some believe that there can be no return to the regions at a time when the peoples of Europe are seeking to unite. For them, regionalism means weakening the basic structures of the nation-states from within and, insofar as the latter are subjected to what they consider to be dynamics for national breakdown, European construction would be weakened and called into question. Opposed to this, there are those who believe that European construction is an obstacle for the regions, as an integrated Europe would inevitably lead to another form of political, economic, and cultural centralism even more redoubtable than that of the nation-states. In my opinion, compatibility and opposition constitute the two objective component parts of the current dynamics of the relations between regions and European integration. For the peripheral regions, which are less highly developed or are faced with serious problems due to the deterioration in their productive machinery, demographic potential, and capacity for technological innovation, the current European integration movement is a source of both fear and hope. The fear is that current trends in the process of European integration, unless corrected, may aggravate the divergences between the peripheral and central regions. The hope emerges as the peripheral regions become aware that the European communities are a component part and an essential dimension of their future. It is precisely at the European level that the positive and negative factors influencing their future development operate. They therefore expect much of Europe, not only in terms of solidarity, but also in terms of promoting more active participation in European construction from the political, economic, and cultural viewpoints. (In this connection, note the final declaration of the first convention of the peripheral regions of western Europe organized in Galway, Ireland, by the Council of Europe in October 1975.)

The European dimension is also necessary to the central nonperipheral regions. The economic and social forces of these regions have greatly shaped the process of European integration. Thus their future development is heavily bound up with the survival of the European "market." At the same time, they have become more sensitive to the regional dimension; devolution and decentralization are no longer considered to be in opposition to efficiency and profitability. The central nonperipheral regions seem to appreciate more flexible and decentralized state management. The nation-state appears to these central regions both too large and too small—too small as an effective macroeconomic regulator given the increasing interdependence of economies, too big to resolve problems that will be more effective and socially accepted through local participation. Yet, in both central and peripheral regions, there are also those who believe that solutions must be found at the nation-state level. For them, regionalist demands and European integration constitute real dangers to the nation-state, its unity, and its survival.

Regionalism and European construction are not necessarily either complementary or mutually exclusive. Convergent tendencies are as strong as divergent tendencies. Which will prevail in the long term? The problem remains to be faced. Responding to it is hardly easy. Nevertheless, it can be stated that the compatibility of regionalism and European integration is possible. It will depend on the will of Europeans.

NOTES

1. The words autonomy, sovereignty, and independence, although clearly defined by legal experts, have been debated in their practical application by historians. Their application will vary in each historical case.

2. In Flanders, nationalist demands have taken the form of a claim to domination over a Belgium that is becoming destabilized.

3. The existing literature is particularly abundant and constantly increasing. See Michael Hechter, *Internal Colonialism, The Celtic Fringe in British National Development 1536–1966*, (London: Routledge & Kegan Paul, 1975); T. Nairn, *The Break-Up of Britain: Crisis and New Nationalism* (London: Left Books, 1977); "Les Minorities Nationales en France," special issue of *Les Temps Modernes*, 305 (August-September 1973); S. Salvi, *Le Nazioni Proibite*, (Firenze: Valecchi, 1973); Riccardo Petrella, *La Renaissance des Cultures Regionales en France*, (Paris: Editions Entente, 1978); S. del Campo, M. Navarro, and J.F. Tezanos, *La Cuestion Regional Espanola*, (Madrid: Cuâdernos para el Dialogo, 1977); P. Elton Mayo, *The Roots of Identity*, (London: Allen Lane, 1974).

4. Derek Urwin teaches at the University of Bergen, Norway, Department of Political Sociology.

5. I dealt briefly with this aspect in "Langues et Société," *Annuaire Européan*, 24 (1976).

6. See Eugene Webb, *Peasants into Frenchmen: The Modernization of Rural France, 1970–1974*, (Stanford: Stanford University Press, 1976); François Furet and Jacques Ozouf, *Lire et Ecrire. L'Alphabetisation des Français de Calvin à J. Ferry*, (Paris: Seuil, 1977).

3

THE RISE AND FALL
OF SCOTTISH NATIONALISM

Jack Brand

In October of 1974 the Scottish National Party (SNP) won a third of the Scottish votes, while ten years earlier it had attracted only two percent and, in years before that, many fewer. The upsurge of nationalism in Scotland in the 1960s and early 1970s is one of the few success stories of British politics. Like all success stories, it has had its sad chapters and, like many other British economic and social stories, the end may be a sad one. But it was exciting while it lasted.

Table 3.1 shows that the nationalist movement in Scotland started as a very marginal party. With a mixture of scorn and humor, Spaniards would have called it a *grupusculo*. Table 3.1 does not show the results before 1939, but they tell the same story. Since 1928 the National Party has struggled on. Sometimes it made a little splash, but the ripples soon cleared away. Why did the SNP reach the senior league in the 1960s? Why was it able to change the course of Labour Party policy and make Scotland a central question in British politics? Why did it crash to the humiliating results of 1979? All these questions have had different answers. When all are given, the SNP still commanded in 1979, its bad year, the support of 504,259 Scots, 17.3 percent of the Scottish electorate.

It is the aim of this chapter to explain these events in terms of some recently developed theories of nationalism. I shall conclude that there is at least one crucial element that is touched on, but not fully developed, by several of the theories.

TABLE 3.1

Scottish National Party Votes and MPs

Election Year	Votes for SNP	SNP Vote as Percent of the Scottish Vote	SNP MPs
1945	30,595	1.2	—
1950	9,708	0.4	—
1951	7,299	0.3	—
1955	12,112	0.5	—
1959	21,738	0.8	—
1964	64,044	2.4	—
1966	129,112	5.1	—
1970	306,796	11.4	1
February 1974	632,032	21.9	7
October 1974	836,628	30.4	11
June 1979	504,259	17.3	2

Source: *The Times House of Commons* (London: Times Books, published after every election).

POPULAR CULTURE AND NATIONALISM

That crucial factor may be called the culture of the people. The relationship between culture and political movements is no new theme. The first stirrings of a national movement are often shown by the work of a poet or by an historian who recreates the past or reminds us of it. In Ireland the modern phase of nationalism certainly was associated with an important literary movement around Yeats and Gregory.[1] In the Basque country Arana led Basques to be proud of their cultural heritage. In many places a past was recreated and epic poems were written in antique styles. In Finland the Kalevala taught Finns that they had a past of which to be proud. It must be admitted, however, that we are speaking about "high" culture. Novelists and, even more so, poets and, even more so, philologists and historians write for a limited audience. Their work may be transmitted in a watered down form through schools and in other popular forms and this is important, but it is not the type of culture I am speaking about here.

Here we are interested in culture in a sense much closer to that of the anthropologists. What are the norms by which people live in everyday life as well as at times of great crisis? What are the institutions and who are the individuals they respect or hold in affection? Do they share a type of humor, do they share hopes and tastes, or do they at least recognize that these hopes and tastes are shared by the majority of the other members of the community? If they do, this sharing also sets up a boundary between those who do and those who do not take part in it—essentially, a marker of where the community begins and ends. The boundary may not be strict. There are many levels and degrees to which the community may be entered, but there is still the awareness that the boundary is there. It may be important in different spheres of life or it may not be crucial at all.

In order to use this notion of culture for a political purpose, we must go further. Cultures exist in many places without implications for the building of a nation. In the north of England, for example, the Tynesiders have a distinctive lifestyle and popular culture. This has taken a political form in the sense that local government is aware of the needs of Tyneside as a region, one expression of which was hostility toward Scottish devolution. On the other hand, it cannot be said that the Tynesiders have a nationalist movement. The same could be said about other regions of England or of Spain in comparison with the Basque country, Catalonia, and perhaps Galicia and Andalusia. When does a regional feeling become a feeling of national community?

A short, rather unhelpful answer to this is: when some of the popularly accepted symbols take on important political meanings. It is possible that a regional culture could become so threatened by outside forces that it would use these ideas of a nation to increase its political power. But in most examples of modern nationalism something more complicated has happened. Virtually all of these movements have been able to use their history as a once independent or quasiindependent people to reestablish their claims. "Use their history" is accurate because nationalist historiography is like every other. Perhaps more than most others, it creates or recreates or interprets the past to establish the future. Many peoples, such as the Basques, had a past in the Middle Ages when a system of formal rights gave them self-government. Medieval sovereigns were not able to maintain the same spread of power enjoyed by modern governments. Some peoples go back even further to the days when their ancestors (or supposed ancestors) were a distinct group in the "Volkwanderung" or the Barbarian flood into the Roman Empire. Whether this memory is based on myth or fact, it is a vital ingredient in the making of a national community. It can be created by a small devoted nationalist movement. The crucial point is that it must be perceived as true by the people.

In these terms Scotland is extremely fortunate. There is a distinctive Scottish culture with a basis as popular as football teams, the comics, and the great industrial sprawl on the Clyde, with all the myth making that goes with it. The Red Clyde is a Scottish myth whether Scots hate it or love it.[2] On top of all this is the consciousness that Scotland was, until 1707, an independent country with its own completely independent political system, its own parliament, and its own king. The fact that from 1603 the Scots shared their king with England did not exclude the most bitter hostility and, on occasion, outright war. For Scotland, deeply embedded in this popular culture and not in any need of manufacture were all the popular symbols of a nation. It is a central consideration in the understanding of Scottish nationalism that national consciousness never left Scotland. It did not have a full political expression until the twentieth century, but Scotland was part of "The United Kingdom." In law, the treaty of 1707 was one entered into by two independent parties. Even when nationalism was at its most quiescent in the latter half of the eighteenth century or the first half of the nineteenth, Scots were conscious of being Scots and of their history as a nation with its own state. This is the step not taken by the theories of Hechter and Nairn.

Evidence of this consciousness of nationality is widespread, particularly in the late eighteenth century poets such as Burns who began to write nationalist verse. At the beginning of the nineteenth century, Walter Scott's novels were full of references to the past of Scotland as a nation-state. Victoria indulged herself in the Highlands of her day. Finally, in the 1840s, the first of the nationalist or protonationalist organizations was founded: the Society for the Vindication of Scottish Rights.[3] The history of the country was taught in Scottish schools, not to a high level but enough to give a picture of Scotland's past. Perhaps the most essential feature of that picture given to school children was of Scotland as a small, poor country that fought off successive attempts by the English to absorb it. Scattered through the history were references to epic leaders, such as William Wallace and Robert Bruce, who fought for the maintenance of the kingdom. The institutions of that separate state had a tangible form in the Royal Palaces such as Holyrood and in the other peculiarly Scottish institutions such as the separate legal system and the distinctive Calvinist church. When Scotland came into the Union with England it was not by way of conquest but as a result of an international treaty: the Union of the Parliaments of 1707. The country was a partner with England, not her possession.

No doubt the details of this history were sketchy and inaccurate. Nevertheless, this was and is the understanding Scots have of Scotland's past. This is the essential ingredient that has to be added to the economic processes—perhaps the process of internal colonialism—if one is to explain why nationalism arose when it did.

THE ECONOMIC EXPLANATION:
A POOR COUNTRY BECOMES POORER

Although the memory of Scotland's national past is important, I do not suggest that the economic situation is unimportant. On the contrary, Hechter and others who have written about internal colonialism have identified serious aspects of the problem.

It should first be said that Scotland was a country on the periphery of Europe. It was not blessed with any obvious natural resources and well over half its land area lay in the highlands, giving almost impossible conditions for the development of a vigorous agriculture. There was a herding economy based upon the traditional black cattle, but the comparison with English development, both in terms of arable farming and the wool trade, is very unfavorable to Scotland. This comparison is one of the basic facts of Scottish life. Scotland shares an island with a country that is considerably larger in land area and ten times bigger in terms of population simply because the land of England will support more people. Among the other advantages the English enjoy is their easier access to European markets. In total, the facts of geography have led to a situation in which England has and does enjoy major economic advantages over Scotland both in terms of resources and communications.

It was not always so. In the nineteenth century Scotland was one of the first parts of Britain to be industrialized. Natural advantages, such as the local availability of good coking coal and iron ore together with a river for shipbuilding, meant that heavy engineering became the core of the economy in central Scotland. For about fifty years Scottish industry was extremely prosperous. In the years since 1919 this prosperity has dwindled. Glasgow and the whole industrial complex around the Clyde is now one of the areas of Britain known for large unemployed population, acres of urban blight, poverty, and a seeming inability to recover anything of its old prosperity.[4]

What happened? First the natural resources that made Clydeside industries so prosperous gave out. The coal and iron ore deposits were exhausted and more expensive raw materials had to be imported. More than this, since the end of World War I there were economic crises. Heavy industry regularly suffered most from recession. For both these reasons, the economy of the West of Scotland, the industrial heartland, was in serious difficulties. To make the condition even more serious, manufacturing industry and business as a whole was passing out of Scottish hands.

In part, this was a worldwide process of takeover by multinationals, but in Scotland there was a peculiar problem. The British source of finance and the headquarters of business is London. English-based firms began to buy into Scottish business until a large sector of the Scottish economy was made up of branches of British parent companies. When economic conditions became difficult, as they did for example in the 1930s or the 1960s, the first parts of these businesses to be closed down were the subsidiaries. The branch factory economy of Scotland was one of the first to be hit. This process gave rise to the concept of internal colonialism.

Later I shall argue that this process of impoverishment was critical to the rise of nationalism. First, however, I should like to put it in the context of some other cultural features that have been important to other nationalist movements.

THE PLACE OF LANGUAGE

Language has been one of the most consistent indicators of a national community. Stalin and others considered it one of the central features of a nation's life. In the Basque country and Catalonia, it has been a cause for which people were willing to die. In Belgium, it has split virtually all of the established parties and even threatens the nature of the state. It is quite easy to see why scholars have given language this importance, but in Scottish nationalism it has almost no importance at all.

Northwest Scotland is the home of a small Gaelic speaking population. It is true that this was once the language of the majority of Scots, but that was the Middle Ages, and Gaelic has been a declining language since then. It is also true that the early nationalists in the few years after World War I were keen to develop Gaelic as the language of the people. They were a tiny movement when Nationalism became more important in Scotland—for example, when the National Party of Scotland was founded in 1928, very few saw the future of Scotland as a Gaelic speaking commonwealth.

In terms of the leaders of nationalism in Scotland, at least the intellectual leaders, there was a much more important attempt to establish Scots. A language distinct from English, although clearly related to it, had been the speech of the majority of Scots before the Union of the Crowns in 1603. After this, it gradually lost importance. The aristocracy followed the court and English soon became its language. Even the Church of Scotland, otherwise completely distinct from the English Church, used the King James version of the Bible written in English. Although Scots remained as an important element in the language of the Courts of Law, it was gone by the middle of the nineteenth century. In its place were left a few dialects.

One of the characteristics of nationalist literature in the nineteenth century was to recreate a national or standard language out of the dialects. Norwegians took part in such an enterprise as did the Czechs. The best known attempt at this in Scotland was made by the poet Christopher Grieve, who wrote under the name of Hugh Macdiarmid. In the 1920s and 1930s he created "synthetic Scots" or Lallans. He and a few others wrote a certain amount of poetry in it but, although some of it was very good, the movement was not successful in reestablishing the language, even for poetry. There is only one well-known novel in Lallans, and it was not used for everyday speech even by its greatest supporters.

Scottish nationalists speak English. This does not reduce the fervor of their nationalism any more than it did for the American nationalists of the eighteenth or later centuries.

THE IMPACT OF MODERNIZATION

From what has been said about the growth of industry, it will be seen that the process of modernization started in Scotland at the end of the eighteenth century. If modernization means the break-up of the traditional society and the traditional economy, then it is certainly true that more and more Scots came from the rural areas of the highlands and lowlands to work in new industries, mostly concentrated in the Clyde valley around Glasgow. In place of the old networks supplied by the village or the clan, an urban society grew up. Most still lived in poverty, but new relationships grew up and a new attitude toward the world emerged. For many, this meant the culture of the slums of Glasgow or Ayr or Paisley. Fewer people helped to build a petit bourgeoisie, and a tiny but crucial group became the capitalists of nineteenth century Scotland.

Gellner has underlined the importance of modernization to nationalism.[5] He suggests that nationalism is a movement of modern or modernizing societies. In the traditional society, the horizons of most people are the boundaries of their villages or of the immediate areas with which they are familiar. In a modern society, the traditional networks and the traditional sources of authority are swept away, or, at least, they become less salient. People look for new legitimators, and they may accept new models of society and the polity. Such a model is the nation-state, including the ideology of nationalism.

Applied to Scotland, there are many powerful features of this explanation. There are also many problems. One is that national identity and support for a separate state on the basis of this identity predated modernization. As previously stated, there was considerable feeling against the Union in 1707, and, at the time of the Wars of Independence in the fourteenth century, this was also quite distinct, as can be seen from the Declaration of Arbroath of 1320.

> But if he [the king] were to abandon this task, wishing to subject us or our realm to the King of England or the English, we should instantly set ourselves to expel him as the betrayer of his own rights and ours. For so long as one hundred men of us remain alive we shall never submit under any conditions to the yoke of English domination.

Another doubt about the exact relationship between nationalism and modernization arises because nationalism has been strong at various times in the areas where there has been least modernization. Thus in the 1880s the Highland Land League was one of the foremost organizations calling for Home Rule. Perhaps more important, the Western Isles was the first SNP seat to be won at a general election, in 1970, and, in the disaster of 1979, it was one of only two seats left to the party.

It is better to modify Gellner's model and replace the notion of modernization as the condition for nationalism with any process that disrupts traditional structures of society. Invasion by an army speaking a different language and having different customs would be just such an occasion. This was the case for Scotland in the fourteenth century. Similarly, life was changing for Scotland at the end of the seventeenth century and the beginning of the eighteenth when the Union of the Parliaments took place. The whole of the seventeenth century was taken up with religious disputes. There was the major social upset of the revolution in 1688. More than in England, this deeply penetrated Scottish society. For a great many Scots, the Darien disaster was also extremely important, and the relation with England seemed closely associated with the scheme. The old order of Stuart kings and many traditional aspects of society were gone. The weakness of Scotland's economic position was clearly emphasized.

THE POLITICAL RELATIONS OF ENGLAND AND SCOTLAND

It was upon this changing world that a union of the Scottish and English parliaments was imposed. Whether one accepts the proposition that there was a nationalist consciousness, there can be no doubt that the union was very unpopular in many quarters. This was partly the result of the circumstances immediately surrounding the debate. It also followed the pattern of the relationship between the two countries for centuries. There had been a continuous English policy to absorb its poorer northern neighbor or at least to dominate it. The majority of Scots seemed to oppose these English attempts, although there had often been an "English" party that believed union would be to the advantage of Scotland or at least to its members' advantage. Still the overwhelming feeling of hostility toward England certainly was in evidence at the time of the union debate. In Edinburgh the mob was out every night threatening politicians who were in favor of union. In Glasgow dragoons had to be installed and rioting broke out again when they were withdrawn. Burgesses and other notables from towns in the rest of Scotland made their hostility clear.[6]

In the century and a half after union the situation changed. There were certainly Jacobites who supported the risings of 1715 and 1745 in the hope of reestablishing Scotland as it had been before 1707. Most supporters of the House of Stuart seem to have been more interested in placing the Pretender on the throne of Britain rather than in the details of the Scottish settlement. Moreover, the effect of the revolts seems to have been to increase the fear of lowlanders for the unpredictable highlands. It is certainly true that in the second half of the century the general trend was a decline of any Scottish consciousness with a political content. Claims that working class movements such as the "Radical War" of 1820 were nationalist seem to have no serious foundation. In place of a real political movement came romantic patriotism, best exemplified by Walter Scott. Implicit in this was the understanding that the independent Scotland was a state of the past. Nothing could revive it for the modern world.

The death of political nationalism did not bring the end of Scottish consciousness. On the contrary, there was a great vogue for Scotland. Scott's vision was extremely important. Queen Victoria and Prince Albert encouraged the fashion by their devotion to the highlands.[7] Even at the end of the century when the tradition had declined into the "Kailyard" school of Scottish *kitsch*,[8] Scots were still conscious of Scotland as a distinct entity within the United Kingdom. Scottish regiments were put into the kilt again to boost recruiting. Jacobite songs became the staple of polite drawing rooms, and the more fortunate Scots made modest fortunes in the empire or, at least, from the empire.

By the end of the nineteenth century, however, some forms of nationalism were beginning to raise their heads again. I have referred to the Society for the Vindication of Scottish Rights. Scott's emphasis on the historical symbols of Scotland raised public awareness of these symbols. As the wave of romantic nationalism crossed Europe, its early effects in Scotland were limited to demands such as one that the Scottish form of the Royal Arms be used there. It is easy to ridicule this sort of demand, but this was the beginning of a political consciousness.

One can appreciate the importance of these developments when one recalls that this was also the time when Ireland became a major problem in British politics once more. In the 1880s the Liberal Party accepted the idea of home rule for Ireland. It was not long before some Scots also demanded home rule. In Scotland it became part of the Liberal program, supported by Liberal leaders including prominent business leaders and aristocrats. The Scottish Home Rule Association was found to press for a Scottish parliament, and it was led by major figures in Scottish politics. In the short run, however, the Scots did not gain home rule, but were given some administrative devolution.

Apart from the question of purely symbolic claims, Scottish political consciousness was called forth by a more specific consideration. The second half of the nineteenth century saw the development of the welfare state. Inevitably there was more and more parliamentary business, and one of the implications of this was that specifically Scottish business was treated hastily. Often there was no proper recognition that particular conditions existed in Scotland; the distinctive nature of Scottish housing and of the poor law regulations are examples of this. For practical purposes the affairs of Scotland were conducted by English departments. For these reasons, Scottish members of parliament began to press for a secretary for Scotland. In spite of strong Whitehall and Westminster opposition and largely through the agency of Lord Rosebery, the office of Secretary for Scotland was established in 1885. This was the beginning of a process in which the Scottish Office was set up as one of the major departments of state with a secretary of state, one of the senior members of the British Cabinet, at its head. It is worth pausing to say how distinctive this development is. There is now a Welsh Office as well as a Scottish Office, also with its cabinet minister. The Scottish development provided a model for Wales. These two are significant departures from the functional basis which characterized the rest of the British administration. Their existence illustrates the extent to which Scottish political interests and, to a lesser degree, Welsh political interests had to be accommodated at the end of the nineteenth century. From being a movement associated with a few political romantics, Scottish political consciousness became a characteristic of the Liberal elite. The Liberal Party in Scotland placed home rule at the top of its political agenda, and it was as a largely Liberal organization that the first Scottish Home Rule Association was set up in 1885. When the ardor of the senior Liberals began to cool, the Young Scots was established on a famous European model but also as the youth wing of the Liberal Party in Scotland. Home rule became associated, in general, with the more advanced form of radicalism.

In this context it is not surprising that the early Labour movement in Scotland supported home rule. The political sympathies of most Scottish trade unionists in the late nineteenth century was with the Liberal Party. In addition, the Crofters Movement in the Highlands learned a great deal from the Irish land reform movement, which was wholly identified with home rule.[9] Thus the Crofters (MPs) were among the foremost of the Scottish representatives to advocate devolution of an advanced kind. The Scottish Labour Party and the Scottish branch of the Independent Labour Party also took up home rule at a very early stage.

From the 1880s to the beginning of World War I, home rule was a lively political issue. In this period eight bills or motions were introduced into the House of Commons, and seven of these had the overwhelming support of the Scottish members.

In many ways World War I was a watershed in British politics. For Scottish nationalism, too, it had this quality. One effect was the shelving of a Home Rule Bill that looked as if it had a great chance of success. Another was the serious weakening of the Liberals to the extent that they could not seriously be considered as capable of forming a government. The Labour Party took its place and, at first, carried on the radical tradition of supporting home rule. There was, however, another similarity between the two parties. While their Scottish sections honestly supported the idea of a parliament in Edinburgh, the commitment of the party as a whole was much weaker. If this had not been so, Scotland would have had devolution before 1914. In the case of Labour, it could have been done before 1930. Nevertheless, it was Labour Party supporters who founded the second Scottish Home Rule Association (SHRA) in 1918. They saw themselves as making the same sorts of demands as their predecessors before the war. By 1928 most of their active members had recognized that they would never get home rule from the Labour Party as it was constituted then. After a great deal of debate, they left the association and helped to found the National Party of Scotland, whose program was independence for Scotland rather than home rule. The association collapsed, and the Scottish political movement took up the stance of full nationalism: a demand for an independent Scotland rather than one that would simply have a parliament to debate domestic affairs.[10]

The other Scottish political group to come out of the war had never had any illusions about the possibility of getting home rule from a London government. The Scots National League (SNL) was founded in London by expatriate Scots, many of them Gaelic speaking highlanders. They founded their demand on a "classic" nationalist position. The Scots were a nation. They had a natural right to govern themselves. Part of this claim was based on the distinctive culture of Scotland, especially of Gaelic Scotland, which had long ago been the culture of the whole of Scotland. Its collapse had been due to alien English influence, and this decline should now be reversed. For the SNL, not only the nation but also the culture had to be restored. The two were indistinguishable.

In 1928 the SNL and the SHRA came together with the Scottish National Movement—a body rather similar to the SNL—to form the National Party of Scotland. The mediator in their union was the Glasgow University Student Nationalist Association led by John MacCormick.

If one compares the growth of nationalism in Scotland with a similar growth elsewhere, it is striking that students have played such a small part. Their role was a major one in Germany. In many of the Slav countries the same is true. Practically the only occasion when they became important in Scotland was in 1928. The circumstances were special. The traditional Scottish universities have a rector elected by the students. In the 1920s and 1930s the candidates were major politicians, and the elections for this largely honorific office were very political. John MacCormick was a young law student who organized a nationalist student society. As its candidate, it put forward Robert Bontine Cunninghame Graham. Cunninghame Graham came from a family of Scottish gentry, but he became an "advanced" Liberal and, in 1888, a founder member and president of the Scottish Labour Party. He sat in Parliament as a radical Labour member. Apart from this, he was a well known writer of the Conrad school and a romantic figure with a commanding presence.

The fact that stunned Glasgow and indeed much of Scotland was that Cunnginhame Graham came in second in the election, scoring 978 votes against the Conservative candidate who happened to be the prime minister, Stanley Baldwin.

Many people contributed to this result, most importantly John MacCormick. In doing so, he assured himself a place in the councils of any nationalist movement. He was not a good organizer, but he was a man who inspired real love among his friends (and hatred among his enemies), and he was one of the best political speakers that Scotland has ever produced. MacCormick was, in fact, a type of charismatic leader. Until 1942 he dominated the nationalist movement. It was on his insistence that the National Party of Scotland merged with the more conservative Scottish Party. Although he believed that independence was the final goal, he was prepared to work by stages, and this precipitated a bitterly fought struggle with the fundamentalist nationalists among his colleagues.

The argument represents a common dichotomy within nationalist movements. On the one side is the "true believer" with a deep feeling of grievance for his country's wrongs and a clear idea that the dominant ethnic group in his state carries the blame for the condition of his nation. On the other side—MacCormick's side—are those who are as deeply committed but less willing to see matters in terms of oppressors and oppressed. For this reason, they are less likely to demand complete independence for their nation as an immediate aim.

The effect was to split the SNP in 1942. MacCormick led a large portion of the members off to form what became the Scottish Convention. The SNP had a brief flurry of good by-election performances during the war, which culminated in the winning of Motherwell by Dr. Robert MacIntyre in 1945. However, MacCormick's Convention movement actually made the running. In 1949 the Scottish Covenant was drawn up, binding its signatories to work for home rule. A very large number signed the Covenant. The total was never propery audited, but it is estimated to have been between one million and two million. Tremendous enthusiasm was aroused, meetings were held all over the country, and, in the end, nothing was achieved.

The basic problem was that the Scottish Convention, or the Covenant Association as it became, was an all-party group. No one was going to put up candidates who might threaten the major parties as the Nationalist might have done. Petitions and shows of unity made good newspaper copy, but the politicians were unimpressed. With MacCormick's death in early 1961, the association finally collapsed.

Precisely at this time the SNP began to enjoy new strength. In the 1950s there was little development. Activists were reduced to a handful, and, at one point, there were only two branches in the entire country. The first stirrings can be dated from the Bridgeton by-election of 1961. Ian MacDonald, partly through sheer hard work, won 18.7 percent of the vote. What happened after the election day was an important as what happened before. Macdonald devoted himself fulltime as the national organizer. He traveled around the country setting up branches and servicing them. In 1962 there was similar encouragement at a by-election in West Lothian. At the General Election of 1964 there were 15 Nationalist candidates, as opposed to 5 in 1959. In the election of 1966 that number rose to 23, and in 1967 two by-elections genuinely stirred public interest. At Glasgow Pollok the SNP vote was so strong that the Labour majority collapsed, letting in the Conservative. A few months later Winnie Ewing won Hamilton, where the Labour majority had been the largest in Scotland.

There was immediate consternation in all the party machines, and support for the SNP began to flow in. At the municipal elections of the following year 103 gains were made.

After this spectacular performance, it is important to notice that there was a crack in the SNP fortunes. They lost most of the local government seats, and their performance at the national election in 1970 was poor, winning only one seat. The reasons for this change are speculative, but one cannot ignore the fact that the performance of the councilors was not good. It was particularly bad in Glasgow, where it was given the most publicity by a critical press. One concludes that a weaknes of the party was its lack of experience, and very little had been done to improve political education, even for those who might take public office. The party gave the impression of being amazed that it had gotten to where it was. There was a very serious failure of leadership at all levels. Instead of paying serious attention to this, there was a great deal of personal squabbling within the movement and argument over policy issues not immediately relevant to the job in hand.

After 1970 the picture changed. In 1971 it was announced that large quantities of oil had been discovered in the North Sea. The party mounted a campaign to claim this oil for Scotland. If Scotland were independent, it was argued, she would be a rich country. It was no longer possible for British nationalists to deny Scotland's right to independence by saying that Scotland could not afford it.

No one can truly say whether this oil campaign had the impact. It probably had some, but several pieces of research show that there was not much belief that oil was going to make an enormous difference in the Scottish standard of living. Perhaps the effect was indirect and worked through the way that the oil campaign stimulated the activists. For whatever reasons, the SNP proportion of the poll kept going up until, at the national election of October 1974, they won 30 percent of the vote.

This result had serious implications for British politics. By the October election, the Labour Party had accepted a policy of devolution. It was not an easy decision to take, since many militants saw this as a sell out to the enemy: the SNP.[11] Nevertheless, the 1974 Labour administration started its period of office committed to Scottish and Welsh home rule. They honored this commitment by introducing two bills. One fell for constitutional reasons, but the other—the Scotland Bill—became law in an amended form. It was amended in such a way that the government was forced to hold a referendum in Scotland on whether there should be a Scottish assembly or parliament and, moreover, 40 percent of registered Scottish electors would have to vote for it if the act were to be implemented.

Since the late 1940s about three quarters of Scottish voters were believed to support devolution. Polls taken in the early 1970s confirmed this, and, although there was irritation at the forty percent rule, it was not thought to raise a serious difficulty. In the event, it did. Support both for devolution and for the National Party leaked away in 1978 and 1979. By-elections in which the SNP was expected to do well, such as Garscadden and Hamilton, did not turn out to be successes. At the referendum on March 1, 1979, only 32.8 percent of registered Scottish electors voted for devolution. Although fewer, 31 percent, voted against, it was not politically possible for the Labour government to implement the act. Too many of its own backbenchers and ministers were hostile. In June the government fell at the General Election, which had been precipitated by Nationalist MPs voting against it. In that election, the 11 Nationalist members were reduced to 2 and, the proportion of Nationalist votes in the country fell to 20 percent.

CONCLUSION

The SNP has gone through some bad times, and, although it may recover its strength, we must still explain why its support weakened. In doing so, we gain insight into the nature of the Scottish movement.

The opinion studies of devolution all show that this was and is a policy supported by most Scots, but also that it was and is not one of the most important issues. Economic issues, such as prices and unemployment, dominate This, then, was an initial weakness. What appears to have happened in 1978 was that the issue of devolution became confused with that of complete independence. When people came to cast their votes in the referendum, many either felt that the argument was about independence or separation or that devolution would be the first step toward separation. This clearly affected the number voting yes and the vote of the SNP.

It was well known, even when the SNP was doing well, that the vote for that party responded to the feeling of economic weakness as much as to constitutional solutions.[12] Many people seem to have voted Nationalist because they believed it would make Westminster give more aid. Fewer gave devolution, let alone independence, as a reason for voting. In these circumstances, it is less surprising that voters deserted the Nationalists when the constitutional option had to be faced.

On top of this was the problem that the SNP did not seem to have a clear idea of what would improve Scottish life and the economy.

At the moment of writing, the Scottish National Party has slipped considerably in popular support. It does well when a poll gives it 20 percent of the sample, but it is well to remember that the SNP is still one of the major parties in Scotland, and it still has the potential of regaining its former position.

NOTES

1. See M. Brown, *The Politics of Irish Literature* (London: Allen and Unwin, 1972).

2. See R. K. Middlemas, *The Clydesiders* (London: Hutchinson, 1965).

3. See H. Hanham, *Scottish Nationalism* (London: Faber, 1969).

4. See R. H. Campbell, *Scotland since 1707* (Oxford: Blackwell, 1965).

5. See E. Gellner, *Words and Things* (London: Gollanz, 1959).

6. See W. Ferguson, *Scotland 1689 to the Present* (Edinburgh: Oliver and Boyd), p. 50.

7. See *Letters of Queen Victoria*, 2nd series, iii, (London: John Murray, 1926), p. 47. ·

8. See G. Blake, *Barrie and the Kailyard School* (London: Arthur Barker, 1951).

9. See J. Hunter, "The Gaelic Connection," *Scottish Historical Review* 54 (October 1975): 178–204.

10. See Jack Brand, *The National Movement in Scotland* (London: Routledge, 1978), especially chap. 11.

11. See Michael Keating and David Bleuman, *Labour and Scottish Nationalism* (London: Macmillan, 1979).

12. Brand, *Nationalist Movement*, p. 161.

5

WALES IN THE 1980s

John Osmond

As Wales enters the 1980s, it continues to present a series of paradoxes in its political development. At the very period when the factors most associated with Welsh identity—language, religion, and political radicalism—are declining, interest in Welshness maintains an increasing momentum. Underlying this is the paradox of Welshness and Welsh identity itself. The historian Gwyn A. Williams argues that the essence of Welshness is Britishness: until this is understood, both in its historical and contemporary sense, analysis of Welsh politics will not come to terms with reality. Nationalists who deny the place of a British identity are, as he puts it, "spitting in the winds of the world." But herein lies more paradox. For at the same time, Williams is also able to say:

> The British nation and the British state are clearly entering a process of dissolution, into Europe or the mid-Atlantic or a post-imperial fog. Britain has begun its long march out of history.

And he adds:

> How ironic it seems then, that in Referendum, General Election and European Election during 1979, it was the Welsh who registered their country as the most passionately and totally British of all the regions of the United Kingdom of Great Britain and about half of Northern Ireland. We Welsh look like being the Last of the British. There is some logic in this. We were, after all, the First.[1]

THE BRITISH CONNECTION

Williams goes on to trace the historical emergence of Wales and to emphasize the importance of British connections in defining Welsh identity. The process took the form of movement and countermovement. So it was, at the head of a largely Welsh-speaking army, that Henry VII picked up Richard III's fallen crown off Bosworth Field in 1485. In fulfilment of the long-promised legend, Henry named his first son Arthur, and the Welsh gentry, the Uchelwyr, flocked to London to become British. The phrase *British Empire* was invented in 1580 by a Welshman, Dr. John Dee, mathematician and chief scientific adviser to Elizabeth I. It was in 1536, of course, that Henry VII's Act of "Union" incorporated Wales into England, proscribing the Welsh language in the process. Yet, before the century was out, Elizabeth I had authorized the translation of the Bible into Welsh, accomplished by 1588, and it was through this medium that nonconformist religion was imported into Wales from England in the following centuries.

Also imported into Wales, with a kind of explosion from the end of the eighteenth century onward, was industrial capitalism. Until this period the Welsh numbered no more than 400,000, often less. But, by the early 1900s, the height of the Welsh industrial revolution, the number had increased fivefold. What these statistics mean is that modern Wales is largely a creation of the industrial revolution concentrated between the years 1870–1911. In 1851 Wales had a population of just over one million, with two-thirds in the countryside. Just sixty years later this population had doubled, and two-thirds of it was now concentrated in urban areas. The pell-mell expansion of coal mining in the southern valleys brought a mass exodus of some 400,000 people out of rural Wales into urban Wales. These people, incidentally, were overwhelmingly Welsh-speaking so that, until the 1920s, Welsh was the majority language in large areas of industrial Wales. This exodus was quickly followed by an influx from outside Wales. In the decade 1901–11 the south Wales coal field attracted 129,000 people, most of whom came from England. In this period Wales was attracting immigrants at a rate almost as high as the United States—an annual rate of 4.5 per 1,000, as against 6.3 per 1,000.[2]

If the dominant social and economic movement of this period was from England into Wales, politically the influence was the other way around. The old Liberal Party dominated British politics, and it, in turn, was strongly influenced by Welsh elements, most notably Lloyd George. As chancellor of the Exchequer in 1909, he laid the foundation stones for the welfare state and then went on, during World War I, to become the most powerful prime minister Britain would ever have. Lloyd George's career retains an immense psychological significance in Welsh politics because of the way in which he fused Welsh and British aspirations. He had been, of course, a leader of the Cymru Fydd (Young Wales) movement of the 1880s and 1890s. But, though a forerunner of modern Welsh nationalism, there is no doubt that its aim was simply to promote equal participation for the Welsh in the British political system. As one of the movement's adherents made clear at the time:

> It is recognized not only that the union with England is inevitable, but that it provides the best opportunity that Wales could have to deliver her mission—if mission she has—to the world. The one condition that is insisted upon is that the connection shall not be made closer at the expense of Welsh nationality.[3]

It was World War I that saw the fullest participation of Wales in British affairs, in the most horrific way possible. With Lloyd George in the lead at the apex of British Imperial power, Welshmen enlisted in the thousands. Wales contributed 13.82 percent of her population compared with England's 13.3 percent, Scotland's 13.02 percent, and Ireland's significantly lower 3.87 percent. The Welsh percentage represented approximately 280,000 men, two-thirds of the country's adult male population between 20 and 40 years of age. The experience marked the end of nineteenth century Wales and the certainties that went with it. It marked the end of Cymru Fydd nationalism defined as collaborating Liberalism in league with suffocating nonconformity. And it provided the opening for the politics of hard nationalism: the founding of Plaid Cymru in 1925 and the confrontation with the British state that ensued.

But it was many years before this opening could be exploited to any great degree. The hemorrhage caused by World War I was surpassed in its impact on Welsh society by the devastation wrought by the depression of the 1920s and 1930s. Welsh industry was based too narrowly on the primary production of coal and steel. Coal production was geared almost entirely to the export sector of the British economy, and, when the main markets in Europe and North America were lost in the years after the war, this dependence proved fatal. Welsh unemployment reached 38 percent in 1932, forcing mass emigration from both rural and industrial parts of the country. Wales lost 450,000 people through emigration between 1921 and 1939, most of them going to England. In Gwyn A. Williams' judgment the depression plays the same social role in Welsh history as the famine in Irish.

At the very time of this mass emigration into England, a political current of socialist ideology was flowing the other way. Although it was given a distinctly Welsh flavor, most notably by personalities such as Jim Griffiths and Aneurin Bevan, socialist ideology—certainly the state centralist variety of the Webbs—was imported into Wales from England.

Early on, there were attempts to counter this brand of socialism with more decentralist forms in line with what can be termed the radical/nationalist tradition.[4] Certainly leaders such as Keir Hardie, (MP) for Merthyr 1900–15, and Arthur Henderson, Labour's general secretary who in 1918 pledged the party to the "widest and generous measure of Home Rule" for Wales, found no problem in accepting it. There was a glimmer, too, of real socialist commitment to decentralized community and workers' control in the south Wales coal field in the years leading up to World War I. It was significant, for instance, that the program outlined in "The Miners Next Step," published in the *Rhondda* in 1912, rejected any schemes for nationalizing the mines. Placing them in the hands of the state, it was claimed, would inevitably result in their return, through the back door, to the coal owners.[5]

But as soon as Labour became regarded as a party of government, after 1923, such commitments and ideas rapidly lost ground. The attractions of parliamentary power politics and the centralized control of the party machine at the all-British level which that entailed proved overwhelming. In the 1931 General Election, Labour was almost wiped out in England; in Wales it lost only one seat. This was a lesson that the party has never forgotten and that accounted for much of the Labour opposition to the Welsh Assembly wielded so effectively in the 1979 referendum. For the assembly implied in the long run a smaller number of Welsh Labour MPs at Westminister, thus reducing the party's chances of forming a government. After all, but for Wales there would have been no Labour government in 1950 (majority seven) or in 1964 (majority five). And without Welsh support there would not have been even a minority Labour government after February 1974, and Labour would not have been maintained in office after October 1974.

It is true that in the late 1950s a significant element within the Labour Party in Wales began to give more attention to Welsh aspirations and the related ideas of decentralization. The results were the creation of the Welsh Office in 1964, followed by the devolution proposals in the 1970s. But those pushing these policies within the Labour party were always a minority. They only succeeded so far as they did because of the Nationalist threat in the background. As Jim Griffiths, the first secretary of state for Wales, put it, the post had been created primarily out of a "recognition of our nationhood."[6] But the real test was the referendum in 1979. In that campaign the Labour Party revealed its true colors when a dissident minority of Welsh MPs succeeded in mobilizing the greater part of the party in Wales against its own government's proposals. This was an episode of immense significance to the future of Labour Party in Wales. It demonstrated that, for the established parliamentary and local government power centers of the party at least, Welshness and Welsh politics were of no account when British interests were at stake. Their attitude was well articulated early on in the parliamentary debates leading up to the referendum by Neil Kinnock, MP for Bedwelty:

> If I had to use a label of any kind, I should have to call myself a unionist. I believe that the emancipation of the class which I have come to this House to represent, unapologetically, can best be achieved in a single nation and in a single economic unit, by which I mean a unit where we can have a brotherhood of all nations and have the combined strength of working class people throughout the whole of the United Kingdom brought to bear against any bully, any Executive, any foreign power, any bureaucratic arrangement, be it in Brussels or in Washington, and any would-be coloniser, either an industrial coloniser or a political coloniser.[7]

On one level the argument inherent in this analysis is a pragmatic one about where best to concentrate the forces working on behalf of "working people." As the "Labour No Assembly" manifesto, published in Wales during the referendum campaign, made clear: "We believe that the conquest of the economic and social wrongs in our system can be best secured by maximising the strength of our movement through the democratic power of a majority Labour government ruling through Parliament."[8] Of course, the opposing view is that the role of socialists at the center is merely to add a gloss of respectability to a system that cannot work in the direction they want. This view maintains that lasting and fundamental change can never be imposed from the top downward. It has to be won by the people themselves, from the bottom upward, at the work place and at every level at which decisions are made, particularly at the Welsh, Scottish, and English regional level in Britain. The efforts of the Labour Party at the British level are seen merely as resulting in the creation of a *state* capitalist structure, breathing new life into the capitalist system in the process. As Tom Nairn has put it:

> Labourism stands not for class and nation—that is the ideological halo— but for class-in-nation; or more exactly, for nation-over-class. Labour is (to employ one of its own historic programme-words in a different sense) the *Nationalisation* of class...
> Labourism constitutes, perhaps, the most important element in the astonishing homogeneity of modern Britain. In effect, the most dangerous seam of civil society, the division between the classes, runs through it rather than outside it and is constantly "healed" (that is, kept closed) by the very structure and world view of the party...
> The Labour-Left almost never stands for class *against* nation, for the material reality of which Labourism is the mystical shell. Were it so, the Labour Party could not exist in its actual form, and would certainly never have survived the trials of the past 20 years without a split.[9]

A WELSH IDENTITY

The interconnections between Wales and England have created an extremely complex background for contemporary Welsh politics and the issue of Welsh identity. Surveys that have been carried out on the question are not particularly enlightening. Opinion Research discovered in 1968, for example, that 69 percent of the people of Wales thought of themselves as Welsh, 15 percent as British, 13 as percent English, and one percent as Irish.[10] But such surveys have not probed the crucial question of Welsh dual identity: the fact that most people think of themselves as both Welsh and British, in differing proportions according to circumstances and the subject under discussion. Such split feelings of varying intensity are not easily verified by objective tests. Nevertheless, ambivalence over identity runs like a fault line through Welsh society and was played on by the opposing forces in the 1979 referendum campaign. The nerve was touched in stark terms by Enoch Powell during the "No Assembly Campaign" eve-of-poll rally:

> Whatever may be true of Scotland, at no time in the last thousand years—and maybe longer still—has it been possible to draw a line on the map along O-fa's Dyke, and pointing to the west of it, to say "that is Wales." The whole history of England, as long as it has been a nation, has been penetrated and interfused with Wales and the Welsh...the heritage and the achievement of the Welsh people is nothing less than the heritage of Britain itself.[11]

Yet Powell's (uncharacteristic) confusion of the terms "England" and "Britain" reveals a fundamental flaw in the concept of Britishness. For, although the term has specific meaning within Wales—and in Scotland and Northern Ireland—in England it is hard to define except in relation to Englishness, so much so that outside of Wales and Scotland (Northern Ireland is more complex), it is difficult to escape the conclusion that "British" simply means "English." The final authority on the English language, Fowler's *Modern English Usage*, is explicit on the point:

> It must be remembered that no Englishman, and perhaps no Scot even, calls himself a Briton without a sneaking sense of the ludicrous. How should an Englishman utter the words *Great Britain* with the glow of emotion that for him goes with *England*? He talks the *English* language; he has been taught *English* history...he has heard the word of an *Englishman* and of *English* fair play, scorns certain things as *un-English*, and aspires to be an *English* gentleman; he knows that *England* expects every man to do his duty...in the word *England*, not in *Britain*, all these things are implicit [my emphasis].[12]

An intriguing attempt to argue that in the concept of Britain there is something more than being Welsh, English, or Scottish has been made by an expatriot Welshman, Daniel Jenkins, in his book *The British, Their Identity and Their Religion*, published in 1975 as the devolution debate was gathering pace. His central assertion is that, "Intelligent Scotsmen and Welshmen find it easy to be good Scotsmen and good Welshmen and at the same time to participate fully in the wider life of Britain."[13] But when he comes to specify those elements that characterize British, as opposed to Scottish or Welsh, identity, he can only list moral qualities that are the essence of English romanticism: reserve, respect for privacy, the ideal of the "gentleman," modesty, fair play, and the social style that derives from them. As R. Tudur Jones has commented:

> The Scots and the Welsh must not be allowed to opt out of a united Britain because they can enrich these qualities. In every case, the typical quality is part of the English ideal and it is argued that the Welsh and Scots are to play the role of contributors to the English quest for moral perfection. Dr. Jenkins seems quite unaware of his own metropolitan perspective. The standard is set in London. London finds difficulty in reaching it. The Welsh and Scots should consider it their Christian duty to assist their English brethren by throwing in their own contribution. On the other hand, the glaring weaknesses of the Scots and the Welsh can be partially cured, if only they hang on to England's apron strings and reject the temptation to become parochial.[14]

The essence of the matter, of course, is the refusal of the English to participate in the idea of Britishness in any meaningful way. This has long been a dilemma for the majority of the Welsh people who have been attached to Britishness as a dimension beyond Welshness. And as it becomes more and more evident that Britishness is under long-term attack—from the shedding of empire that gave it primary meaning, from spiraling economic decline, and from the growth of competing identities (Europeanism, Welsh, Scottish, Irish and, most underestimated, English)—so the dilemma intensifies.

It is precisely because Britishness is being eroded by these forces that the issue of Welsh identity is being brought more sharply into focus. The crisis of Welsh identity—as defined by the combined retreat of language, religion, and Liberalism, now followed by Labourism—has been well documented. Less articulated is a parallel insecurity induced in people living in Wales by the slow collapse of confidence in Britishness. The most important element in the collapse is unquestionably Britain's accelerating economic decline relative to other countries. As Wales moves into the 1980s, Welsh people face the prospect of declining living standards relative to those experienced within Britain itself in the recent past. This is despite the windfall of oil in the North Sea. The pace of the decline and the nature of the political reaction that will accompany it are uncertain. So far as Wales is concerned, nationalism has tended in the past to do best at the polls when the economy has been relatively buoyant, for example in the 1960s. On the other hand, times of austerity have tended to produce a conservative reaction against change. One key question for the politics of the 1980s is whether the state of the economy will become so bad that people will be encouraged to abandon security and seek change. That is a question relevant for politics throughout Britain. But it is particularly relevant in peripheral areas such as Wales and Scotland where not only the prospects for economic decline are most severe, but also where indigenous political alternatives are readily at hand. More so than in the immediate past, the politics of Wales in the 1980s are dependent on the course of events in Britain as a whole.

AN INTERNAL COLONY?

Ideology is important not only for interpreting political movements, especially nationl movements, but also for providing an impetus for political action itself. Any ideological framework for Welsh politics must take account of the interrelationship of Wales with the rest of Britain, which has projected British identity so forcibly into the consciousness of Welsh people so much so that, by now, this is one factor that distinguishes them most from the peoples of the rest of Britain. Failure to take this into account is a fundamental flaw in probably the most influential ideological initiative in Welsh politics of the 1970s, the concept of "Internal Colonialism." Nevertheless, following the publication of 1975 of Michael Hechter's work on the subject's application to Britain, it achieved remarkably swift currency in Welsh debate.[15] Within months of the appearance of Hechter's book, for example, the President of Plaid Cymru, Gwynfor Evans, published his *A National Future for Wales*. The third chapter is headed "Wales A Colony" and quotes liberally from Hechter's description of an internal colony, as follows:

> Commerce and trade among members of the periphery tend to be monopolised by members of the core. Credit is similarly monopolised. When commercial prospects emerge, bankers, managers and entrepreneurs tend to be recruited from the core. The peripheral economy is forced into complementary development to the core, and thus becomes dependent on external markets. Generally this economy rests on a single primary export, either agricultural or mineral. The movement of peripheral labour is determined solely by forces exogenous to the periphery. Typically there is great migration and mobility of peripheral workers in response to price fluctuations of exported primary products.

Economic dependence is reinforced through judicial, political and military measures. There is relative lack of services, lower standards of living, and higher levels of frustration, measured by such indicators as alcoholism among members of the peripheral collectivity. There is national discrimination on the basis of language, religion, or, in general, ethnicity. Thus the structural differences between groups are causally linked to cultural differences.[16]

This account of Wales' relationship with England has proven attractive to those wishing to reconcile Welsh nationalism with socialism. For, if the theory of internal colonialism is correct, it means that class divisions within Wales fade into insignificance compared with the exploitation of Wales as a whole by the British state. Moreover, the theory enables Welsh nationalists to establish links between their movement and Third World anticolonial movements. Mainstream British internationalist socialist thinking has no difficulty in reconciling the socialist and nationalist aspirations of Third World independence movements. So, by analogy, if Wales were placed in a similar position, the same ideological union between socialism and nationalism could be consummated.

Unfortunately, however, the theory of "Internal Colonialism" as set out by Hechter is seriously flawed in its application to Wales. Consequently, the nationalist ideological position built on it has not corresponded to reality. The process, again, has been paradoxical. The nationalist motivation for seizing upon "Internal Colonialism" as a way of describing the plight of the Welsh people has been precisely because this enables linkages with socialism. Underlying the idea of socialism in this context has been the wish to appeal to the urban industrialized south and northeast of Wales whose English-speaking majority population has so far resisted large-scale adherence to the national cause.

But the central tenet of the internal colonialism thesis, as the previous quotation from Hechter makes clear, is that the economic differences between core and periphery are "causally linked to cultural differences." This factor distinguishes internal colonialism from other forms of economic exploitation that characteristically apply between the prosperous centers and outlying areas of all countries, as well as between classes.

The problem is that once cultural differentiation is introduced as a causal factor in such relationships, the issue is driven back to definitions of the cultural markers involved. In Hechter's case these hinge on language, religion, and voting patterns. But these are markers that serve only to dissipate any communal sense of identity between the people of Wales as a whole. Of course, the markers do provide a foundation for the concept of ethnicity as an accurate term for describing the condition in which such factors combine. But by definition, so far as Wales is concerned, the ethnic group that emerges from the analysis can only be a minority of the population suffering the exploitation that is evidently occurring. Paradoxically then, nationalist theorists, by resorting to internal colonialism as a means of unifying socialism and nationalism as a prerequisite for mobilizing widespread support, have only succeeded in emphasizing the national movement as a minority cause in Wales. Hechter's theory of internal colonialism, resting as it does on bogus cultural explanations for economic exploitation, is an intensely divisive influence in the important effort underway in Wales to effect a union between socialism and Welsh nationalism,[17] for it has encouraged the nationalist movement to think of itself in ethnic terms. Yet, by definition, the term "ethnic nationalism" suggests political group consciousness of only one, usually immigrant, group that does not constitute a demographic majority in a contested region. Welsh nationalists, of course, claim a common heritage for the people of Wales as a whole and seek autonomy for the nation as a whole. This is not "ethnic nationalism" (if, indeed, nationalism is a proper epithet to attach to ethnicity), but just nationalism, without qualification.

This argument is reinforced when a further aspect of Hechter's exposition of internal colonialism in relation to Wales is examined. Not only does he insist that the Celtic peripheries have been materially disadvantaged in a systematic manner, but also that internal colonialism is characterized by weak political integration of the periphery into the state, symbolized most potently by the persistence of nationalism in Wales and Scotland. However, the periods of nationalist advance and retreat in recent Welsh history do not coincide with background economic and cultural conditions relating to the internal colonialism analysis, rather the reverse.

There is no doubt that in the last 100 yearsWales has been a relatively disadvantaged region within Britain. There is no doubt either that while Wales' position in this respect steadily worsened up until World War II, since that time the position has been steadily improving. Yet the performance of the nationalist movement has not corresponded to these developments according to the pattern the internal colonialism thesis would suggest. The years up to World War II saw the consolidation of the class-based Labour movement in Wales with the forces of nationalism playing an insignificant role. On the other hand, since World War II, Welsh nationalism has steadily increased its support and achieved some electoral success.

Indeed, far from being a product of weak political integration, Welsh nationalism has thrived in those areas in Wales where the British state has been most active. The two most effective forms of government activity in this respect have been the extension of welfare provision and nationalization immediately following World War II and the expansion of regional economic policy and planning in the 1960s. Plaid Cymru responded by campaigning strongly on economic issues, pressing the case for Wales to be treated as a unit both for economic planning and in the new nationalized industries. The establishment of the Welsh Office and the all-Wales approach to economic planning which that entailed from 1964 onward lent credibility to these demands. So, too, did the creation of the Wales Trade Union Congress (TUC) in 1973. In 1970 Plaid Cymru published its Economic Plan for Wales, a comprehensive document that, among other recommendations, called for a Welsh Development Authority. In 1975 the Welsh Development Agency was duly created, albeit with less than adequate powers. If the link between such activity and the growth of nationalism be doubted, it should be enough to point to the two areas of Wale where Plaid Cymru has most developed since World War II: the quarrying areas of Gwynedd in northwest Wales and the mining valleys of Mid Glamorgan in the south. These are the two areas where economic problems have been most serious, and the government has responded by singling them out as Special Department Areas, with additional incentives for incoming industry to the rest of Wales.[18]

This noncorrelation of nationalist resurgence and typical indicators of an internal colonial relationship is recognized by Hechter himself. He suggests that during times when straightforward nationalist activity was attenuated, the drive was still present but directed through more mainstream forces:

> The apparent vacillation in the strength of Welsh and Scottish nationalism is puzzling. How can a social movement, such as nationalism, "die" after 1921, then suddenly reappear forty years later? Nationalist movements take root because the issues they raise have salience for political actors. This salience apparently disappeared after 1921. How can this be explained? Did circumstances in Wales and Scotland change so drastically that these needs were eclipsed by others, of totally opposite direction? Or did political actors take their nationalism and place it in the hands of candidates of national (i.e., British) parties?[19]

But this begs the question. Were the politics of Liberalism in Wales, followed from the 1920s onward by the politics of Labourism, an expression of Welsh national identity? Or were they, more simply, a pragmatic means for containing any political expression of Welshness as a separate force and, more insidiously, absorbing any such potential into a British expression? The latter view has been consistently and forcibly expressed by Plaid Cymru. Indeed, it was precisely because the founders of the party held this to be the case that they took the initiative they did in 1925. Their judgment was eloquently borne out by the behavior of the Labour Party in Wales in the years leading up to the 1979 Welsh Assembly referendum and by its conduct during the campaign itself. Shortly afterward, a study of the campaign concluded:

> The Labour Party in Scotland and Wales with varying degrees of reluctance has moved a long way since 1973, but it remains a self-consciously centralising force. The devolution proposals were presented with the avowed intent of safeguarding the integrity of the United Kingdom.[20]

The Labour Party is the most instinctively British nationalist of all the political movements active in the United Kingdom. By comparison, the Conservative Party and even the National Front are English parties. The Labour Party contains the class divisions of British society that might otherwise threaten to fracture the British consensus. And the Labour Party, so far this century, has successfully integrated Wales and Scotland into the British system and has been the most hostile opponent of Britain's integration into the European Economic Community—so much so that, in the February 1974 General Election, Enoch Powell, a lifelong Tory, urged his Wolverhampton supporters to vote Labour.

In Wales the Labour Party, above all else, represents the British side of Welsh identity. Even those in the Labour Party who advocated devolution did so precisely because they saw it as the most effective means of keeping Britain united. As James Callaghan, then prime minister and MP for Cardiff South East told Labour's 1976 annual conference, "My political instincts tell me that the successful implementation of devolution offers us, as a party, the best way of keeping the United Kingdom united."[21] Hechter is simply ducking the issue when he attempts to argue that, in the period from the early years of the century to the mid-1960s, Welsh nationalism was an underlying force diverted into Labour party ranks.

Hechter's central theme is that there is a causal relationship between cultural differentiation and economic exploitation. Yet, Welsh nationalism emerged as a political force in the 1960s at the very time when culturally differentiating factors were most steeply in decline. The retreat of the Welsh language and nonconformism have been well-documented. But even more serious for Hechter's analysis has been the rapid change in the Welsh economy. An essential part of Hechter's cultural differentiation of Wales from England was the overwhelming reliance of the Welsh economy on three basic industries: farming, coal mining, and steel making. But, since World War II, there has been a massive decline in these industries together with a steady diversification of the manufacturing base, a twin process that is continuing as Wales enters the 1980s. The numbers employed in the Welsh farming industry dropped from more than 80,000 in the early 1950s to just 20,000 in 1980; coal miners from 115,000 to

27,000; and steel workers from 65,000 in 1970 to barely 30,000.[22] Halving employment in the Welsh steel industry within ten years was a reeling blow. And, at the end of 1979 came the shock announcement that more was to follow with a major cutback at the two remaining major Welsh plants, Port Talbot and Llanwern, with the loss of 12,000 jobs and probably more. These redundancies would also place in jeopardy 11 of Wales' remaining 37 collieries (there were 211 in 1948) and the jobs of some 8,000 miners since their main market would be lost.

Though the Welsh economy has diversified greatly, with tertiary industries, for example, increasing their share of Welsh employment from 6 percent to 36 percent between 1960 and 1980, this has been unable to keep pace with the mounting redundancies in coal and steel. So it is probable that in the early 1980s unemployment will rise by as much as 50,000, pushing the percentage up from the 8 percent level of the late 1970s in Wales to around 15 percent. These figures do not take into account two further factors: that large numbers of young people are due to swell the queues looking for jobs during the 1980s and that investment in the high-growth technology sector of the economy tends to result in fewer jobs. As has already been stated, unemployment levels reaching toward 20 percent could trigger a major destabilization in Welsh politics. But, if that occurs, it will not be the result of Hechter's cultural division of labor between core and periphery. It will be because the periphery will start losing confidence, on a larger scale than has so far happened, in the core's ability to generate labor for the periphery at all. In this way, the periphery will be driven back to ideas of self-reliance.

This judgment points to an alternative approach to explaining the emergence of Welsh nationalism as a force of some political consequence since the 1960s, an approach that is, incidentally, taken up by Hechter himself at one point. This is that, so long as Wales remains tied into the centralized British state economic and political system, it will never be able to develop a balanced infrastructure and industrial profile. This is not so much the result of any neocolonial relationship as a straightforward consequence of centralized state capitalism. As Hechter puts it:

> Though the partial industrialisation of Wales and Scotland did permit the structural integration of these regions into the national society, principally through the establishment of national trade unions and the Labour Party, persisting economic stagnation in the periphery has shaken much confidence in the class-based political organisation. There is a new awareness that no state-wide political party will commit sufficient resources to achieve development in the periphery. Nationalism has reemerged in the Celtic periphery largely as a reaction to this failue of regional development.[23]

This failure is more than the proven inability of government-sponsored regional economic policies to tackle the problems of peripheral areas.[24] It is the deeper consequence of the debilitating centralist logic of the capitalist-run economy, especially the state-capitalist variety that characterizes the British system. The experience of the state-run steel industry, which as the 1980s opened precipitated Wales' latest economic crisis, bears eloquent testimony to this view. In the early 1970s the British Steel Corporation (BSC) undertook a fundamental review of its long-term plans. The outcome was a strategy for concentrating large-scale crude steel making on a half dozen large sites by 1980, compared with 30 or so centers in the late 1970s. This was an extraordinary strategy since it flew in the face of countervailing economic forces that were clearly visible at the time, so much so that the essential question is how any management could have arrived at so disastrous a policy.

To begin with, the policy entailed projecting demand for the BSC's steel at somewhere between 33 million tons and 38 million tons by the early 1980s (some figures stretched the demand as high as 44 million tons). These projections assumed three important conditions: that the British economy would be in a state of buoyant growth by the early 1980s; that overseas producers in countries such as Japan, Korea, and Brazil would not be able to undercut the BSC on its prices; and that the BSC would be able to deliver its product regularly, on time, and at consistent quality. All three assumptions have proved wildly wrong. By 1980 Britain was battening down the hatches for a prolonged recession, there was massive import penetration by foreign steel into the British market, and the BSC's output was hovering near 15 million tons.

The second part of the BSC's policy was to concentrate crude-steel making on a few large-scale sites, involving massive capital outlay. The alternative was to spread steel making among a larger number of existing smaller sites that were better suited to the production of specialized steels. If this course had been taken, the BSC could have better withstood competition from abroad, could have adjusted more easily to falling demand, and would have faced less capital outlay and caused less traumatic upheaval to its work force, its prime asset, and the many communities dependent on the industry. These considerations are so compelling that the essential question is how the BSC management arrived at such misjudgment.

The answer is to be found in the renationalization of the steel industry in 1967 and its subsequent organization and reorganization.[25] These three stages in the industry's evolution provide the key to the BSC's strategy that proved so disastrous for Wales. Each was accompanied by intensified centralization of control over the industry. And therein lay the essential motivation. The complete centralization of decision making in the corporation's London headquarters made inevitable the choice of a few large steelworks, large-scale production, and massive capital outlay instead of a greater number of smaller steelworks, producing a smaller volume of more specialized steels, and involving less capital outlay. The choice was a logical outcome of the centralization of power in the steel industry: a small number of large works could be more easily controlled and governed from the center than could a greater number of smaller ones.

This perspective is recognized in general terms by Hechter in his discussion of the emergence of Welsh and Scottish nationalism. He concludes, "The most recent crystallisation of Celtic nationalism may ultimately be understood as a trenchant critique of the principle of bureauractic centralism."[26] But this is a product of state capitalism, not internal colonialsm, a judgment borne out by Gwyn A. Williams:

> It is apparent that Wales and the Welsh, as distinctive entities, cannot survive the capitalist mode of production in its present historic phase. A tiny Welsh nation may survive in a marginal and impotent bunker; a vivid Welsh-language culture should survive if only in aspic. But the continuous reproduction of Wales and the Welsh over generations requires the elimination and the transcendence of the capitalist mode of production. If capitalism in the British Isles lives, Wales will die. If Wales is to live, capitalism in the British Isles must die.[27]

This is recognized, too, by leading Nationalist thinkers, such as R. Tudur Jones. As he has put it, Plaid Cymru demands "the freedom to be responsible, not the license to be separate. And this demand is made not only to curb and reform the economic policies of the centralised state in London but also in order to withstand the depradations of capitalism upon the social life of the nation."[28]

THE REFERENDUM

In the first year of the new decade Kenneth O. Morgan had temerity to give his new history of Wales between 1880 and 1980 the title, *Rebirth of a Nation*.[29] Yet only a year before, in March 1979, proposals to set up a Welsh Assembly had been overwhelmingly defeated in a referendum, by four to one. A few months later the Conservative Party, traditionally regarded as most hostile to Welsh national aspirations, scored an outstanding victory in the General Election the referendum precipitated. Its share of the vote in Wales jumped from 23.9 percent in October 1974 to 32.1 percent. This result put Plaid Cymru in third place behind the Conservatives in the southern valleys, upset the politics of rural Wales with the Conservatives winning Anglesey, Montgomery, Brecon and

Radnor (and causing Plaid Cymru president Gwynfor Evans to lose his Carmarthen seat to Labour), and destroyed Labour's claim to speak for the whole of Wales.

Nevertheless, Morgan insists that despite these events the century up to 1980 saw a progressive development of Welsh institutions that took Welsh identity beyond reliance upon language and religion. He sees twentieth century Welsh history as pivoting round the painful accumulation of embryonic institutions. The process began in 1872 with the foundation of the University of Wales at Aberystwyth. In the late 1880s elected local government was established, followed by the Welsh Intermediate Education Act of 1889 and the Central Welsh Board of Education in 1896. The Welsh Department of Education in Cardiff opened in 1907, the National Library in 1916, the Welsh Board of Health in 1919, and the National Museum in 1922, the year of disestablishment with the creation of the Church of Wales.

After World War II the onrush of state intervention, most notably welfare provision, was accompanied by the extension of Welsh institutions into the political arena. In 1947 the Advisory Council for Wales was established, followed by the appointment of a minister for Welsh Affairs attached to the Home Office in 1951. Through the 1950s a campaign gathered strength for the establishment of a full-scale Welsh Office, which was finally achieved, together with a secretary of State in the Cabinet, in 1964. By 1980 the Welsh Office had grown into a major spending department—its budget exceeded $1,000 million—with responsibility for industry and economic planning, housing, health, education, roads, agriculture, and local government. Another important advance was the creation of the Wales TUC in 1973 and the formation of all-Wales local authority associations in the wake of the reorganization of local government in 1974. At the same time there was a proliferation of important nominated bodies that lent weight to Welsh identity, such as the Welsh Water Authority (1974), the Welsh Development Agency (1975), and the Land Authority for Wales (1975). Despite the 1979 referendum result, this institutional development continued. The first meetings of the Parliamentary Select Committee on Welsh Affairs were held in 1980, and from 1981 the Welsh Office is to be responsible for distributing central funds to local authorities from a block grant of some $600 million negotiated directly with the Treasury.

But the most important institution established during the 100 years— the one from which most of the others flowed—was Plaid Cymru, the Welsh nationalist party. In itself, the party, founded in 1925, has remained only a small element in Welsh politics and has grown slowly, achieving around 10 percent of the Welsh vote in the 1970s (8.1 percent in the 1979 General Election). But Plaid Cymru is far from being purely a political expression. It is a movement in the broadest sense, and its influence has penetrated practically every corner of Welsh life, often in terms of provoking an adverse reaction but, in doing so, breaking down indifference.[30] The future of Wales as a national entity is bound up with the future of Plaid Cymru and, in particular, the direction the party takes following the watershed experience of the 1979 referendum. The history of the party up to 1979 and the constitutional path it had charted in the 1960s led the majority of the leadership to accept the proposed assembly and assist in its advocacy. The logical beginning of this response was the Carmarthen by-election victory in 1966, after which Plaid Cymru became caught up in the parliamentary system. The gradualism that this dictated was far from alien to the party's leaders who, if they stopped to analyze it, felt they were merely facing up to reality. So the details of the devolution settlement contained in the 1978 Wales Act were irrelevant: as long as what was on offer applied to the whole of Wales and differentiated the country to some extent from England, it was acceptable as a step in the right direction. More than this, the assembly proposals were undoubtedly a logical extension of the institutional definition of Wales that had been gaining momentum throughout the century.

There were two flaws in this approach, however. First, the development of bureaucratic institutions at the Welsh level was still in its infancy. The process had not gone far enough to establish the consciousness amongst the people of Wales that would have allowed the qualitative leap that democratic control implied. It is not difficult to prescribe the conditions under which such a consciousness will materialize. What is needed is a fuller development of Welsh-based communications, especially television. This remains a key issue for the 1980s and partly explains the enthusiasm Plaid Cymru found for a campaign on the allocation of the fourth television channel to Welsh language programs in the wake of the referendum. Not only would this enable an integrated Welsh language service to be developed, but it would also clear the other channels so that the same could be undertaken for the English language in Wales.

The second flaw in the gradualist nationalist approach, a flaw that became only too evident during the referendum campaign, was the idea that progress toward self-determination could be achieved through the agency of an unwilling Unionist party. The main themes exploited by the antiassembly forces in the campaign were reflected in opinion polls that sought out the issues. A month before polling, of those who said they would be voting against the assembly, 23.5 percent believed it would involve extra cost, 19.1 percent thought it would create another tier of bureaucracy, 18.4 percent thought it would be a first step toward the break-up of the United Kingdom, 15.4 percent said it would cause uncertainty and damage the economy, and 4.6 percent believed it might result in Wales gaining benefits at the expense of other areas of Britain. At this stage Labour voters were evenly divided on their support of the assembly. Later they were to swing decisively against it. So it was highly significant that the sample as a whole was unclear where the Labour government, the Labour MPs, and the trade unions stood on the issue.[31]

They were right to be confused. Though the official line of the government and the party in Wales was in favor of the assembly, neither mounted an effective campaign. The government did not even distribute a leaflet explaining its policy as it had in the European Economic Community (EEC) referendum campaign. Moreover, a large proportion of the party's activists, from MPs downward, were actively campaigning against. Of the 23 Welsh Labour MPs, 12 supported the assembly, but no more than 6 of them were at all effective in the campaign. On the other side six "rebel" Labour MPs (labeled the "gang of six") campaigned vigorously against. After the result was declared, a leader of the "All-party Wales for the Assembly Campaign" (without which there would have been little organized support for the Assembly), Dai Francis, a Communist and former secretary to the South Wales Miners, accused the Labour Party of "organised sabotage."[32] The lack of any effective Labour organization in favor of the assembly in all but a handful of the 36 Welsh constituencies meant that virtually total responsibility for running the campaign on the ground fell on the Nationalists, who were often to be seen delivering Labour pro-assembly leaflets.

The underlying forces that surfaced so fiercely against the assembly in Wales were an unrestrained unleashing of Unionist reaction borne on a current of general antigovernment sentiment at a time of industrial unrest and economic insecurity. This last factor should not be underestimated. A wave of strikes in the public services that badly affected rubbish collection, threatened to close hospitals, and left the dead unburied in some areas bred widespread hostility toward the Labour Movement, which was ostensibly pressing for devolution. More importantly, it created an atmosphere inimical to appeals for reform. It is not the most favorable time to press for radical change when the popular press is calling hysterically for the declaration of a state of emergency. And, symbolically, many pro-assembly canvassers found themselves picking their ways to the doorsteps through piles of uncollected rubbish on one side and piles of snow on the other.

Similar circumstances, though probably not such widespread hostility in the Labour Movement, applied in Scotland where the "Yes Campaign" nevertheless managed to secure a narrow majority. What accounted for the difference? A brief analysis of the reasons, which for convenience are summarized under five headings, reveals much about the Welsh condition.

English Penetration

The Welsh and English economies are far more interfused than are the English and Scottish. The major Welsh road and rail systems run east-west out of England. Welsh industry is overwhelmingly controlled from outside, to a greater extent than in Scotland. A Welsh-Council commissioned report, published in 1973, found that a majority of Welsh firms of all sizes were controlled from outside. Of those employing between 500 and 1,000 people, 78 were controlled from outside Wales and 16 inside Wales; of those employing more than 1,000 people, 42 were controlled from outside and only 7 inside.[33] Coupled with these factors have been bigger migration movements in and out of Wales, so that some 18 percent of Wales' 2.8 million population was born outside the country.

Media

Compared with Scotland there is nothing approaching a locally based media in Wales. Many people in southeast and northeast Wales, the most highly populated parts of the country, tune their television sets to English transmitters, largely because of the Welsh-language content of the broadcasts from Welsh stations.

Newspaper readership figures are difficult to gauge, but, at most, no more than 25 percent of the Welsh working class reads a daily newspaper originating in Wales. One estimate has put the circulation of Welsh daily newspapers at 386,000, compared with a circulation of 704,000 for London daily newspapers in Wales.[34] In Scotland, on the other hand, there are several mass circulation Scottish dailies and also a popular Sunday newspaper. The treatment of Welsh issues in the London papers that reach the large majority of Welsh readers is minimal. The two most popular, *The Sun* and the *Daily Mirror*, both tabloids, managed to underplay the devolution issue while trivializing and sensationalizing it. *The Sun*, on February 8th during the referendum campaign, ran a center-page spread that presented a cartoon depicting a manic, kilted Scotsman and an equally wild Welsh woman in national costume sawing the figure of Brittania in half. The spread, headlined "Disunited Kingdom: Danger Ahead," was written by the paper's political correspondent, who concluded his article thus, "If the Assemblies are a success the break-up of the U.K. will be on its way. If they are a flop we are stuck with one more cumbersome heap of bureaucracy." The first devolution item during the referendum campaign in the *Daily Mirror* was on the eve of poll. It consisted of an exceedingly brief news report predicting the rejection of the assembly proposals in Wales. The report was relegated to the corner of page seven, which was dominated by a picture of two topless girls, one Scottish, the other Welsh.

Linguistic

The impact of the Welsh language on the referendum, indeed on political attitudes generally, is difficult to assess, but any subjective analysis must give it a profound role. The language has been lost to the majority of Welsh people in two short generations, with incalculable psychological implications so far as suppressed guilt feelings are concerned. This can result in irrational responses occasionally bordering on the psychotic. During the referendum campaign itself, there was an unspoken agreement between the contending sides to avoid exploiting such a divisive issue. But the subsoil had been unscrupulously tilled in the years leading up to the campaign. For example, in a typical speech in the autumn of 1978, Leo Abse, Labour MP for Pontypool, gave vent to the following:

> The way is being prepared to ensure that only the Welsh speakers will be able to rise to the top in the huge Civil Service that devolution would bring. The referendum will give the opportunity to English-speaking Welshmen to cry halt to these maneuvres and the attempt to make the English-speaking Welshman an exile in his own land. The Nationalists, by insisting on Welsh being spoken in the Assembly, will ensure the creation of a Welsh-speaking bureaucratic elite who will attempt to impose a false homogeneity upon our marvellously various Wales.[35]

Any rational assessment would question the ability of the 20 percent minority of Welsh speakers to impose their wishes on the majority (rather, the reverse). But there is no doubt that language played an important role in the referendum. The opinion polls did not register the factor, but neither did they probe it. In a very real sense, opinion polls only tell what people think they ought to say and certainly not what they might be ashamed of saying. Significantly, the referendum question that faced the people of Wales in the voting booths on March 1, 1979—"Do you want the provisions of the Wales Act 1978 to be put into effect?"—was printed in both English and Welsh.

Citizenship

A great deal has been made in this chapter of the development of Welsh institutions during the twentieth century. Despite their importance, they have yet to be consolidated into Welsh life. The point is made by contrast with Scotland. Much of Scottish national consciousness is based on the survival since 1707 of an interlocking institutional framework, in particular the separate Scottish legal system and Kirk. Moreover, institutions such as the Scottish Office and Scottish TUC have a longer history than their counterparts in Wales, which have only recently been created. As a result, Welsh loyalties tend to be more regional, within Wales, than applies in Scotland. In turn, this has limited the development of a sense of Welsh citizenship—a concept very much bound up with institutions—and the sense of responsibility that goes with it.

Nationalist Support

The previous four factors go a long way to explain why, in the October 1974 General Election, Plaid Cymru was only able to win 10.8 percent of the Welsh vote, compared with the Scottish National Party's 30.4 percent. In turn, these varying levels of nationalist support were directly reflected in the referendum results in both countries. It is impossible to assess the strength of support for the Welsh Assembly on a parliamentary consti- tuency basis since the results were given county by county. But observers present at the count throughout Wales reported that support was greatest wherever Plaid Cymru had made an impact, either at parliamentary or local government levels.

Because of their fear of being identified with nationalism, Labour prodevolutionists confined the advocacy of their case during the years running up to the referendum campaign to the intellectually satisfying, but emotionally arid, democratic argument. But it was highly significant that the pressure of the campaign itself pushed them to make an economic case for an assembly, a case that, had it been argued from the start (in the 1960s) and pressed consistently, might have spelled success for the devolution cause.[36] However, this case implied a fundamental criticism of the central Labour government's ability to tackle Wales' economic problems and so was difficult for Labour Party people in Wales to make. Moreover, the case was intruding directly on Nationalist ground and so was highly dangerous—indeed, potentially divisive, of the Labour Party in Wales. Thus it is of some importance that, albeit near the end of the referendum campaign, the official Labour Party, Wales, Pro-Assembly Campaign began advancing the claim that an assembly would result in economic benefits for Wales: 1) by wielding greater political "clout" on behalf of Wales to ensure fairer (by definition, more) allocation of resources from the center for economic development, housing, education, and health services, and 2) by mobilizing the political will within Wales to improve economic planning and coordination through the machinery already set up, making it more aggressive and adventurous in planning, capital formation, and job creation. Prodevolutionists had the Welsh Development Agency, which would have been responsible to the assembly, particularly as the machinery through which nationally inspired energy could be channeled.

These declarations, vehemently disputed by opponents of the assembly within Labour's ranks, only came in the closing weeks of the campaign—too late to have any impact on the result. But their long-term implications for Welsh politics may be profound, since they were a major concession to the Nationalist case. Equally important, the accumulation of institutions at the Welsh level, however embryonic, still points toward the need for democratic control. As one observer of Welsh nationalism put it following the referendum:

> The Welsh Office, the Welsh Development Agency and the Wales TUC are perhaps the most important of the many institutions that continue to provide both the arena and, to some extent, the protagonists in the struggle. Pro-Assembly people who, in the aftermath of the Refer- endum, stated that the issue would not die simply as a consequence of the Referendum results were criticised in some quarters for being poor losers. In fact, they were not declaiming their own unwillingness to drop the issue (most, probably, will do so) as much as they were acknow- ledging the large degree of devolution that already exists. It is recog- nised, given the nature of bureaucracies, that such devolution is practically irreversible, and that these devolved institutions continue to provide a stimulus for ever more devolution. (It is noteworthy that even anti-Assembly people frequently declared themselves in favour of devolution.) Thus, the need for some sort of accountability to the Welsh people by the institutions that regulate so many facets of their lives will persist. The loss of the Assembly means, most probably, that the Labour Party has lost an initiative in the struggle to bring this decision-making under Welsh control. The most likely candidate to assume such an initiative at present would seem to be Plaid Cymru.[37]

END OF THE WELSH METAPHOR

As Wales enters the 1980s, the metaphor of it as a nonconformist, radical, one-class single-party society, complete with a Welsh veneered collaborating elite working at long-range in London, is rapidly becoming untenable.[38] Together the referendum and General Election in 1979 accelerated the disintegration of this most favored Welsh myth. In its place is the prospect of a prolonged period of fragmentation, polarization, and instability in Welsh politics. Outside events will, of course, play a part in determining the outcome: the continuing British economic decline, the path of European integration, Irish politics, the developing situation in Scotland, the expression of English as English consciousness in a variety of forms. All these, and more, will react with events in Wales. But it is in Wales that the main drama will occur.

Since the industrial revolution, the nationality of Wales has been prevented from developing into widespread nationalism by the remarkable achievement of, first, the Liberal party and, then, the Labour Party in smothering conflict and locking the country firmly into the British system. The period of Liberal supremacy climaxed with the party winning 29 out of 35 Welsh seats in the 1906 General Election. There ensued a rapid decline, but Labour moved rapidly to fill the vacuum, and its success story culminated in the 1966 General Election in which it won 32 out of 36 Welsh seats. In this sense, both the Liberal and Labour parties have been major centralizing forces in the British political system, fully engaging Wales and, to a lesser but vitally important extent, Scotland in mainstream British politics. They have done so only at the expense of differentiating the two countries and, particularly, Wales by their sheer predominance. But that was necessary to contain any internal conflict that might have developed between the metropolitan industrial enclaves and the more rural hinterlands.

By the 1980s, however, the social background that enabled the Liberal and Labour parties to emerge in the way they did in Wales has largely disappeared. The nonconformist ethos, an essential strand in the development of both parties in Wales, is by now vestigial. More important, the special economic conditions of Wales, of an economy based on agricultural, coal, and steel production, has, as we have seen, largely broken up. (In political terms, it is noteworthy that the last miners' MP from Wales retired prior to the February 1974 general election.) Nation- alism has soaked up whatever radical input the Welsh language injected into the Liberal and Labour parties. In short, the conditions that provided the foundation for the metaphor of Welsh/British incorporating radicalism had largely disappeared by the beginning of the 1980s. Wales had modernized and Welsh politics were beginning to catch up.

Even before the 1979 General Election, it was possible to discern the emerging landscape. The election merely brought it into sharper focus. Labour had already retreated from its 1966 hegemony of 32 MPs (out of 36) to winning only 23 at the October 1974 General Election, with its share of the Welsh vote dropping from 60.4 percent to 49.5 percent. Excluding the uncontested Cardiff West seat of the speaker of the House of Commons (which must be vulnerable in any case), following the election Labour had 21 seats and 46.9 percent of the Welsh vote. As Labour retreats into its southeast Wales valleys stronghold, the potential for further rapid erosion of its position decreases. But it does stand to lose

Swansea West, Cardiff West (once the speaker, George Thomas, goes), Flint East in northeast Wales, and a Gwent seat if the Boundary Commission decide to merge Bedwellty and Abertillery and compensate by giving Newport a second seat that the Conservatives would be likely to pick up.

This would leave Labour with a core of perhaps 17 or 18 seats by the mid-1980s and its Welsh strength nearly halved in 20 years. By then, even these remaining seats may be looking vulnerable if the towering Labour majorities in the valleys are pared by the development of multiparty politics, with the Conservatives, Plaid Cymru, and possibly the Liberals all polling a significant share of the vote. In this event, the multiparty politics of rural Wales, which has already undermined Labour's hold there, would have spread to industrial Wales as well. Certainly recent elections, and not least the 1979 Conservative surge in the valleys, point in this direction.

Since the early 1960s and until 1979, the Conservatives had been winning seats while their overall Welsh vote declined. In 1966 the party won 27.9 percent of the vote and three seats; in October 1974 only 23.9 percent of the vote, but eight seats. They had secured their grip on peripheral Wales most affected by English immigration and urban influences. For the rest of Wales, the appearance was of a continuing attachment to radicalism in the Lib/Lab mold. But it was only appearance. In 1979 the Conservatives demonstrated their capacity to intrude into the Welsh heartland with a vengeance and pushed their overall Welsh vote up to 32.2 percent, electing 11 MPs.

Though the Welsh Liberals (federated with the English and Scottish Liberal parties) had improved their performance from 6.3 percent of the Welsh vote in 1966 to 15.5 percent in October 1974, the 1979 election showed the party's fortunes to be crumbling. Its share of the poll dropped to 10.6 percent (electing only 1 MP), but, more importantly, the election campaign demonstrated the poverty of the Liberal's organization and policies in Wales. In most constituencies the party only has a scratch organization, brought to life for elections, and in others the organization is in disarray because of feuds and splits. In wide stretches of Wales the inheritance of Liberalism has been Conservatism.

The future of Welsh politics hinges around the development of Plaid Cymru. The loss of Carmarthen and the fall in overall support to 8.1 percent of the Welsh vote in 1979 may only be temporary, but there is no doubt that its stronghold—where it has elected 2 MPs and managed to displace Labour almost completely as the radical force—is Gwynedd in northwest Wales. The challenge it faces in the 1980s is to begin performing the same exercise in southeast Wales from a position where it has now been forced into third place electorally behind the Conservatives. But Plaid Cymru's strength, in contrast for example to the Liberals, is that it has a tradition and commitment to fighting at the local level. The probability is that henceforth it will concentrate in this area. The events of 1979 should force Plaid Cymru to shift its center of gravity, both in terms of organization and policy, toward the southeast.

All this is likely to create a three-party pattern in many of Labour's southern Wales strongholds as the 1980s draw to a close, with the vote shared among Labour, Conservatives, and Plaid Cymru. Politics would then become confrontational on class and national lines in constituencies that have not experienced a real political battle for generations. Labour and Plaid Cymru would compete for the radical vote against a strengthening Conservative tide.

The first point to note about this scenario is that it involves a fundamental break with the whole tradition of Welsh electoral politics since the 1880s. Labour is in decline, but there is no clear successor to take over the role of centralizing Wales into the British political system. The Conservatives would like to assume the responsibility, but they are likely to be frustrated by Plaid Cymru.

The second point to consider is the resources of the contemporary Labour Party in Wales. Its main attribute is its control of the major power centers, particularly in local government, with all the patronage that that entails. But it is an aging party with a poor organization that is not used to fighting battles against strong opposition. Its local government power is being eroded by the Conservatives, Plaid Cymru, and independent groups such as the Ratepayers. The more thoughtful members of the party believed the Welsh Assembly provided its main hope for rejuvenation since it would have been forced to set up new machinery to fight the assembly elections and, equally important, to develop new policy-making initiatives at the Welsh level. Some moves had been made in the latter direction through increased importance of the party's Welsh executive committee and annual conference in the preparation of the devolution policy itself. But the referendum results discredited that policy (in immediate political terms) and, in so doing, weakened these progressive arms of Labour in Wales, both in the eyes of the party centrally in London and in the Welsh constituency organization.

Finally, the fulfillment of the scenario suggested will depend on the way Plaid Cymru exploits its opportunity. There is a strong argument to indicate that the support so far achieved by Plaid Cymru is somewhere near its maximum because of the constraints placed on it by linguistic and class factors. The problem of language for a party like Plaid Cymru is clear enough. Its response is likely to be an increased effort at identification with English-speaking Wales by concentration on social issues and by allowing militancy on the language question to pass even more into the separate but related hands of Cymdeithas yr Iaith Gymraeg, the militant

Welsh Language Society. Interestingly enough, the referendum result may ease this shift since it effectively removed short-term inhibitions on the Society's activities. Shortly after the referendum result was declared, one of the Society's leaders, Rhodri Williams, just released from a six-month prison sentence for damaging television installations, commented:

> The referendum result will have a significant bearing on future language society policy. Personally, I see our policies moving towards the intensification of our campaign on a broader spectrum... In the past we have had pressure on us to keep quiet during election campaigns, during the referendum too, asked not to rock the boat, not to threaten the chances of those trying to bring about change through the ballot box. I don't think we'll see that kind of pressure being brought again.[39]

Following the 1979 referendum and General Election, Plaid Cymru became involved in organizing a campaign of protest against the new Conservative government's decision to renege on a commitment to establish the new fourth television channel in Wales for mainly Welsh language broadcasts. Instead, the new government cynically resolved to split Welsh language broadcasting between the new commercial fourth channel and BBC 2. The nationalist response was to organize a widespread campaign of refusal to pay television licenses until the commitment to establish an integrated Welsh language service on one channel was made to ensure balanced and peak-hour programming was reinstated. This activity on behalf of an objective so clearly related to the Welsh language might seem to contradict the judgment that Plaid Cymru will tend in the future to place less emphasis on the linguistic issue in favor of concerns more central to English-speaking Wales.

However, the fourth television channel question is more central to Welsh political development than its connection with the language might suggest. To begin with, it presents a classic example of the way troublesome Welsh issues are handled by the central government. Demands for an improved television service for Wales as a whole had been made since the 1960s; the English-speaking population was just as affected as Welsh speakers, since Welsh language programs would displace programs in the English language on the main channels. In the early 1970s a broad consensus across party lines developed in Wales in favor of allocating the fourth channel to the Welsh language as the best solution to a profoundly complex problem. Numerous reports set up by the government came to the same conclusion, but each year there were delays because of financal constraints, so it was asserted. Meanwhile, in Wales, the campaign intensified with many members of Cymdeithas yr Iaith Gymraeg serving prison sentences for taking direct action on the issue. Finally, in the 1979 General Election, both Labour and Conservative parties committed themselves to setting up the fourth channel for a Welsh language service by 1982. The Conservatives won the election and, within a matter of months, began to dilute the commitment. Plaid Cymru had no choice but to respond. Moreover, the party's leadership has increasingly come to the view that, on a whole range of issues, the main obstacle in their making a successful appeal to the Welsh people is the lack of a properly integrated Welsh media operating in a Welsh context. In this sense, the fourth television channel campaign strikes at the root of the problem. As a resolution approved by the Plaid Cymru inspired National Broadcasting Conference held in Aberystwyth in late 1979 put it:

> We refuse to live in a mass society forced to accept messages produced by someone else, in a direct language or culture belonging to someone else. We declare once more that the campaign for a Welsh and Welsh-language television service is part of a wider popular fight for the right to communicate with each other on the mass media.[40]

The class issue is, in many ways, one of greater complexity than the linguistic issue for Plaid Cymru. A Marxist, who in late 1979 left the ranks of Plaid Cymru to help found the Welsh Socialist Republican Movement, Gareth Miles, has expressed the problem in the following terms:

> As the British Empire crumbled in the post-war years, and as England declined in political and economic importance, there was a growth of national consciousness among the Welsh petty-bourgeoisie and working class, which is reflected in the increased electoral support for Plaid Cymru in the past decade and in the limited though significant achievements of Cymdeithas yr Iaith Gymraeg and other movements seeking to promote the use and development of the Welsh language in education and public life.
> It does not, however, seem likely that Plaid Cymru will succeed in transforming itself into a dynamic mass movement in the near future, since mainstream Welsh Nationalism is still thoroughly petty-bourgeois in outlook and philosophy and too inhibited by its origins and history from taking the decisive left- or rightward turn which would seem necessary if it is to achieve the much longed-for "break-through."[41]

But two factors are likely to combine to force Plaid Cymru to change its orientation more quickly than Miles' suggests. The first was the experience of the referendum itself, which dealt a severe blow to those in the party who advocated gradualism and a generally conservative approach to constitutional change. For the immediate future at least, the referendum result decisively blocked gradual moves toward greater self-determination within the British state system. This should encourage those elements in Plaid Cymru who seek more radical methods with less emphasis on parliamentary politics.

There was a sense in which, deep down, the leadership of Plaid Cymru in the 1960s and 1970s did not believe that the anglicized Welsh working class was capable of expressing itself in Welsh national terms. Because of this, it may have been deluding itself, as much as the centralist socialists in the Labour Party, into thinking that change can be effected from the top downward—in this case by a Welsh-speaking nonconformist petty-bourgeoisie imposing its values on the English-speaking majority in Wales. The referendum result gave a lever to the growing, mostly younger, and generally left-orientated elements in the party who had long been pressing for greater effort in the anglicized working-class areas of Wales. Too much should not be made of this since Plaid Cymru had been steadily, if slowly, moving in that direction since the 1960s. Nevertheless, the referendum result added momentum to the shift.

The second factor likely to aid the further movement of the party in this direction is the worsening economic outlook for Wales. On the day of the referendum result came the news of another 2,000 redundancies in the Welsh steel industry, amid accusations that the announcement had been delayed until after the poll. But that was only the beginning. By early 1980 an employment crisis in the Welsh steel and coal industries of immense proportions was looming. The British Steel Corporation announced its intention of drastically slimming down Wales' two major steel plants at Port Talbot and Llanwern with the immediate loss of 11,000 jobs. The Wales TUC estimated that within three years 15,000 jobs would be lost in the Welsh steel industry; 15,000 jobs in the Welsh coal industry; and a further 21,000 jobs in related service industries: a total of 51,000 jobs lost on top of an existing unemployment level that averaged 85,000 through 1979. Set against planned cutbacks in public expenditure, particularly the reduction of regional assistance by a third in 1982, the Wales TUC predicted an unemployment level of 150,000 by the end of 1981, some 15 percent: "There is a very real danger that the BSC's proposals combined with government's doctrinaire refusal to intervene, will plunge the whole of industrial Wales into becoming an industrial wasteland."[42] Circumstances such as these are likely to move Plaid Cymru into a more aggressive left-wing posture, with a new emphasis on direct community and factory involvement.

So the referendum and General Election of 1979 precipitated an accelerated development of Welsh politics in the 1980s in a number of important and related areas: they assisted the growth of the Conservative Party, hastened the decline of the Labour Party from its previously hegemonic position, and encouraged the radicalization of Plaid Cymru. The combined result should be a destabilization of Welsh politics. There will be no obvious successor to the Liberal and Labour parties to pursue their role of firmly co-opting Wales into the British state system. The growth of the Conservative presence, at local and parliamentary levels, will increase the class polarization in Welsh politics. Injected into this will be the even more divisive national issue in the presence of Plaid Cymru.

If Plaid Cymru develops in a way to combine the class and national issues and take on the Conservatives as the major progressive force in Welsh politics, Wales will assume an instability within the United Kingdom that probably would have been prevented if the Welsh Assembly had gone ahead. In a very real sense, the assembly as presented in the 1979 referendum campaign stood for the survival of the old Welsh metaphor. The referendum signaled its end. This will be sad news for those, perhaps romantic, nationalists who sought to recover a Wales built in their own image, in which the deracinated mass society of industrial Wales would be leavened by the impulses from a healthier rural Wales. But for those who deal with realities rather than images, the referendum result should be welcomed as extinguishing such cozy projections. For such projections would have eliminated any possibility of a truly self-determined future for the greater number of the people of Wales.

NOTES

Note: Election statistics are based on "Parliamentary Elections 1959 to 1979," (Cardiff: The Labour Party Wales, Transport House, 1 Cathedral Road).

1. Gwyn A. Williams, "When Was Wales," (BBC Wales Annual Lecture, Cardiff, November 1979).

2. See Brinley Thomas, "Wales and the Atlantic Economy," in *The Welsh Economy, Studies in Expansion*, ed. Brinley Thomas (Cardiff: University of Wales Press, 1962), pp. 1–29.

3. W.L. Williams, *Cymru Fydd, Its Aims and Objects* (Cardiff: , 1894), p. 51.

4. See, for example, Ioan Bowen Rees, *The Welsh Political Tradition* (Cardiff: Plaid Cymru, 1962, republished 1975).

5. Unofficial Reform Committee, "The Miners' Next Step," in the *Rhondda* (London: Pluto Press, 1973, republished 1912 with an introduction by R. Merfyn Jones).

6. "Functions of the Secretary of State for Wales and Constitutional Changes in Wales," *Hansard*, Welsh Grand Committee, First Sitting, December 16, 1964, col. 10.

7. *Hansard*, February 3, 1975, p. 11.

8. "Facts to Beat Fantasies," Labour No Assembly manifesto, (Blackwood: Gwent, February 1979), p. 1.

9. Tom Nairn, *The Left Against Europe?* (London: Penguin, 1973), pp. 51–54.

10. Richard Rose, "The United Kingdom as a Multi-National State," in *Studies in British Politics* 3rd ed., ed. Richard Rose (London: Macmillan, 1976), p. 127.

11. Enoch Powell, speech at the Temple of Peace, Cardiff, February 2, 1979.

12. H. W. Fowler, *A Dictionary of Modern English Usage* 2nd ed. (New York: Oxford University Press, 1965), p. 139.

13. Daniel Jenkins, *The British, Their Identity and Their Religion* (London: SCM Press, 1975) p. 132.

14. R. Tudur Jones, "The Kiss of Death," *Planet* 30 (January 1976): 12. See also his *The Desire of Nations* (Landybie: Christopher Davies, 1974).

15. Michael Hechter, *Internal Colonialism: The Celtic Fringe in British National Development, 1536–1966*, (London: Routledge & Kegan Paul, 1975).

16. Gwynfor Evans, *A National Future for Wales* (Cardiff: Plaid Cymru, 51 Cathedral Road, 1975), p. 29. The quotation is taken from Hechter, *Internal Colonialism*, pp. 33–34.

17. See, for example, *Planet* 37/38 (May 1977), which contains the proceedings of a conference held in Aberystwyth during November 1976 on "Socialism and the National Question."

18. This point is also made by Charlotte H. Aull, "Nationalism After the Referendum," *Planet* 49/50 (January 1980): p. 22. See also her "Ethnic Nationalism in Wales—An Analysis of the Factors Governing the Politicization of Ethnic Identity," (Ph.D. dissertation, Duke University, 1978).

19. Hechter, *Internal Colonialism*, p. 215.

20. J. Barry Jones and Michael Keating, "The British Labour Party as a Centralising Force," (Studies in Public Policy No. 32, Center for Studies in Public Policy, University of Strathclyde, 1979), p. 38.

21. *The Times* of London, September 29, 1976.

22. *Welsh Digest of Statistics* (Welsh Office, HMSO Cardiff, published annually).

23. Hechter, *Internal Colonialism*, p. 265. Further discussion of the application of Hechter's theories to Wales can be found in Graham Day, "The Sociology of Wales—Issues and Prospects," *Sociological Review*, 27 (August 1979): p. 88, which raises similar questions to the ones put here.

24. For an analysis of the application of regional economic policy to Wales see John Osmond, "The Failure of British Regional Policy," in *Creative Conflict—The Politics of Welsh National Identity* (Cardiff: Collegiate Centre of Theology, University College, 1979), p. 94.

25. For a full account of this process see John Osmond, *The Centralist Enemy*, (Christopher Davies, Wales, Ltd., 1974), Chapter 2.

26. Hechter, *Internal Colonialism*, p. 310.

27. Williams, "When Was Wales," p. 46.

28. R. Tudur Jones, "Christian Nationalism" in *This Land and People: A Symposium on Christian and Welsh National Identity*, eds. Paul H. Ballard and D. Huw Jones (Cardiff: Collegiate Centre of Theology, University College, 1979) p. 94.

29. Kenneth O. Morgan, *Rebirth of a Nation: Wales 1880–1980* (Oxford: Oxford University Press, 1980).

30. There is by now a massive literature on Plaid Cymru. A usefully brief recent summary with further references can be found in Denis Balsom, "Plaid Cymru: the Welsh National Party," in *Multi-Party Britain*, ed. H.M. Drucker (London: Macmillan, 1979), p. 42.

31. *Western Mail*, February 10, 1979. For a full account of the opinion polling carried out and of the campaign generally, see J. Barry Jones and Robert A. Wilford, "The Welsh Veto: The Politics of the Devolution Campaign in Wales," (Studies in Public Policy No. 39, CSPP, University of Strathclyde, 1979).

32. *Western Mail*, March 3, 1979.

33. Cyril Tomkins and John Lovering, "Location, Size, Ownership and Control Tables for Welsh Industry," (Welsh Council sponsored report, HMSO Cardiff, 1973).

34. Jones and Wilford, *The Welsh Veto*, p. 45.

35. *Western Mail*, September 29, 1978.

36. See, for example, *Western Mail*, February 15, 1979. Also, "Referendum Study Papers," 1, 3, 5, and 6, Wales for the Assembly Campaign, (Cardiff: University of Wales Press, February 1979).

37. Charlotte H. Aull, "Nationalism After the Referendum," p. 70.

38. An earlier version of this section, "End of the Welsh Metaphor," appeared in *Planet* 48 (May 1979): p. 12.

39. *Western Mail*, March 27, 1979.

40. Resolution approved by the National Broadcasting Conference, Aberystwyth, October 13, 1979.

41. Gareth Miles, "A Half-Baked Nation," (Autumn 1978). Publication forthcoming in

Identity and Ideology: Socialism and Nationalism in Wales, eds. John Osmond, J. Barry Jones, and Peter Stead. See also Gareth Miles and Robert Griffiths, *Socialism for the Welsh People* (Cardiff: Arcade Y Faner Goch, 21 Howard Gardens, September 1979). In late 1979 and early 1980 a revived Mudiad Amdyffyn Cymru (Welsh Defense Movement) began destroying by fire a number of unoccupied holiday homes in rural Wales. At the time, a founder of this movement, who served a ten-year prison sentence following its activities in the late 1960s, John Jenkins, was quoted, "The choice before Wales in the 1980s is either to develop as a large English suburbia based on Cardiff or to develop as another Northern Ireland to achieve our demands." (*Sunday Times*, January 20, 1980).

42. "Save Steel—Save Pits—Save Wales" (Wales TUC campaign broadsheet, January 1980).

5

EUZKADI: BASQUE NATIONALISM IN SPAIN SINCE THE CIVIL WAR

Robert P. Clark

On October 25, 1979, voters in three of the four Basque Provinces of Spain—Alava, Guipúzcoa, and Vizcaya—went to the polls to vote on the proposed regional autonomy statute that, if approved, would grant them the rights of self-governance, which had been denied them since 1876. More than 832,000 voted in favor of the statute; a mere handful (47,000) voted against. Yet, about 620,000 (or 40 percent of the eligible electorate) abstained from voting, thus making the election an ambiguous expression of Basque nationalism. Did the abstainers stay away from the polls out of apathy, or because the proposed statute was too radical, or because it was not radical enough?

The mere fact that the Basques were casting ballots on this subject less than 4 years after General Franco's death, 40 years after the end of the Spanish Civil War, and more than 100 years after the end of the Second Carlist War that ended Basque regional autonomy made the referendum an event of transcendent importance, not only for newly democratic and industrially developed Spain, but also for all persons interested in the resurgence of ethnic nationalism in the industrial democracies of western Europe.[1]

Euzkadi, the name given to their homeland by Basque nationalists since the latter decades of the nineteenth century, stretches inland from the eastern end of the Bay of Biscay, following roughly the lines of the intersecting mountain chains, the Pyrenees and the Cantabrian.[2] The Basque Provinces of Spain and France occupy about 20,600 square kilometers, about the size of the state of New Jersey. On the French side of the border, in the three provinces of Labourd, Basse Navarre, and Soule, about 200,000 Basques live on about 3,000 square kilometers. Thus about 90 percent of the total Basque population and about 85 percent of the total Basque land area are concentrated on the Spanish side of the frontier.

BASQUE IDENTITY

The Basque region of Spain is made up of four provinces: Vizcaya and Guipúzcoa, situated on the littoral of the Bay of Biscay on the north slope of the Cantabrian Mountains; and Navarra and Alava, on the south slope of the mountains, where the land turns to gently rolling hills and eventually becomes the Ebro River Valley. The region as a whole contains about 17,600 square kilometers, about 3.5 percent of Spain's entire territory. Of this amount, Navarra accounts for about 10,400 square kilometers, about 59 percent of the total. The other three provinces range between 2,000 and 3,000 square kilometers each.

The ecology of the Basque homeland—coastline, mountains, and plains—has played a central role in determining the shape of Basque social, economic, and political life. To the north of the mountains, topography and climate combined to direct the people outward toward the sea, rather than south toward the interior of the Iberian Peninsula. A maritime culture, adventurous and daring, was the consequence. As the society developed, its south flank was protected from invaders by the rugged mountains of the Cantabrian range. The southern plains, in contrast, fostered the growth of a cattle and farming culture, one that looked inward both to Spain and to itself rather than outward to a world of commerce and exploration. At least for the last 1,000 years, this geographical division has broken the Basque region into two distinctive subregions, with the coastal provinces more ethnically Basque and less interested in contacts with Spain and the interior provinces more closely tied to the polity and economy of the rest of the peninsula. To this day, these differences persist and intrude sharply into the political calculations of both Basques and Spaniards. With the important exception of Navarra, however, the geographical definition of Basque ethnonationalism is clear and understood by most of the concerned parties. Whether Navarra should be included within an autonomous Basque region remains a serious point at issue between Basque nationalists and Spanish political leaders.

Moving beyond geography, our working definition of ethnic nationalism focuses on a commonly held historical and cultural tradition. The two principal questions to be asked here, then, are how many of the residents of the Basque Provinces consider themselves to be ethnic Basque, and what is the nature of the cultural and historical tradition to which they are heirs?

The first question is not an easy one to answer. To begin with, the Basque population, which in 1970 was about 2.3 million (about 7 percent of the population of Spain), is distributed in a highly unequal manner. Densely populated Vizcaya Province accounts for about 45 percent of the Basque population (1 million) and Guipúzcoa for about 27 percent (0.6 million). The sparsely populated interior provinces together are roughly equal to Guipúzcoa in population. Of the 500 or so independent townships (*municipios*) in the region, only 5 contain more than 100,000 people, but these five hold more than 40 percent of the total Basque population. At the other end of the spectrum, more than 70 percent of the townships contain fewer than 2,000 people, but they make up only about 8 percent of the total population. The overall weight of midsize towns or cities of betweeen 10,000 and 100,000 population is relatively slight. Indeed, much of Basque politics has turned on the struggle between the rural areas and small towns on the one hand and the major cities of Bilbao, San Sebastian, Vitoria, and Pamplona on the other.[3]

People of demonstrable Basque ethnicity are also distributed in an unequal fashion throughout the region. Since the 1950s, between 20,000 and 25,000 Spaniards on the average have migrated annually to the Basque region from other parts of Spain, so that today only about 65 percent of the Basque population is indigenous to its province of residence. In Navarra, where industrialization has proceeded much more slowly, about 80 percent of the population is native born; but in Alava, Vizcaya, and Guipúzcoa, the percentage of native born drops to about 60 percent.

Since genetically transmitted characteristics that set Basques apart, such as blood type or incidence of Rh negative factor in the blood, are too subtle and diffuse to identify Basques from non-Basques, language has become one of the most important distinguishing features of ethnicity. Language usage will be discussed later. I shall only mention here that speakers of the Basque language, Euskera, are also distributed highly unequally throughout the region. According to a recent study by Pedro de Yrizar,[4] about 19 percent of the total regional population can speak Euskera, although that percentage increases to nearly 30 if one considers only the indigenous population of the region. Usage of Euskera tends to be highly concentrated in Guipúzcoa (about 44 percent of the total population, 68 percent of the indigenous population) and Vizcaya (13 and 22 percent, respectively), with relatively few speakers in Navarra and Alava. In all, nearly 92 percent of all Euskera speakers live in either Vizcaya or Guipúzcoa. Usage of the Basque language tends to be concentrated in small towns and villages and declines sharply as one approaches the major cities and provincial capitals.

As we move from ethnic indicators such as language to more overt expressions of ethnic sentiment, one very valuable source of information

comes from a 1975 survey of several Spanish regions by Spanish sociologist Salustiano del Campo and his associates.[5] Del Campo found, for
example, that about 29 percent of his respondents from the Basque region
felt no identification at all with the region, about the same level of regional
"rootlessness" as evidenced in the two other areas of Spain that have
attracted great waves of migrants: Madrid (35 percent) and Cataluna (32
percent). It should be noted that del Campo's survey of the Basque region
included only Alava, Guipúzcoa, and Vizcaya and expressly excluded
Navarra. Among native born Basques, however, a plurality (40.7 percent)
named the Basque region as the most important focal point of their self-
identities, while Spain was a clear second place (31.6 percent). On a
somewhat different subject, more than half of the native born Basques in
the del Campo study applied very stringent criteria to whether a person
should be considered "Basque": 2.6 percent said he or she had to speak
Euskera, and 9.4 percent said that both criteria had to be satisfied. Finally,
53.5 percent of the native born Basques believed that the Basque region
was a persecuted and punished region by the Spanish government (in
contrast to only 16.3 percent in Cataluna).

One final measure of Basque nationalist sentiment can be found in
the returns of the four elections held in the region since General Franco's
death: the two parliamentary elections in 1977 and 1979, the municipal
elections of 1979, and the referendum on the autonomy statute of 1979.[6]
Basque nationalist voters were offered several options in the first three
elections. The more moderate Basque Nationalist Party (PNV or Partido
Nacionalista Vasco) captured the center of the ethnic political spectrum,
while the Basque socialist parties were arrayed through the left of the
spectrum, all the way to and including parties that were pro-Euzkadi ta
Askatasuna (Basque Homeland and Freedom or ETA). Combined, these
two forces in Basque politics won an increasing share of the total vote: in
1977, about 472,000 votes or 35.6 percent; in the 1979 parliamentary
elections, about 525,000 votes or 43.2 percent; and, in the municipal
elections, 659,000 votes or 55.3 percent. This latter election, by the way,
marked the first time that Basque nationalism had won a majority of the
votes in any election in the Basque region. Finally, in the autonomy statute
referendum later in the year, 832,000 voters cast their ballots in favor of
regional autonomy, about 60 percent of the eligible electorate and about
one-third of the total population of the region.

This brief excursion into the demographic and electoral data of the
Basque region suggests that, of the total population of the region,
somewhere between one-third and one-half feel Basque ethnicity to be
the primary source of their identity. When one recalls, however, that more
than one-third of the total population of the region is not native born, it

then becomes apparent that a sense of Basque ethnicity among *Basques* is much higher, aproaching perhaps 80 percent.

BASQUE HISTORICAL TRADITION

Cave paintings and other remnants of the civilization suggest that there were people living in what is now the Basque region as long ago as 20,000 B.C., although we cannot be certain that these people were indeed the ancestors of the present-day Basques. We do know, however, that there were Basques living in the area between 5,000 and 3,000 B.C., making the Basques one of Europe's truly ancient cultures. Until about the tenth century after Christ, however, the Basque area remained a relatively disorganized and violent region, dominated by small tribes of fierce mountain people who resisted encroachment by outsiders. First the Celts and then the Romans, the Visigoths, the Franks, and the Moslems came close to controlling the Basque tribes, but the area was mountainous, uninviting, and lacked obvious resources that would make conquest worthwhile. Thus, for the first 1,000 years or so of the Christian era, the Basque region remained a virtual backwater in the ebb and flow of the historical currents of the Iberian Peninsula.

This state of affairs was altered permanently by the rise of the Kingdom of Navarra in 905 A.D., an event that gave political and economic coherence to the Basque region and, for the first time, made it worth a struggle to retain this independence. Nevertheless, Navarra began to slide into disorder almost immediately after its first generation of leaders, and, little by little, the Basque Provinces fell under the sway of the emerging power in the peninsula, the Kingdom of Castilla. This process of disintegration and reintegration was fundamentally completed by 1512, when the border between Spain and France became permanent.

From this period (actually beginning in the twelfth century) until 1876, the relations between the Basque Provinces and the central government were carried on under the jurisdiction of the foral law system, wherein each province (and, indeed, each township) was granted substantial powers of self-governance by the reigning monarch. In the case of Vizcaya Province, the Spanish monarch could not assume authority over the Vizcayans until he had traveled to Guernica and had sworn fealty to the province before the famous oak tree of that city. Given the tensions between centralism and regionalism, there was no other way in which an emerging Spanish state could have managed its relations with the outlying areas except through the *fueros*.

In the 300-year period from 1512 to 1814, several major events shook the foundations of the Spanish state and altered forever its relations with the Basques. While the definitive changes would not come until the nineteenth century, the seeds of change were sown in the preceding three centuries. The first of these events was the discovery of the New World and the demands it placed on Spain for increased commerce, trade, and industry. In all this, the Basques were to play a key role. Their ports and their earlier history as sailors and adventurers placed them in a key position to lead the exploration and exploitation of the western hemisphere. The resultant economic prosperity produced a new economic class, a new bourgeoisie called *jauntxos* or "little lords," the first class in Basque society that had an explicit interest in ties with Spain. The second event was the French Revolution, which not only spread the ideas of the enlightenment to the Basque elite just across the border, but also interrupted the nascent Spanish liberal revolution at a key point in its development. As a result of these trends, there arose a crucial conflict of interest between centralism and regional rights, a conflict that would not be solved despite the more than 130 years of bloody internal struggles.

The long struggle between centralism and regionalism in Spain began with the adoption of the liberal centralizing Constitution of 1812 and continued unmitigated through to the promulgation of the Constitution of 1978, which allows for the establishment of regional autonomous communities. Along the way, the milestones of this struggle included the two Carlist Wars (1833–40 and 1873–76), the dictatorship of Primo de Rivera (1923–30), the fall of the monarchy and the creation of the Second Republic (1931–36), the Spanish Civil War (1936–39), and the dictatorship of Francisco Franco, which ended with his death in 1975.

The net effect of all these historical currents was to raise the importance of the Basque region in the industrial development of the rest of Spain. As a consequence, successive Spanish governments determined to override the ancient foral laws protecting the Basque region and to incorporate the region into the Spanish economic system. Not surprisingly, certain social and economic classes in the Basque region reacted negatively to these efforts, and the result was the spawning of the Basque nationalist movement in the 1890s. After about a generation of growth and development, Basque nationalism became the single most important political force in the region and was its dominant element during the turbulent years of the 1930s. The collapse of Spain into civil war in 1936 produced temporary regional autonomy for the Basques, but their defeat at the hands of the insurgent military forces of Franco and others (which included the infamous German bombing of the city of Guernica in April 1937) drove the Basque government into exile in France.[8] The combination of the bloodshed of the Civil War and the ferocious oppression of the Franco dictatorship made Basques even more aware of their ethnic heritage and bound them more tightly together as an underground political force. When the Franco years were over and Spain emerged to try democracy once again, the Basque nationalists were among the first to organize their political parties and to test their strength at the polls. The outcome of these tests will be detailed later.

ROLE OF LANGUAGE

Modern ethnic nationalisms place great stress on their attempt to save near-dead languages that have been assaulted by the dual enemies of political centralism and cultural homogenization. The Basques are no exception to this general pattern. Their distinctive language, Euskera, has been not only the rallying point for Basque nationalists since the 1890s, but also one of the first features of Basque culture to be attacked by Spanish governments in their attempts to incorporate the region by force into the life of the rest of the country.

While no one seems to know with any precision exactly how many people have spoken Euskera at any given moment in history, one conclusion can be drawn from a comparative analysis of various sources: in global terms, the number of Euskera-speaking persons has changed very little in the past 100 years, despite the fact that the population of the Basque provinces has grown several times over during the same period.[9] In 1860, out of a population of about 750,000, more than 50 percent (about 400,000) spoke Basque; by 1930, when the population had nearly doubled to 1,200,000, the Euskera-speaking population had grown but slightly, to 500,000 or about 41 percent. As noted earlier, in 1970, out of a population of about 2,300,000, the total of Basques speakers had declined slightly, to 455,000 or slightly less than 20 percent.

These changes in the use of Euskera over the past 100 years are the product of an interplay of two kinds of forces: purposive governmental policies designed to reduce the use of the language and impersonal social forces, such as industrialization, immigration, and modernization, that are less the outcome of human preference and more the blind workings of aggregate human populations in transition.

The policies of the Spanish government toward the Basque language can be divided into three phases since the end of the Civil War. From the fall of the Basque region to the insurgents in 1937 until the early 1950s, the policy was one of total suppression of the language.[10] Use of Euskera in public was illegal, as was the teaching of the language. Priests were denied the right to use the language in sermons, and all public documents, such as birth and marriage certificates, were altered to erase Basque names. No mass media were allowed to operate in Euskera, and the publication of books, magazines, and newspapers in Basque was prohibited. From the early 1950s onward, however, Spanish policy was gradually liberalized. After Vatican II permitted the use of the vernacular in Mass, Euskera was used for the religious ceremonies of the church. After 1968, the teaching of the language in Basque language schools (called *ikastolas*) was permitted, although not encouraged. Cultural works could be published in the language if the themes did not stray too far toward politics.

During the latter half of the 1970s, the newly democratic government of Spain has launched a new policy toward all regional languages. (Spain is, today, the second most populous multilingual state in the world, after the Soviet Union.) The 1978 Constitution makes regional languages "co-official" with Spanish in each language's respective region. In 1979, the Spanish Ministry of Education accepted responsibility for financial support for *ikastolas*, and instruction in Euskera was made obligatory in those areas (primarily Vizcaya and Guipúzcoa) where the language is still a functional medium of communication. In other areas, such as Alava and Navarra and some of the larger cities, language instruction will be optional and introduced gradually. The recently approved Basque autonomy statute gives to the regional government authority over language and education, however, so it is assumed that there will be increased official encouragement of residents of the Basque region to become functionally bilingual.

Despite these positive signs, the social pressures of modernization (immigration of non-Basques to the region, industrialization, urbanization) have combined to erode the use of Euskera. Within the region, migrants from small towns and rural areas to the larger industrial cities like Bilbao usually cast off their native tongue and adopt Spanish. By the time their second or third generations have grown to maturity, the language has practically disappeared from the family unit. In the small towns of Guipúzcoa and Vizcaya, it is not unusual to find 95 percent of the population either bilingual or monolingual in Euskera only. In the industrial suburbs of Bilbao, however, the situation is reversed and hardly anyone speaks Basque, even in the home. The large-scale migration of non-Basques into the region since the Civil War has certainly aggravated this trend. Even in the small towns and villages where the accepted language is Euskera, immigrants from the rest of Spain usually remain ignorant of the language. As the Basques enter their newly won autonomous status, one of their top priorities will certainly be to find ways to reverse these trends and to make Euskera a functioning medium in an industrial society.

It is frequently alleged that distinctive ethnic languages make symbolic ethnic politics easier by clearly drawing the line between "us" and "them." To illustrate the workings of this phenomenon in the Basque context, I have assembled some data on the relationship between the use of Basque and the voting strength of the Basque Nationalist Party in the three elections since Franco's death. These data are portrayed in Figure 5.1.

While the fit between Euskera speech and PNV vote is not a perfect one, the relationship still seems strongly supported: as the rate of Euskera usage declines, the share of the vote won by the PNV declines as well. Given this kind of finding, is it any wonder that Basque nationalists have striven so mightily to save their distinctive language or that the Spanish government might at one time have tried to suppress it out of existence?

BASQUE ROLE IN SPANISH ECONOMIC DEVELOPMENT

The Basque and Catalan cases have always confounded prevailing theories of the resurgence of ethnic nationalism in industrial states, since many of these theories are designed to explain ethnic reawakening in deprived or disadvantaged areas of prosperous and highly developed economies. Thus, for example, the theory of "Internal Colonialism" was advanced to explain ethnic nationalism in the Celtic fringe of Britain: Ireland, Scotland, and Wales.[11] According to this and other theories, ethnic nationalism is awakened by the obvious discrimination against a particular ethnically distinct region of a rich country, leaving the ethnic region poor, underdeveloped and deprived. What makes the Basque case so confusing is the relative wealth of the Basque Provinces compared with the rest of Spain. Since the industrial boom in Vizcaya following 1876, the Basque region has customarily been among the richest areas of Spain. With only 3.5 percent of Spain's territory, the Basque region contains from 10 percent to 15 percent of the country's energy, between one-quarter and one-third of its weapons industry, 17 percent of the nation's bank assets, about one-third of its ship yards and shipping lines, and two-thirds of its integrated steel mill capacity. In 1969, the provinces of Guipúzcoa, Vizcaya, and Alava ranked first, second, and third respectively in terms of per capita income, and Navarra ranked seventh (out of 50 provinces). Collectively, the 4 Basque Provinces rank first in per capita income among Spain's 14 economic regions.

Why, then, should Spain's richest region be precisely that region most desirous of separating from the larger state? One answer heard frequently has to do with the unequal impact of Spanish taxation and public spending in the Basque Provinces. From 1968 through 1973, for example, the Basque Provinces paid to Madrid in taxes an annual average of 22 billion pesetas more than the value of public services received by the region from the Spanish government, a sum equal to slightly more than 10 percent of the total annual regional income of the four provinces.[12] Moreover, the

FIGURE 5.1

Distribution of Vote to Basque Nationalist Party

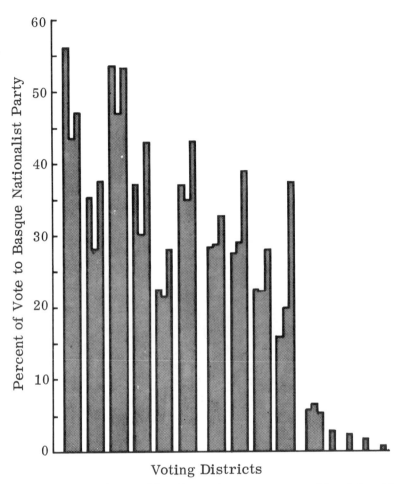

Note: The 15 voting districts of the 4 Basque Provinces are arranged from left to right in descending order according to the percent of their populations that speak Euskera. The three bar graphs portray for each voting district the percent of their votes won by the Basque Nationalist Party (PNV) in 1977 and in the two elections of 1979. The six voting districts to the left have Euskera usage rates above the mean, while the nine districts to the right have percentages of Basque speakers below the mean. I have separated Navarra from the other four low Basque-speaking districts because of the historically weak position of the PNV in Navarra. In the three elections in question, the PNV has not even presented candidates alone in Navarra, preferring to contest elections there in coalition with other parties. (The vote for the PNV in Navarra is depicted in the figure as my estimate of *their share* of the coalition vote. In any case, the vote percentages are so small as to be insignificant.)

Source: Compiled by the author.

argument continues, most of the funds spent by Spain in the Basque region went to pay for the instrumentalities of Spanish oppression: the parliamentary Guardia Civil and the police; the courts, prisons, and other institutions to maintain public order; the bureaucratic apparatus needed to maintain the Spanish presence in the region; and the public educational system that, according to Basque nationalists, was little more than a Spanish propaganda instrument.

Even granted the distorted emphasis of Spanish public spending on the administrative apparatus of a police state, I am inclined to look elsewhere for an explanation of the Basques' desire to free themselves from Spanish domination. Seldom taken into account are the very great benefits derived by some Basques by virtue of their access to the Spanish labor, capital, and trade markets. During the late 1960s, Vizcaya Province received a net inflow of funds from the rest of Spain amounting to between 3 billion and 4 billion pesetas annually, while Guipúzcoa received a net inflow of between 1.7 and 2.0 billion pesetas per year.[13] These funds flowed back into the Basque region essentially as return on Basque investments in the rest of Spain. Such net capital flows amounted to about 5 percent of the provincial income of Vizcaya and Guipúzcoa, thus offsetting considerably the disequilibrium in public taxation and expenditures. Furthermore, virtually every industrialized state experiences some degree of regional inequity in the flow of public funds. Absolute equality in taxation and spending would be not only impossible to achieve but probably undesirable in any state dedicated to some kind of income redistribution. It seems to me, rather, that the resurgence of Basque ethnic sentiment stems from the peculiar role Basque wealth has played in the economic development of Spain, and, most importantly, from the differential (and discriminatory) way in which this role has redounded to the economic benefit of a few Basques of the economic elite and to the economic disadvantage of, first, the Basque lesser bourgeoisie and, subsequently, the Basque working class. The following section is devoted to a summary of this explanation.[14]

In his analysis of ethnic nationalism in Britain's Celtic fringe, Hechter suggests that an awakening (or reawakening) of ethnic sentiment occurs in an industrializing country when the burdens of economic growth are distributed unequally and in such a way as to lead people to believe that they are discriminated against because of their cultural preferences (religion, language, and so forth). In this light, then, the first step in trying to unravel the confusion surrounding Basque ethnic nationalism is to observe that the revival of ethnic sentiment penetrated Basque society in a highly uneven manner. Different economic classes became caught up in renewed ethnic fervor according to the way in which they were involved in the industrialization effort, the differential impact of the burdens of

Spanish economic development, and the timing or sequence of policy choices in Madrid and elsewhere.

The argument is seen most clearly when one distinguishes between the first phase of Basque industrial development, between 1876 and the Civil War, and its second phase, from the beginning of the Franco period to the present.

Following the Second Carlist War in 1876, there took place a number of extremely important economic changes in the Basque Provinces. At the close of the war, the formal law system that had governed Basque-Madrid relations for centuries was definitively eliminated and with it a number of important obstacles to industrial and agrarian capitalism in the region. Under the terms of the foral law of Vizcaya, the export of iron ore had been prohibited. After 1876, Vizcayan ore became highly prized in Great Britain, not only because of its proximity but also because its low phosphorous content made it valuable for the newly discovered Bessemer process for manufacturing steel. British capital flooded into Vizcaya to exploit the iron ore deposits and to develop accompanying industries. In the 1860s, total iron ore production in Vizcaya was about a quarter of a million tons annually. In 1876, this figure doubled to almost a half million tons; in 1877, production doubled again to more than a million tons; and by 1899, Vizcaya was producing nearly six and a half million tons of ore annually, more than 80 percent for British markets. Of the 180 million tons of iron ore imported by Britain between 1874 and 1914, 130 million came from the Iberian Peninsula, nearly all of which came from Vizcaya.

Other economic developments occurred in the Basque region as a consequence of the derogation of the *fueros*. For centuries, customs duty-collection stations had been placed at the Ebro River between the Basque country and the rest of Spain, rather than at the Basque ports. During the eighteenth and nineteenth centuries, these collection stations were moved back and forth between the Ebro and the Bay of Biscay, depending on the strength of the government in Madrid. After 1876, the stations were moved for the last time from the Ebro to the ports, such as Bilbao and Pasajes, in Guipúzcoa. The effect on Basque society was twofold. Now shielded behind high Spanish tariffs and having access to the Spanish market, Basque industry could begin to expand production for a home market of some size. On the other hand, the Basque middle class and working class, accustomed to purchasing imported goods duty free, now had to pay higher prices for items brought from France, Britain, and the rest of Europe.

The third major development following 1876 had to do with the tax structure in the Basque Provinces. As a consequence of the abolition of the *fueros*, the Basques were henceforth required to pay an increased share of taxes to Madrid. Out of respect for the vestiges of regional sentiment, however, Spain agreed to negotiate the overall tax burden with each province, and the results were enshrined in an economic accord called the *concierto economico*. The *concierto* prescribed the overall level of taxes, but left to the provincial assemblies the task of collecting the sums agreed upon. The distribution of the tax burden under these agreements is revealing for what it tells about the allocation of political power in those days. The most heavily taxed items were farmland and livestock, which bore between 65 and 70 percent of the total tax burden. Highly regressive sales taxes on staple consumer items such as flour and salt accounted for from 10 to 12 percent. Industry's share of the tax load ranged between 5 and 7 percent. There was no tax on income or wealth.

The total effect of these changes on Basque society can hardly be exaggerated. As industry grew, floods of workers migrated from the fields and small towns of the Basque region to the major cities and, from the rest of Spain, to the Basque Provinces. All of the well known ills of early rampant industrialization—slum housing, sweat shop conditions, pollution, and so forth—began to afflict the Basque world. At the same time, a modified form of agrarian capitalism began to appear in the Basque countryside, adjusted to fit the reduced size of the tillable plots in the mountainous region. The small farms were absorbed into larger units, frequently owned by outsiders or absentee landlords. The departure of young workers from the farms and towns to the cities also disrupted traditional Basque family life. Finally, the advent of large scale capitalism in the Basque country began to separate the Basque bourgeoisie into two segments: the elite, who cooperated with Spanish politics and British capital for their own benefit and who turned their backs on their Basque ethnicity, and the lower middle class and professionals, who found themselves disadvantaged in the struggle over the benefits of industrial growth and who turned increasingly to their ethnic heritage for psychic comfort and political power.

The origins of the Basque nationalist movement can be understood only in this transitional class context.[15] There were, to summarize the preceding paragraphs, three groups of people who were forced to pay a high price for the industrialization of the Basque region: the lesser bourgeoisie and professionals lost out to their elite counterparts, who were willing and able to forge alliances with Spanish and British interests; the small farmers and townspeople saw their way of life disrupted by the advent of agrarian capitalism; and the Basque proletariat migrated to the urban slums to take low paying jobs under dangerous conditions, and its efforts to organize for self-defense were thwarted by the antilabor policies of the Spanish government and by competitive Spanish workers, who were unorganized and available to work under brutalizing conditions whenever the Basques downed tools and went out on strike.

POLITICAL MOBILIZATION

The Basque Nationalist Party, founded in 1895 by a Bilbao journalist named Sabino de Arana y Goiri, was (and is) the reflection of these class interests.[16] From its inception, the party has been middle class and bourgeois in its orientation and moderate in its policy proposals. In the beginning, the party relied for support on the lower middle class, small farmers, and the townspeople of Vizcaya and Guipúzcoa. Since this was a most religious constituency, the party was from the outset a confessional party with decided ties to the Roman Catholic Church. Only in the years since Franco's death has this relationship changed, with the party no longer espousing an official state-supported religion. Since its constituency was predominantly ethnically Basque and since the consequences of industrial development seemed to bear almost exclusively on those who retained their ethnic identity, the party was founded as an ethnic party, whose intention it was to unite across class lines all persons who shared this ethnic identity. Finally, since its constituency was predominantly Euskera speaking, the party made the Basque language the focal point of its political program and created most of the symbols that continue to represent Basque political and ethnic nationalism. These included the flag, the party motto ("Jaun Goikua eta Laggi Zarra" or "God and the Old Laws"), and even the very name of the new regional unit: Euzkadi.

Perhaps the most significant thing about the PNV in these early years was its relationship to the ethnic Basque labor movement. The Basque working class at the turn of the century and even until the post-Franco period had to make a political choice between class and ethnicity. During the last years of the nineteenth century, the Spanish unions had moved into the major industrial areas such as Bilbao and had organized the Spanish workers there, but Basque workers played little role in Spanish unions. Whether deliberately contrived or not, relationships between Basque and Spanish workers were strained, often to the breaking point. They were quartered in different zones, and industrial managers and their own leaders pitted them against one another as if their ethnic differences overrode their class similarities. On the other side of the coin, the only party that spoke for Basque was the PNV. Since it had developed nearly a generation ahead of the Basque labor movement (the first Basque union was formed in 1911) and since the PNV had a monopoly on the ethnic symbolism of Basque politics, Basque workers had little alternative but to be absorbed into the essentially middle class party. No party spoke for Basque wokers per se. As things turned out, Basque workers split fairly evenly, with a major segment joining the Spanish labor movement out of class interests and a significant portion (perhaps the largest single union) joining with the PNV and attempting to make it a broader and less bourgeois party.

Until the 1950s, the PNV was synonymous with Basque nationalist politics. Throughout the first third of the century, it was the only party to challenge the Spanish parties at the polls and gradually came to be the single most powerful party in the Basque region, although, even at its height in the 1930s, the PNV never won more than about one-third of the votes in the four provinces (more nearly half in Vizcaya and Guipúzcoa). The party was especially strong at the municipal level, and, during the 1930s, it controlled the vast majority of the town councils in Vizcaya and Guipúzcoa and somewhat fewer posts in Alava. When the region was granted its autonomy after the outbreak of the Civil War in October 1936, the PNV won control of the new autonomous government in the person of its president, José Antonio Aguirre. Throughout the Basques' long night in exile, the PNV and the government in Paris were the voice of Basque nationalism abroad and its organizational structure in the anti-Franco underground.

RADICALIZATION

Not all Basques agreed with the approach of the PNV, however. Too gradualist, too moderate, they said, and accused the party and the government of betraying the struggle or selling out to capitalism or to the United States. During the 1950s and early 1960s, other groups emerged to speak for Basque nationalism in a more radicalized and more class-conscious context. To understand this new development, the role of Basque wealth in the second phase of Spanish economic development, beginning with the rule of General Franco and extending beyond his death, must now be discussed.

Spain in the 1940s was, to put it simply, still an underdeveloped country. In 1942, the nation's per capita GNP was only about $340 and growing so slowly that it would reach $500 only in the mid-1950s. In 1940, more than 60 percent of Spain's work force was still employed in agriculture, and the country's agrarian sector had not yet experienced the capitalist revolution that must occur in order for industrialization to take place. In the 1950s, half of all Spanish farmland was concentrated in one percent of the holdings, the average size of which was about 50 hectares, while the other half was held in 99 percent of the holdings, the average size of which was less than half a hectare. The larger estates were exploited very inefficiently with an absentee landlord class and a peasantry only slightly removed from the living conditions of serfdom.

Whether General Franco actually wanted large scale industrial development or not, and the evidence is cloudy on this point, the fact remained that Spain could not regain its stature in the world of nations until it had gone through the arduous process of industrial growth so necessary to the maintenance of national power. Franco's problem, however, was that he rode at the head of a coalition of interests, individuals, and institutions that agreed upon little except their fear of what would happen to Spain if Franco failed in his effort to restore order and national unity. By no means was the coalition in accord on the need for, or desirability of, industrial development. Some coalition partners, such as the Falange, supported radical modernization that would inject Spanish state power into the industrializaton process. Others, such as the more moderate technocrats of the Catholic lay order Opus Dei, advocated a capitalist bourgeois reform of the country's archaic economy, leaving it open to the fresh winds of liberalism and competition. A few of the coalition members, such as the monarchists and the armed forces, were relatively indifferent to the issues of economic modernization so long as their particular interests remained unaffected. There were some coalition partners, however, such as the large landed aristocracy from the south, who opposed economic development and all of the changes it would bring with it.

In order to keep this coalition intact, Franco guided Spain through a series of economic and social changes that few, if any, industrial nations have been able to duplicate. In essence, Franco modernized the Spanish industrial economy while leaving intact the traditional, antimodern, and precapitalist structure of agrarian Spain. During the 1950s, the Spanish economy grew at the rate of 3.5 percent annually; during the 1960s, manufacturing grew at three times that rate. In the 1960s, Spain was the fastest growing economy in Europe and second only to Japan among the industrialized countries outside the Soviet bloc. By 1975, per capita GNP had risen to nearly $1,300. Nevertheless, the agrarian sector was still much the same as it had been in the nineteenth century: 3.5 percent of all owners possessed 61 percent of the land.

The Spanish government managed to accomplish this near-miracle in economic development by means of a two-pronged strategy. On the one hand, Spain was the fortunate recipient of huge quantities of foreign exchange that flowed into the country without any concomitant structural changes inside the country. The principal sources of this windfall were military and economic aid from the United States in return for the use of several bases on Spanish territory, a remarkable influx of tourists who flocked to "sunny Spain" in numbers that exceeded the nation's population in 1973, and the remittances of earnings of Spaniards who had gone to other European countries, particularly Germany, for jobs when they were scarce in Spain itself. The billions of dollars earned by the Spanish economy each year during the 1960s enabled the country to purchase abroad badly needed products, including food, without making many structural changes. The second prong of Franco's strategy was to shift the burden of development onto the two major sectors of Spanish society that were not represented in his governing coalition: the industrial proletariat throughout the country and the already industrialized regions of Euzkadi and Cataluna. The effect was to place a double burden on the Basque working class, both as workers and as Basques.

Spain's economic problems at the beginning of the Franco era were, in fact, two sides of the same coin: the relatively backward state of the economy generally and the high concentration of industrial wealth in a small fraction of the nation's territory. Spain's leaders believed that both problems had to be solved more or less concurrently. Wealth would not be distributed more equally until there was more of it to distribute; the overall level of economic production would not increase until the entire nation shared in the prosperity of the Basques and Catalans.

To deal with this problem, Spain's leaders considered two separate kinds of solutions. The first, the *globalista* approach, concentrated on increasing industrial production wherever and however that might be accomplished, without much concern for the geographic distribution of the industry. Those areas that already had an industrial base should be pushed to do more, even if that meant denying resources to the poor regions. In turn, workers from poor regions would be attracted to the industrial areas by the newly opened job opportunities, solving thereby the dual problems of insufficient labor in the north and restive unemployed workers in the south. The second policy, called the *regionalista* approach, reversed the priorities of the globalist strategy. The regionalists called for skewing public investment toward the poor regions to increase those areas' industrial potential, even if it meant denying resources to the Basques and Catalans. Public investment in social infrastructures (schools, hospitals, roads, housing, and so on) and in industrial parks would spur growth in formerly poor regions, and local workers could stay in their homes and still find jobs. Not surprisingly, the Spanish government chose elements of both policies, and thus encouraged both increased industrial production and employment in the already industrialized areas of the Basque region and Cataluna while simultaneously diverting public funds south and west into those regions that were still impoverished.

The effects of these dual policies were disastrous for the Basque workers. The globalist policy sought to squeeze more industrial production out of the Basque region and attracted thousands of Spanish workers into the region to compete with Basques for scarce employment. At the same time, the Basque region was denied the resources needed to deal with the ills of industrial growth: pollution, cramped housing, urban decay, pressures on schools and hospitals, and many others.

The consequence of all these factors was the radicalization of the Basque working class, who found itself oppressed not only because for being Basque but also because of class. This was an entirely new phenomenon in Basque and Spanish politics, and the traditional political organizations found themselves unable to respond to these interests. The PNV continued to focus its attention on political and cultural matters, while Spanish socialists and communists were unable to deal creatively with the demands of the restive Basques. Not surprisingly, then, the answer was to forge an entirely new political entity, the Basque socialist movement.

Basque socialism consists of two elements: the revolutionary armed insurgent force, Euzkadi ta Askatasuna (Basque Homeland and Freedom or ETA) and the several political parties that have contested elections in the Basque region since 1977, known collectively as the *abertzale* (Basque for Patriotic) left.

The history of ETA dates from 1952, when a small group of college students in Bilbao began to meet in a series of discussion sessions that today would be called "consciousness raising."[17] At first, their meetings represented primarily frustration at the inability or unwillingness of the PNV to wage a more active campaign against Spanish domination. Their agenda in these early days was study, discussion, and the formulation of a coherent ideology that would lead them into a more activist strategy. During the mid-1950s, the PNV, through its youth branch, attempted to bring the group of students, now called "Ekin," into the larger and more moderate body, but these efforts failed late in the decade, and, in 1959, the new group split off definitively to form Euzkadi ta Askatasuna.

ETA at the outset was neither violence-oriented nor particularly revolutionary. Its leaders described the movement as "patriotic, democratic, and nonconfessional." Prior to 1968, the organization devoted itself to building an organization, recruiting members, robbing banks to gain the funds to finance its operations, and numerous propaganda activities carried out entirely for effect, with little or no damage done to anyone. Spanish countermeasures were particularly harsh, with numerous detentions and members sent into exile. As a result of the pressures of clandestine activity and the natural kind of developments in the life of an underground movement, ETA became increasingly radical during the 1960s, both in regard to the use of violence and the ultimate aim of the organization. In addition to independence for the Basque region, the militants added a number of reforms leading to a revolutionary brand of socialism. Through the course of the 1960s, ETA experienced a number of internal struggles over ideology and over control of the organization. ETA-BERRI (new ETA) quarreled with, and eventually split from, ETA-ZARRA (old ETA); ETA-Sexta (named after the Sixth Assembly of the organization) split from the parent body, then known as ETA-Quinta (for the Fifth Assembly); and ETA-militar (military ETA) had differences of opinion with ETA-politico-militar (political-military ETA). There were numerous smaller schisms as well. As a general rule, the splits were over ideology (the degree or brand of socialism), alliances with Spanish groups of similar persuasion, or the use of violence in the struggle. The series of splits have kept the organization weakened and less effective than it would have been if it could have dedicated its energies to a single strategy against Spain.

The first death associated with ETA activity took place in 1968 when a young ETA member named Echebarrieta was killed by a member of the Guardia Civil when he refused to stop at a roadblock. In retaliation, ETA assassinated a hated police chief named Meliton Manzanas, whose killing led to the famous Burgos trial of 11 Basques in December 1970. From 1968 through 1973, ETA was charged by Spanish authorities with 8 killings, but the count rose steadily thereafter (36 in the two-year period 1974/1975 and 19 in 1976), dipped slightly in 1977 (to 11), but rose sharply once again in 1978 (at least 60) and again in 1979 (more than 100). In all, about 234 people had been killed by ETA by the end of 1979. A few of these killings were spectacular: the bombing of the automobile of the Spanish premier, Admiral Luis Carrero Blanco, in 1973; the daylight machine gunning of the president of the Provincial Legislature of Guipúzcoa, Juan de Araluce, in San Sebastian in 1976. I know of only one incident, however—the 1979 bombings of the Madrid airport and two railroad stations—in which ETA deliberately set explosives in crowded public places and caused the death of noncombatants. In the great majority of incidents, ETA went out of its way to protect noncombatants from harm.

The violence done by ETA can only be understood in the context of the institutionalized violence of the Spanish police state under General Franco. Spanish countermeasures against ETA consisted of the declaration of "states of exception" in order to suspend constitutional guarantees, the use of military courts martial to try civilians, and the detention and imprisonment of Basques for the expression of political dissent. From 1960 to 1977, a state of exception was declared to be in effect six times in the Basque Provinces for periods ranging from two to six months. One Spanish journalist estimated that as many as 8,500 Basques were affected by these measures through arrest, torture, imprisonment, or exile. During one such state of exception, in 1975, Amnesty International investigated charges of police state violations of human rights and found hundreds of cases of illegal detention, of imprisonment without notification of family or attorneys, and of brutal torture. Once placed under arrest, accused ETA members were tried by military rather than civilian courts and thus were denied the protection of constitutional guarantees of the accused. They were systematically denied right of cross examination and of confronting their accusers and witnesses, their confessions extracted under torture were admitted as evidence, and their attornies were harassed and denied access to evidence and witnesses. I know of not a single case in which an ETA member accused of an act of terrorism was tried by a civilian court and convicted. There were, of course, many ETA members imprisoned, and the Spanish prisons contained hundreds of Basques throughout the Franco period. From 1968 through 1975, the number of Basques arrested each year for political crimes never diped below 315 and rose as high as 862. During the Franco years, Basques constituted an estimated from 15 to 20 percent of all persons in prison for assassination, bank robbery, or terrorism. This despite the fact that residents of the Basque Provinces (including many non-Basques) account for only from 7 to 9 percent of all crimes in Spain (a percentage much more nearly in accord with the 6.9 percent of the total Spanish population living in the Basque Provinces). It was not without reason, then, that when Basques spoke of terrorism in the Franco years it was as likely to be the organized terror of the Spanish state as the more random and less violent terror of ETA.

Once Spain had passed out of the Franco period and parliamentary democracy began to function once again, Basque socialism began to assert itself as a new political force in the Basque Provinces. After political parties were allowed to organize, Basque socialists founded a number of small parties and labor unions, many of which passed out of existence for lack of support.[18] In the elections of 1977, these parties grouped together under the banner of an organization called the Basque Socialist Coordinating Council (KAS), which was composed of two labor unions and three socialist parties, including the politicomilitary wing of ETA. The ideology of the KAS consisted of intransigent opposition to any ties with Spain, advocacy of a union of all seven Basque provinces including the three in France, and a general social revolution in both France and Spain. The KAS contested the 1977 elections under the label Euzkadiko Ezkerra (EE) and won a little more than five percent of the total vote of the region and one seat in the Cortes. All *abertzale* socialist parties combined won about 11 percent of the vote in 1977.

By 1979, the range of the *abertzale* left had expanded, and a new party, Herri Batasuna (Popular Unity) had emerged even farther to the left and more intransigent than the KAS. In the 1979 parliamentary elections, all *abertzale* socialist parties combined won 21.0 percent of the vote, with Herri Batasuna (HB) receiving 13 percent and three seats in the Cortes, EE wining 6.3 percent and one seat, and the remainder distributed among a number of smaller parties. In the 1979 municipal elections, the *abertzale* left won 25.4 percent of the vote. HB won 11.1 percent in Navarra, 14.5 percent in Alava, 14.8 in Guipúzcoa, and 17.3 in Vizcaya. When one considers that HB is the electoral wing of an armed insurgent force (ETA) accused of terrorism by its opponents, it is easily concluded that the Basques may be one of the most radicalized ethnic minorities in any industrial democracy.

BASQUE NATIONALISM SINCE FRANCO

The four-year period from Franco's death in November 1975 to the Autonomy Statute referendum of October 1979 marked a historical turning point in Basque politics.[19] With Franco gone and Spain entering a period of renewed democratic activity, the Basques had to develop a new approach to politics and a new agenda of political issues. The political institutions and rhetoric that sustained them through the Franco years were clearly inappropriate for the new Spanish political order. Thus, ETA began to stretch its historical role to cover the post-Franco period, even while many moderate Basques condemned its increasingly violent activity. However, as is often the case in democracies, the political process succeeded in raising more issues for the Basques than it resolved. At the end of the four-year period, the Basques found themselves with a new regional autonomy, new democratic institutions, and a new degree of self-control over their own lives and destinies; but they also found themselves beset by a cluster of new problems for which they had had little experience or preparation. Thus, while the four years after Franco brought to a close one momentous era in Basque politics, it also heralded the beginning of another that would be equally demanding and equally significant for the quality of life in the Basque region.

One of the central themes of the post-Franco period was the ease and speed with which political mobilization occurred in the Basque region. After an enforced hiatus of more than a generation, many Spaniards awaited expectantly the beginning of open political competition to see what changes had taken place in the Basque country during the dictatorship and how these changes would affect the expression of Basque political preferences once elections were held.

The milestones in the dismantling of the dictatorship sped by with unexpected rapidity. The process of democratization began during the summer of 1976, when the King appointed Adolfo Suarez as the Spanish premier and gave him the task of guiding the country back to parliamentary procedures while maintaining order and unity. By December 1976, Spaniards went to the polls to vote in a referendum that sanctioned the democratization of the country's political institutions. Shortly thereafter, in early 1977, political parties were legalized and, immediately, more than 170 new parties sought recognition and began to prepare for the first parliamentary elections. Among these new parties was the PNV, which held its first convention in public since the Civil War in April 1977, in Pamplona. Other Basque parties from the socialist left also appeared and prepared to contest the elections. From this point forward, Basque voters were given four distinct alternatives at the polls, and the story of the three post-Franco elections is essentially the story of the rise and fall of these four political groupings.

After a somewhat shaky start in 1977, the moderate PNV had by 1979 regained its position as the single most powerful political party in the region. In 1977, the PNV won only 24.4 percent of the vote and 8 of the region's 26 seats in the Cortes, slightly behind the Spanish socialist party (PSOE) and slightly ahead of the Spanish center-right coalition (UCD). In the 1979 parliamentary contest, the PNV dropped to 22.2 percent of the vote, but still managed to win 8 of the region's 26 seats. By the 1979 municipal elections, the PNV had climbed to slightly less than 30 percent of the vote and won 1,054 of the 2,309 contested municipal council seats.

The second traditional bloc of voting strength in the Basque region, the Spanish left, began strong in 1977, but declined sharply as it failed to adjust to the new demands of Basque voters. In 1977, the PSOE won 25 percent of the vote and 9 seats in the Cortes, but the socialists' claim to be the major party in the Basque region lasted only until the 1979 elections. In 1979, PSOE dropped to 19.4 percent of the vote and 5 seats in the parliament, and to 16.1 percent and only 217 municipal seats in the second election.

The other traditional factor in Basque politics, the Spanish right parties, showed similar declines throughout the two-year period. In 1977, the governing UCD won 16.2 percent of the total Basque vote and 7 of the region's parliamentary seats. In addition, the neo-Francoist Alianza Popular won 3.7 percent and 1 seat. In the 1979 parliamentary elections, UCD's share of the vote rose to 20.4 percent and 8 seats in the Cortes, but, because of the decline of other rightist parties, the overall share of the vote given to conservative parties declined from 27.6 to 22.6 percent. The right fared even worse in the municipal elections a month later, declining to 16.6 percent of the total vote, with UCD receiving only 13.2 percent.

The real surprise in Basque politics was the emergence of the *abertzale* socialist parties, previously discussed. From a relatively modest 11 percent in 1977, the Basque nationalist left rose to 21 percent in the 1979 parliamentary elections and to more than 25 percent in the municipal elections. The result of this trend has been to split the vote of the Basque region into four almost equal groups: the Basque nationalist center and left and the Spanish center-right and left. One senses the inherent instability of such a distribution and should expect, therefore, considerable change over the next several years as Basque ethnicity and class consciousness vie for preeminence in the Basque political spectrum.

Whatever the future holds for politics in the Basque Provinces, the results of the three post-Franco elections are solid evidence of anti-Madrid sentiment in the region. If one considers the sum of Basque ethnic and Spanish left votes as expressing a generally negative attitude toward Premier Suarez and the Spanish governing party, it is worth noting that this sentiment consistently has captured about 70 percent of the Basque vote (71.6 percent in 1977, 69.6 and 76.7 in 1979). Whatever judgment history may make about Suarez' contributions to Spanish democracy, voters in the Basque region have made their opinions known loudly and clearly, and they are not favorable.

We cannot leave this chapter on contemporary Basque politics without some mention of the newly approved Autonomy Statute and what it may portend for politics in the Basque region and in Spain generally. The transition to Basque regional autonomy began officially on December 31, 1977, when the Spanish Minister for Regions announced that his government had decreed the granting of a "pre-autonomy" legal and administrative status to the Basque Provinces. By virtue of this decree, there was established a Basque General Council, whose tasks included the transfer of numerous administrative responsibilities from Madrid to local authorities as well as the development of a draft autonomy statute for eventual approval by the Spanish government. Almost exactly one year later, on December 29, 1978, only one day after the new Spanish Constitution was promulgated, the members of the Spanish parliament from the three Basque provinces of Alava, Guipúzcoa, and Vizcaya met in the historic Basque town of Guernica to approve the draft autonomy statute and voted to send it to Madrid immediately to begin the long process of ratification. Ten months after that vote, on October 25, 1979, the voters of the three provinces went to the polls to approve overwhelmingly the new statute. Throughout these procedures, Navarra remained apart from the regional union, with the option to participate, but unwilling to join in the new autonomous community for reasons that are at once historical, political, and economic.

The new Basque autonomy statute contains these central features:

a Basque parliament of twenty members, representing each province and freely elected by all eligible voters. The functions of the Parliament include approval of budgets and all legislation as well as the selection of the Basque president.

a Basque president who, once chosen by the parliament, will form his or her government or cabinet of councilors, which will constitute the executive branch of the government.

the judicial functions will be left to a superior tribunal of justice, whose composition and mode of selection are yet to be agreed upon.

the law enforcement authorities will be under Basque control, and

Spanish police and Guardia Civil troops will be withdrawn. With this move, one of the principal sources of friction will be eliminated.

the *conciertos economicos* will be reestablished for Vizcaya and Guipúzcoa, where they were derogated following the Civil War. The Basque government will be endowed with the necessary taxation and expenditure authority to raise its own funds and dispense them on public projects.

the Basque government will have exclusive authority over matters affecting social security, health, welfare, labor relations and working conditions, education, culture, media of communication, and environmental protection. The Spanish government will retain ultimate authority over international matters such as trade and customs duties, coinage of money, maintenance of armed forces, and so forth. Authority will be shared in such sensitive matters as the protection of Spanish citizens in the region and the maintenance of public order.

the Basque language will be the official language of the region and will share that distinction with Spanish. No citizen will be discriminated against for his or her failure to speak either of the two languages.

Navarra will have the right to vote on its entry into the autonomous community and will accomplish such a step by means of a vote first by the provincial legislature and then by a popular referendum.

It should not be forgotten that the provisions for autonomous communities in the new Spanish Constitution differ from federalism as it is practiced in the United States, more nearly resembling the practice of devolution as it is used in Great Britain. Accordingly, the principal difference seems to be that, unlike the case in the United States, the Basque regional autonomous community enjoys its status by grant of the Spanish government, and such status can be amended or even withdrawn by Madrid if the Spanish government determines such a step to be in the general interest.

With the approval of the Autonomy Statute and the election of the first Basque parliament scheduled for early 1980, the struggle for Basque autonomy will have come full circle. After more than a century of protest, political mobilization, civil war, and dictatorship, the Basques finally enjoy some measure of control over their own destinies. In company with the Catalans, the Basques have accomplished something quite rare in contemporary industrial democracies: the decentralization of power and administrative authority in a complex modern society. Since the independence of Ireland in 1921, only the French-speaking Quebecois in Canada have succeeded in similar accomplishments. In most other industrial democracies, the trend seems to be quite the opposite, as in Northern Ireland or the erosion of federalism in the United States. What all concerned parties must know, however, is that the real battle for Basque autonomy has only just begun. The new Basque government must now demonstrate that it can truly deal with the many problems that beset its society: high unemployment, scarce energy resources, environmental contamination among the worst in Europe, not enough schools, hospitals, or parks, cramped housing, decaying urban areas, and many others. Until now, these problems have been subordinated to the more dramatic goal of regional self-governance. That goal, the dream of Basque nationalists for 100 years, has been accomplished. Now Basques must decide for themselves how their hard-won freedom will be used.

NOTES

1. The general reader interested in reviewing Basque political history may begin with Stanley Payne, *Basque Nationalism* (Reno: University of Nevada Press, 1975). Since Payne's book ends in 1937, readers interested in a more contemporary treatment may consult my book, *The Basques: The Franco Years and Beyond* (Reno: University of Nevada Press, 1980), which ends with the events of 1978–79.

2. Jose Miguel de Azaola, *Vasconia y su Destino: I, La Regionalizacion de Espana* (Madrid: Revista de Occidente, 1972); the two books by Luis C.-Nunez Astrain, *Clases Sociales en Euskadi* (San Sebastian: Editorial Txertoa, 1977) and *La Sociedad Vasca Actual* (San Sebastian: Editorial Txertoa, 1977), are good places to begin a review of the social, economic, and geographic bases for politics in the Basque Provinces.

3. Talde Euskal Estudio Elkartea, *Euskadi, Ante las Elecciones Municipales* (San Sebastian: Ediciones Vascas, 1978), chap. 1.

4. Pedro de Yrizar, "Los Dialectors y Variedades de la Lengua Vasca: Estudio Linguistico-Demografico," *Separata del Boletin de la Real Sociedad Vascongada de los Amigos del Pais*, (1973).

5. Salustiano del Campo, Manuel Navarro, and Felix Tezanos, *La Cuestion Regional Espanola* (Madrid: Edicusa, 1977). The section on the Basque language is found on pp. 211–16.

6. Robert P. Clark, "Recent Voting Trends in Spain's Basque Provinces," (European Studies Conference, University of Nebraska at Omaha, October 12, 1979).

7. The following is derived from Payne, *Basque Nationalism*, and from the following works: William A. Douglass and Jon Bilbao, *Amerikanuak: Basques in the New World* (Reno: University of Nevada Press, 1975), chap. 1; Martin de Ugalde, *Sintesis de la Historia del Pais Vasco* (San Sebastian: Ediciones Vascas, 1977); Maximiano Garcia Venero, *Historia del Nacionalismo Vasco* 3rd ed. (Madrid: Editora Nacional, 1969).

8. Hugh Thomas, *The Spanish Civil War* (New York: Harper & Row, 1961); George L. Steer, *The Tree of Guernika: A Field Study of Modern War* (London: Hodder and Stoughton, 1938).

9. In addition to de Yrizar, "Los Dialectors," the following is based on these works: Milton M. da Silva, "Modernization and Ethnic Conflict: The Case of the Basques," *Comparative Politics* vol. 7.2 (January 1975): 227–51; Raymond and Françoise Mougeon, "Basque Language Survival in Rural Communities from the Pays Basque, France," in *Anglo-American Contributions to Basque Studies: Essays in Honor of Jon Bilbao*, ed. William A. Douglass, Richard W. Etualain, and William H. Jacobsen, Jr. (Desert Research Institute Publications on the Social Sciences, no. 13, 1977), pp. 107–15; Meic Stephens, *Linguistic Minorities in Western Europe* (Llandysul, Wales: Gomer Press, 1976), pp. 633–64.

10. Beltza, *El Nacionalismo Vasco en el Exilio, 1937–1960* (San Sebastian: Editorial Txertoa, 1977), pp. 133–36.

11. Michael Hechter, *Internal Colonialsm: The Celtic Fringe in British National Development, 1536–1966* (Berkeley and Los Angeles: University of California Press, 1975).

12. Charles W. McMillion, "Spain's Rapid Transition to Industrial Democracy: International Integration and Intra-national Disintegration," (American Political Science Association, Washington, D.C., 1979).

13. de Azaola, *Vasconia*, pp. 143, 549.

14. My analysis draws heavily from Beltza, *El Nacionalismo Vasco, 1876–1936* (San Sebastian: Editorial Txertoa, 1976) and Ortzi, *Los Vascos, Sintesis de su Historia* (San Sebastian: Hordago, 1978).

15. Joseph Harrison, "Big Business and the Rise of Basque Nationalism," *European Studies Review* 7 (1977): 371–91.

16. Jean-Claude Larronde, *El Nacionalismo Vasco: Su Origen y Su Ideologia en la Obra de Sabino Arana-Goiri*, trans. Lola Valverde, (San Sebastian: Ediciones Vascas, 1977).

17. Federico de Arteaga (pseud.), *ETA y el Proceso de Burgos* (Madrid: Editorial E. Aguado, 1971); Gisele Halimi, *El Proceso de Burgos*, trans. Mercedes Rivera, (Caracas: Monte Avile Editores, 1972); Kepa Salaberri, *El Proceso de Euzkadi en Burgos: El Sumarisimo 31/69* (Paris: Rudeo Iberico, 1971).

18. Alberto Perez Calvo, *Los Partidos Politicos en el Pais Vasco* (San Sebastian: Luis Haranburu Editor, 1977); Idoia Estornes Zubizarreta, *Que Son los Partidos Abertzales* (Zarauz: Itxaropena, 1977).

19. Robert P. Clark, "Basque Nationalism in Post-Franco Spain: A Progress Report," (International Studies Association, Toronto, Canada, 1979).

6

DIMENSIONS OF CATALAN NATIONALISM

Oriol Pi-Sunyer

> Existing political state boundaries often do not coincide with historical,
> economic or strategic boundaries. They never fully coincide with
> national boundaries: no state encompasses only one nation and no
> nation is wholly encompassed in one single state.[1]

Some years ago, I was discussing politics with a Castilian friend. As is
common when a Castilian and a Catalan talk about such matters, the
subject of Catalan nationalism soon arose. While we agreed on many issues
(Franco had been dead a few months and both of us hoped that
democracy would prosper), it was clear that my colleague did not really
understand many of the reasons or causes at the root of Catalan nationalist
sentiment. Only partly in jest, he said, "Catalonia must be one of the few
examples of a metropole wishing to secede from its hinterland."

Indeed, Catalonia does not satisfy many of the criteria that characterize a good number of ethnically distinct regions in other states or in
Spain itself. Most obviously, it is hardly a zone of poverty and underdevelopment. Industrialization dates back to the middle of the last
century, the rural sector is dominated by a true peasantry, and Barcelona is
a dynamic city of more than two million inhabitants. While there are very
real economic problems and weaknesses, we are not considering a Corsica
or a Galicia.

One is struck, nevertheless, by the many points of similarity between
Catalan nationalism and comparable movements in other parts of Europe
and beyond. These common features include responses to political and
administrative centralization, issues touching the survival of language and

culture, and questions of group identity in the contemporary world. On closer examination, we shall also learn that Catalans do not perceive themselves as being economically secure.

ETHNONATIONALISM IN THE WORLD OF NATION-STATES

The ethnic-linguistic resurgence in western Europe has occurred within the political boundaries of nation-states sharing traditions of centralized control dating to the age of absolutism. Typically, language has become the measure and symbol of ethnic assertiveness, hence the stress placed on minority language use as an indicator of the relative health of the ethnic community. Nationalist movements vary enormously in their formal political ideologies and the means utilized to achieve desired goals. Actually, to speak of a specific nationalist movement is a simplification, for generally there are different components and approaches encompassed in a given nationalist tradition. As one might expect, it is for the most part violent nationalist manifestations—such as those of ETA in the Basque country—that are reported by the media.

Given this variety of movements—from Welsh to Occitan, from Basque to Breton, some essentially rural, others with a strong urban component, some revolutionary, others reformist—what features do they share in common? And beyond this question, to what degree or in what respects do they reflect factors of structure having a wider dimension? Thus, in many different parts of the world, we find movements that have variously been termed "nationalistic," "liberational," and "fundamentalist." Given that these, in turn, also differ widely in composition and specific historical causality, may some of them be understood as responses to the same underlying causes that have given rise to Western ethnic nationalism?

Two observations are warranted at this juncture. The first has to do with a search for simplicity or, to paraphrase Occam's dictum, "of all explanations that fit, select the simplest." The second observation takes note of certain similarities in the relative positions, within their respective contexts, of Western and non-Western movements of ethnic and/or nationalist affirmation. Thus, the non-Western examples are encountered predominantly in the third world, while the Western ones manifest themselves in zones that may reasonably be termed an internal third world. I am not implying that the answer lies in simple economic determinism, but that one should consider the consequences of inequality, whether economic, political, or cultural.

A number of fundamental changes took place in Western society following World War II. These transformations were interrelated, but may be considered independently. They include:

the decline of old empires and the rise of new power centers;

an erosion in the prestige of many old nation-states;

the emergence of new forms of economic organization, in particular supranational corporations functioning beyond the range of state regulatory authority;

changes in the occupational composition of developed societies, specifically a relative decline in the industrial labor force (generally accompanied by a further reduction in rural occupations) and the growth of service sectors, both private and public;

new or increased expectations among working classes of the developed world and some blurring of traditional class markers;

a rising tempo of resource exploitation and some forms of industrialization, tourism in particular, in the European periphery; and

an unprecedented movement of contract and semipermanent labor from the European fringe lands to the developed cores.

What I am offering is a frame of reference that will permit us to study nationalist movements not as isolates but as political, economic, and cultural responses to broad structural changes. This approach combines theoretical insights derived from "world system" models, concepts of "internal colonialism" and "dependent development," and generalizations respecting the nature of "postindustrial" society.[2]

Within anthropology, I follow several "community outward" approaches that consider local-level phenomena in the light of higher-order political and economic structures.[3] The assumption is that efforts to polarize part and whole, micro and macro, state and community/region, "does violence to the nature of the dynamic relations between them."[4]

For essentially the same reasons, explanations of ethnic nationalism require that consideration of the broader system of supraregional processes that transcend the entity in question. Such an approach does not diminish the importance of solid ethnographic and historical investigation.

Paradoxically, Western society is undergoing a process of cultural homogenization at the same time that deep cleavages and antagonisms disturb civil life. Styles of dress and material culture have achieved a universal quality, at least superficially: people watch the same television programs, consume much the same food, and attend the same sports events. It is also true that many of the surface class and occupational indicators—the worker's cap, the tie and jacket of white-collar employment—have lost much of their significance. And almost everyone seems to own a car. This is obviously a very different world from that depicted in *The Road to Wigan Pier*, but a price has had to be paid, and it is not simply the ubiquitous presence of rock music and the spread of fast food franchises. Racism has emerged in the most unlikely places—it has been the cause of ugly incidents in such traditionally democratic societies as Holland and Sweden and has put into question the tolerance and fair play of police forces in Great Britain.

This situation impinges on ethnic nationalism at several points or levels. In a world of mass consumption and mass ideas, it becomes much harder to maintain cultural boundaries, hence, those features that remain different and have a high symbolic quality (such as language) become all the more important. Furthermore, this sameness does not solve many inequalities, but functions to make them less evident. Ethnic movements are thus not only a response to the historic claims of the state, but also an effort to restore a sense of human proportion, of community.

The fear of being overwhelmed is not simply a matter of language and culture, but also entails anxieties about physical survival. In the not too distant past, many peripheral regions managed in one way or another to retain a certain economic viability. Isolation itself sometimes helped to perpetuate archaic subsistence patterns finely atuned to environmental potentials and limitations. Many of these locations are now faced with spiraling land prices as farms are bought by rich urbanites and resort developments invade the coasts. Even regions of established industrialization, such as Catalonia, are faced with growing external competition and forms of development that increase dependence. I recently noted that,

> The increasingly closer integration of Catalonia into a market economy of continental dimensions has... worked to alter the economic balance: from a developed zone within the Spanish economy, Catalonia is being transformed into an appendage of a much more powerful system.[5]

The play of these global and continental forces makes itself felt on societies and communities that have long formed part of state political orders. The state is the original hegemonic force, and the West is the cradle of modern centralization. The political systems that emerged in postmedieval Europe differed in detail, but shared a similar ethos. At the level of the individual, universalist considerations were displaced by a new political morality emphasizing the primacy of the state and the duties of the subject to this entity. With respect to collectivities, including what we would now term nationalistes, pluralism and a diffusion of power gave way to uniformity and power concentration. The dream of monarchs was to govern without opposition. Thus, with respect to the Spanish situation, the process involved an attempt to Castilianize all of Iberian society or, to quote the memorandum penned by the Conde Duque de Olivares to his master Philip IV:

> The most important thing in your Majesty's Monarchy is for you to become king of Spain: by this, I mean, Sir, that Your Majesty should not be content with being king of Portugal, of Aragon, of Valencia and count of Barcelona, but should secretly plan and work to reduce these

kingdoms of which Spain is composed to the style and laws of Castile, with no difference whatsoever. And if Your Majesty achieves this, you will be the most powerful prince in the world.[6]

This master plan of 1624 did not prove easy to carry out. Portugal achieved its independence, and Catalonia was not reduced until almost a century later, in 1714 following a long military campaign. But, in other respects, the Olivares design is of a kind with others of the period. In different ways but in direct relation to the increasing power of the state, the European peripheries experienced the loss of their formal identity, whether political, legal, or administrative. Legal and political restructuring required the mandatory use of the official language in public affairs, which in turn facilitated the cooptation or displacement of regional elites. With the advent of compulsory education in more recent times, the state had at its disposal a powerful instrument of applied culture change with the potential of influencing all classes of society.

Nevertheless, many regional cultures managed to survive. In part, this survival can be attributed to factors of class and occupation, since peasant communities and economic systems were only partially influenced by the dictates of government. Then again, a certain distance from the centers of power might offer an element of protection in preindustrial societies. But to such "passive" factors we should add "active" variables such as movements of cultural revitalization and nationalism. The "crisis of the state" in the West may thus in part be approached as a problem in the limits of integration. Furthermore, in not a few cases, the memory of prior autonomy or independent status remained alive in ethnic homelands, for not all of these can reasonably be categorized as "failed" nation-states.[7]

In summary, the modern nation-state has been the first and most obvious adversary of regional particularism. The many changes that accompanied political centralization long antedate the economic transformations discussed. What we find today, therefore, is a very complex and overlapping situation entailing different aspects of peripheralization. Furthermore, the concept of a periphery is always relative and constantly raises the question: peripheral to what? We find nation-states that are globally or continentally peripheral in which critical decisions are formulated beyond their own borders, as is true of much of Mediterranean Europe. There are peripheries within peripheral states, and even the most economically powerful core states contain internal peripheries. Finally, all of post-World War II Europe, East and West, may be seen to constitute two, often far from contented, peripheral zones.

A HISTORY OF CATALAN NATIONALISM

In the Middle Ages, Catalonia, Aragon, and Valencia constituted the entity known as the Crown of Aragon. This was a fully independent

Mediterranean power with a thriving commercial and maritime tradition. The dynasty was Catalan, and the economic center of gravity lay in the busy seaboard provinces of which Barcelona was the hub. This early prosperity was based on the export of textiles and iron shipped throughout the Mediterranean in vessels owned by Catalan merchants and insured in Barcelona. Historians will remember that it was Catalans, in the *Llibre del Consolat de Mar*, who codified the first international law of the sea.

With respect to politics, the affairs of the component kingdoms were regulated by their own parliamentary assemblies. These *corts* were the basis of a highly developed constitutional system "in which the conflicting necessities of liberty and order were uniquely harmonized."[8] The underlying political philosophy was founded on the firm understanding that legislative responsibility and fiscal control were to be exercised by the representatives of the people, the *estements* or estates of the nobility, the clergy, and the bourgeoisie. The corts met regularly, and they alone could undertake legislation. As such they functioned as the chief organ of government. Within this structure, royal power was circumscribed and could only be effectively exercised in conformity with the will of the community.

For our purposes, it is perhaps sufficient to note the early evolution of a sophisticated political structure and of a concept of nationhood. In the words of the French historian Pierre Vilar, "Catalonia realized one of the earliest examples of the nation-state in the Medieval West, granted all the reservations that should be made in such a transfer of vocabulary."[9] This system, unchanged in essentials, passed to the heirs of Ferdinand and Isabella. The marriage of these monarchs in 1469 made of two dynasties a single one, but it did not unite the respective dominions of Castile and Aragon. It was only at the conclusion of the War of Spanish Succession, which left the Catalans abandoned by their English allies, that Philip V was in a position to centralize and Castilianize the government and administration of Catalonia. The end of Catalonia as a politically and legally distinct entity occurred at a specific point in time—September 11, 1714—when, following a long siege that left 6,000 defenders dead, Barcelona surrendered to the army of Philip V. By a logic that is difficult for non-Catalans to understand, September 11 is celebrated as the Catalan national day.

Of course, defeat in war and the loss of traditional political institutions did not mark the end of Catalonia as a distinct cultural and linguistic entity. Furthermore, the rural economy survived and even prospered and, while Catalan trade and industry never regained the primacy it had enjoyed in medieval times, it too made some advances. There was a quickening of economic activity during the latter part of the eighteenth century as the markets of Spanish America were opened to Catalan commerce, but this revival ended with the catastrophies of the Napoleonic Wars.

Modern Catalonia is very much a consequence of the economic transformation ushered in by industrialization. By the middle of the nineteenth century, Catalonia had become the workshop of Spain, and Catalan goods, textiles in particular, were being sold in overseas markets. The process of industrialization was destined to have a major impact on all sectors of society. The first workers' association in Spain was organized in Barcelona in 1840. By 1917, almost 30,000 workers in the Barcelona area were enrolled in trade unions, and a further 130,000 workers were members of cooperatives and mutual aid societies. To put these figures in perspective, the number of industrial workers in Barcelona was slightly more than 200,000 in 1919. Thus, quite early there emerged in Catalonia a genuine working class culture: an industrial labor force with organizational capacities that were to be tested in several general strikes.

Industrialization also helped to lay the groundwork for a movement of cultural and linguistic renaissance, *La Renaixenca*. Initially a movement concerned with literary revival and the formulation of modern grammatical and orthographic rules, it merged toward the end of the nineteenth century with *Catalanisme*, a more consciously political philosophy that drew most of its support from the rising bourgeoisie. In common with many nineteenth century nationalist movements, Catalanisme was essentially reformist in orientation. Stress was placed on the reacquisition of some degree of local autonomy and the need to support the Catalan language and Catalan institutions.

By the early decades of the present century, Catalanisme had sufficiently broadened its appeal and base of participation to include not only middle class but also substantial peasant and working class components. As a nationalist philosophy, it influenced the formation of a number of political parties covering the spectrum from conservative to socialist. Needless to say, class interests and nationalist interests did not always coincide, and in the background were issues of state-level political parties and the degree of independence enjoyed by their Catalan affiliates. One should also remember that, as in the rest of Spain, the 1920s and the 1930s were particularly difficult years: a time of growing labor discontent, of economic depression, of increasing political polarization, and, finally, of civil war.

But granted all these problems, it was also a period marked by a growing nationalist consciousness and political progress. Most important of all, Catalonia achieved a significant degree of home rule through the Statute of Autonomy voted into law by the Republican Parliament of 1932.

The statute reestablished a distinct Catalan government, the *Generalitat*, answerable to a legislative body, the Catalan parliament. While Catalan home rule was not a return to the political independence lost in 1714, it provided for significant jurisdiction over culturally critical areas, such as education, territorial organization, natural resource management, and some fiscal control. Suffice it to say that during the 1930s education in Catalan flourished at all levels from elementary school to university. In much the same way, other areas of cultural expression and cultural maintenance—books, newspapers, theater, music—experienced a notable florescence.

In the Civil War of 1936–39, the vast majority of Catalans of all classes supported the Republic that had granted them the autonomy statute. The military, which had risen in revolt against the government, espoused a policy of the most rigid centralization and an image of Spain destined for imperial greatness. The military also attracted to its cause all manner of reactionary elements, including the Spanish fascists, the Falange. With the victory of these forces, Catalonia faced years of the most brutal repression directed at the language, at the culture, and at every form and type of political expression.

An attempt to examine in any detail the policies and events that followed the victory of General Franco is beyond the scope of this chapter. Yet enough must be said so that one may understand the nature of a regime that lasted 40 years and was, from the beginning, dedicated to the eradication of cultural diversity and every form of liberty. Spanish fascism, consciously, clearly, and very specifically espoused a policy of cultural genocide, not only in Catalonia but in all other ethnically distinct areas. With respect to Catalonia, even a partial tabulation is sufficient to provide some idea of the moral, material, and physical cost of this reimposition of centralization by military force. To begin with, there was the destruction of the organs and agents of cultural transmission. The Catalan press, which had numbered some 400 periodicals, was closed down, and for decades no books were allowed to be printed in Catalan. In education, the use of Catalan in the schools and the university was proscribed, and the school system, one of the best in Spain, was taken over by the state. In the first months of occupation, tens of thousands were imprisoned and hundreds faced the firing squad every day. All teachers, professors, and civil servants who could be identified as having worked for the Generalitat were dismissed or jailed; the majority were never reinstated. Obviously, all official business had once more to be transacted in Castilian, and the same requirement was also extended to commercial correspondence and publicity. Street names, some dating back centuries, were changed, and the names of towns, rivers, and mountains—of all the geography—were changed to conform to Castilian spelling. Quite simply, Catalan ceased to be a public language and was only tolerated in purely private communication.

The same fate befell all manner of corporate entities, from music societies, sports clubs, and neighborhood groups to trade unions and political parties. Many of these were simply banned, while others had to incorporate themselves into state agencies. In short, a totalitarian system atempted to control the totality of civil culture; it was not simply the Statute of Autonomy that was abrogated but any entity that might seem to pose a challenge to the state, whether a Boy Scout troop or a choral society.

One might add that before the Franco forces reached the French frontier, some 200,000 individuals chose exile, and a high proportion of these were Catalan intellectuals and professionals as well as political figures, many ordinary people, and the remnants of the Republican army. This huge exodus represented a phenomenal loss of talent and leadership. Many who left never returned.

In the face of such a traumatic defeat and such repressive measures, how was Catalan culture maintained? Initially, the language and the culture survived in the private domain, in the home and in the web of friendship. In due course, however, other opportunities presented themselves. As all of Spain became more closely integrated into the economic currents of post-World War II Europe, the more manifestly repressive features of fascist ideology and policy were attenuated. In the early 1960s, the Spanish government undertook a course of economic development based on the twin pillars of mass tourism and labor migration. By the early 1970s, Spain was attracting some 35 million tourists a year—one tourist to each Spaniard—and about a million Spanish workers were employed in the industrialized countries of western Europe. At the same time, millions of country people from the poorest regions were attracted to the expanding industrial regions of Spain itself, in particular to Catalonia, the Basque country, and the industrial belt around Madrid.

Taken in conjunction, these changes facilitated mobility and communication and offered at least some opportunities for political resistance and cultural reaffirmation. Overt opposition was not possible, but contradictions in the system could be exploited. Toward the end of the Franco regime, all manner of shadow organizations, from trade unions to political parties, were in place. The trick was to develop groups and associations able to skirt the regulations limiting rights of assembly. Typical of such entities were outing and excursion clubs, folk dance and folk song groups, cinema clubs and alumni associations. All such collectivities had one characteristic in common: there was a considerable disparity between purported function and actual aims. Thus a cinema group might be established, and, in fact, movies would be shown, but a period of discussion followed. Since "discussion" could be broadly interpreted, this was likely to range beyond cinematographic techniques and the talents of the actors. The overall approach was described to me this way in the late 1960s:

> The gambit with us has always been the same: take measures and approaches that are very modest and legal and build on them. What we

say is this: "Tread carefully so as not to scare the hare, then catch it before it wakes."[10]

I have sat around dining room tables at which political parties were organized and visited churches that hosted clandestine political conferences. But apart from these endeavors, there was another approach that was to prove very successful. The monopoly that the state exercised over every facet of political life made the system remarkably cumbersome. It thus became possible to infiltrate the state apparatus at such levels as municipal administration and trade union locals (theoretically the preserve of the Falange). As a result, by the time Franco died in 1975, many local-level offices were staffed by individuals hostile to the aims and ideology of the regime.

CATALAN NATIONALISM SINCE FRANCO

On November 20, 1975, General Franco died following a long illness. By the time of his death, the regime of which he was the "maximum leader" was beset by internal contradiction and exuded a musty and anachronistic quality. On the one hand, it had retained the formal political structure of what was termed "unity of command and division of functions" (one-man rule, delegation of administrative tasks); on the other, it aimed at a Western model of development that increasingly linked the economy to external financial interests. It was a monarchy without a king and a regime that purported to defend all that was traditional and eternal in a situation of changing patterns of mobility, values, and expectations. The ideological underpinnings of the system—so-called "organic democracy"—which supposedly eliminated sectoral interests and conflicts of class, were manifestly impractical and irrelevant in a society that was increasingly urban and postindustrial, in habits and aspirations. Franco had won the Civil War, but he had not been able to keep at bay the influences and pressures attending modernization.

Spain did not disintegrate, as some had predicted, following the death of the *Caudillo* (leader). For a year or so, administrations that attempted to change little and acted only when forced to do so controlled the government. But rising pressures and discontents made such gradualism untenable. There followed two general elections, reasonably democratic in form, in June 1977 and March 1979. In both the party of the administration, the Union of the Democratic Left (UCD), won a plurality of the votes and of the seats in the bicameral parliament. This, however, was not the case in Catalonia where the electorate overwhelmingly voted for nationalist and Left candidates.

The period between the elections was dominated by parliamentary consensus politics, known as the Moncloa Pact, that limited the cut and thrust of debate and certainly worked to the detriment of permanent minorities, such as Basque and Catalan nationalist parties. It was claimed, and there was certainly some truth to this, that an element of consensus was necessary to hammer out the details of a new constitutional framework. From these deliberations, a constitution did in fact emerge and was then approved by referendum in December 1979.

The constitution, an exceedingly detailed document, established strict—many would say rigid—guidelines for the granting of statutes of autonomy. However, these statutes—both the Catalan and the Basque—fell considerably short of the historic statutes of 1932 and 1936. One should take note that there was considerable pressure on minority nationalist politicians to agree in substance with the draft proposals. The pressures came not simply from government but also from some state-level opposition parties, in particular the Communists and the Socialists. Thus, Santiago Carrillo, leader of the Spanish Communist Party (PCE), chastised the Catalan Communists as being "too nationalistic," while Felipe Gonzalez, secretary general of the Socialist Workers Party (PSOE), claimed that the issue of nationalities and autonomies might be resolved by the year 2000!

Other factors also impinged on the debates and the implementation of resolutions. In the course of the last five years, there has been a disturbing rise in political violence, much of it attributable to the terrorist activities of the ETA Basque separatists, but also including a growing tempo of right-wing terrorism and intimidation. Many people, and not simply Catalan nationalists, harbor a strong suspicion of the military and its intentions. A military coup is probably not in the cards at the moment, but one amateurish attempt was foiled in 1978.

Finally, one should also take into account a deteriorating economic climate. Early in 1980, the Spanish inflation rate was close to 15 percent, and some 10 percent of the labor force was unemployed. Inflation had run as high as 30 percent in 1979. There has also been a decline in tourist entries and a return of Spanish workers from abroad.

In the aggregate, all these factors help account for the implementation of a new Statute of Autonomy (approved by a referendum of Catalan voters in 1979) that has variously been described to me as "having a very low ceiling" and as "a Statute of fear." This is not to deny that very important political gains have been made over the past few years. The restrictive legislation on the use of language has been abolished, there is a new Generalitat in Catalonia, and all manner of groups and associations are free to function. Slowly, very slowly, the central government is transferring powers and competencies to the Generalitat and to municipalities. A new Catalan parliament was installed in the spring of 1980.

The question at this point is whether these changes have come too little and too late.

SURVIVAL OF THE CULTURAL ENTITY

It may seem paradoxical that the survival of a national identity is posed just at a time when democratic institutions have been reestablished and minority rights—to culture and to language—are recognized in law and form part of a constitutional framework.

If there are anxieties of cultural survival, and unquestionably this is the case, they are in part attributable to factors mentioned here. Forty years of dictatorship played havoc on the capacity of a culture to perpetuate itself. Not only did it shatter institutional structures—educational, political, social, and even recreational—but, to some degree at least, it forced the adoption of others. In the very important area of language maintenance, these 40 years can be viewed as a period in which language skills deteriorated year by year to a point at which, for much of the Catalan-speaking population, a diglossic pattern has been firmly established: Castilian was the language written and read, Catalan the language of domestic usage. This gives rise to a functional separation of language use or, phrased differently, a form of linguistic stratification.

A situation of this type, serious though it may be, is still potentially manageable—one that can be rectified in the future. But a further factor makes recovery harder. The exodus of 1939 and what this meant in terms of the loss of intellectual and political leadership has been mentioned, but far more serious than this loss of talent and people was the massive immigration of Castilian speakers. Initially, these immigrants arrived in relatively small numbers and found a situation in which it was to their advantage to learn the local language and forms of life. In fact, this was not a new phenomenon, since poverty in rural Spain and labor demands in Catalonia had attracted people from other areas since the nineteenth century. Although Catalan ceased to be a language of public life after the Civil War, it still retained a certain prestige and importance: it was the language of the majority and also the language of the bourgeoisie, that is, of the employer class.

The balance began to change quite drastically in the early 1960s. A series of economic factors—expansion of industrialization and tourism, a growth in the service sectors, specific government plans of stabilization and development—triggered an unprecedented rate of immigration. It was also at this point that patterns of settlement increasingly reflected differences in linguistic usage. No longer were new residents to be found intermixed with the old ones but more and more in huge new housing developments inhabited almost exclusively by immigrants or those whose everyday language was Castilian. By the early 1970s, some one-third of the population of Catalonia was of recent non-Catalan origin, and this figure grew to about 40 percent by 1980. By now, the majority of the population of the Barcelona metropolitan area does not speak Catalan as its first language, and many do not speak it at all.[11]

Numbers alone do not tell the full story, for one must also consider significant changes in social context. Together with this demographic change—and one must remember the relative prosperity of Catalonia and the size and importance of Barcelona—there took place a change in class representation. Historically, two types of non-Catalans were to be found in Catalonia: workers and agents of state authority. Workers virtually always stayed, while bureaucrats, military personnel, and the like hardly ever did so. However, as the Castilian-speaking population grew, this attracted middle class sectors who identified themselves as Spanish and often had little in common with their Catalan class counterparts.

At the same time, radio and television—state monopolies—reinforced the image of a unitary Spanish society. Not only was all programming in Castilian, but the media were utilized as potent manipulators of tastes and public opinion. This is obvious enough with respect to news and other information, but it also holds for other programs including those leased from foreign countries: the foreign, the exotic, all was viewed or heard in Castilian translation.

Some of the consequences of these events and of the history that antedates them are easily observable. Catalans speak Catalan among themselves, and Castilian speakers use their own language in the same manner. Together, however, and in this it makes little difference which group is in the minority, the language of communication is almost invariably Castilian. Class, occupation, or education play little role in determining long-conditioned patterns of intergroup relations. Mechanisms of a similar type apply in different contexts. Thus inter-marriage between Catalans and non-Catalans—once viewed by Catalans as the most "natural" form of incorporating others into their own culture—now functions in the opposite direction.

The hard reality, one with which is very difficult for Catalans to come to grips, is that in Catalonia there are two language communities and that, in relative terms, one has been growing and the other declining. This, in fact, has been recognized and clearly stated in a recent article by a group of ethnolinguists at the Autonomous University of Barcelona:

> Therefore, as a consequence of the great migrations of the last decades, the ethnic composition [of Catalonia] has been radically altered to the

point that society is in no sense homogenous, but on the contrary finds itself divided into two large groups increasingly different from one another.[12]

I quote the authors of this article not because I agree with them completely, but because they have been willing to face a current reality rather than explain it away. Too many Catalans believe that the immigrant population will become Catalan in due course, the assumption being that the attractions of the culture, shared experiences, and identity with one's place of origin in the succeeding generations will function to make this population think of itself as Catalan.

There is a certain truth to this hypothesis. Both "new" and "old" Catalans can and do share common experiences and may believe themselves moved by the same symbols, cultural or political. But at the very core of Catalan nationalism, as something that all could share, as something that would differentiate them from other peoples, was the language. This raises what I believe is the key question, the most important cultural and political consideration with which this generation of Catalans must struggle: is it possible to be Catalan without speaking the language? If the answer is in the affirmative, what does it mean to be Catalan once language takes a secondary position as a symbol of identity?

One thing is already obvious: the classic definitions no longer stand up. In the past and regardless of political and cultural oppression, of elites that at times followed interests of class rather than of nation, and of centuries of state control, Catalonia was a bounded entity: it had a homeland, a distinct history, and its own language. In the simplest terms, one who spoke Catalan was a Catalan.

This formula is no longer applicable, certainly not in its entirety. In attempting to resolve the issue of group membership, the current political leadership in Catalonia has come up with a new formulation: "Whoever lives and works in Catalonia is a Catalan," a slogan that sounds eminently fair but makes residence the prime consideration. It may also be faulted on the grounds that, as a measure of collective identity, it leaves out all those Catalans who find themselves beyond the borders of Catalonia. There has also been a good deal of talk about Catalans by "birth" and Catalans by "choice" and many other similar formulations. As a final point, Catalan politicians and intellectuals have traditionally pressed for education in the maternal language, but for many who reside in Catalonia this language is now Castilian.

If there is a lesson to be drawn from the Catalan case, and I believe there is one, it is that even a nationality as well established as the Catalan, one furthermore that has managed to overcome many misfortunes, finds itself today at great risk. The major problem is one of survival in a world where small cultural entities now find themselves highly vulnerable: vulnerable to the state, vulnerable to the hegemonic pressures of finance and the media age, vulnerable to all the structural changes Western societies are experiencing.

NOTES

1. Joseph Frankel, *International Politics* (London: Pelican Books, 1977), p. 100.

2. See Immanuel Wollerstein, *The Modern World System* (New York and London: Academic Press, 1976). On internal "colonialism" and "dependent development," see Andre Gunder Frank, *Capitalism and Underdevelopment in Latin America* (New York: Monthly Review Press, 1967); Michael Hecter, *Internal Colonialism: The Celtic Fringe in British National Development 1536–1966*, (Berkeley and Los Angeles: University of California Press, 1975); Fernando Henrique Cardoza, "Associated Dependent Development: Theoretical and Practical Applications," in *Authoritarian Brazil*, ed. Alfred Stepan (New Haven: Yale Press, 1973), p. 181–202. On the nature of "postindustrial society," see Bevemin S. Kleinberg, *American Society in the Post-Industrial Age: Technology, Power, and the End of Ideology* (Columbus, Ohio: E. E. Merrill, 1973).

3. See John W. Cole and Eric R. Wolf, *The Hidden Frontier: Ecology and Ethnicity in an Alpine Valley* (New York and London: Academic Press, 1974); Sydel Silverman, *Three Bells of Civilization: The Life of an Italian Hill Town* (New York and London: Columbia University Press, 1975); Oriol Pi-Sunyer, "The Politics of Tourism in Catalonia," *Mediterranean Studies* 2 (1979): 46–69.

4. See Jeremy Boissevain, "Introduction," in *Beyond the Community: Social Process in Europe*, ed. Jeremy Boissevain and John Friedl (The Hague: Yale University Press, 1973), pp. 1–22; see also Oriol Pi-Sunyer, "Zamora: A Regional Economy in Mexico," in *Studies of Middle American Economics*, ed. Margaret A. L. Harrison and Robert Wauchope (New Orleans: Publication 29, Middle American Research Institute, 1968), pp. 51–59.

5. Oriol Pi-Sunyer, "The Politics of Tourism in Catalonia," *Mediterranean Studies* 2 (1979): 60.

6. J. H. Elliot, *The Revolt of the Catalans* (Cambridge: Cambridge University Press, 1963), p. 200.

7. Peter Worsley, *The Third World* (London: Weidenfeld and Nicholson, 1973), p. 82.

8. J. H. Elliot, *Imperial Spain 1469–1716* (New York: St. Martin's Press, 1964), p. 15.

9. Pierre Villar, "La Historia Culturel Cataluna Vista Desde Francia," in *Cataluna Vista Desde Fuera*, ed. Baltesar Porcel (Barcelona: Llibres de Sinera, 1970), p. 60.

10. Rafael Ninydes, *Cuatro Idromas para un Estada* (Barcelona: Editorial Cambio 16, 1977), pp. 224–25.

11. Miguel Strubell i Trueta, "Immigracio i Integracio Linguistica el Prioxipat," *Quaderns d'Alliberament* 2 (1978): 252–54.

12. Joan Argente, "Una Nascio sense Estate, un Poble sense Llengua?" *Serra D'Or* 249 (1980): 17.

7

CORSICA AND THE FRENCH STATE

Peter Savigear

Islands are different, and among the European islands Corsica is especially different. A moment of political independence in the middle of the eighteenth century has never been regained. Dependence has been the norm, and the island has not enjoyed the kind of special constitutional arrangement that has been accorded to many of the other islands belonging to the European nation-states, from Sicily to Greenland, from the Azores to the Isle of Wight. Corsican particularism has not been recognized in its constitutional status. Corsica remains part of the metropolitan state of France, as totally a part of France as the departments of the Somme or the Ardeche, the Seine Inférieure or the Bouches du Rhône. It is thus hardly surprising that two centuries of political association with France have been punctuated by demands for the revision of that relationship. These demands have become more insistent in recent years and more violent during the 1970s.

Violence is not a new element in Corsican politics. The recent explosions (300 annually since 1975), injuries, and deaths are not an inherent part of traditional and political life, but reflect a long period of unhappy government reaching back through centuries of civil struggle.°

°There have been several hundred explosions attributed to various nationalist groups in Corsica and on the mainland—298 in 1976, a figure exceeded in 1978 and 1979. Some have been small and others very destructive. The attack on an Air France Boeing 707 and that on the Serri-di-Pigno television station are among the more dramatic, both claimed by the Peasant Front. Three deaths occurred in August/September 1975, all to members of the security forces, and recently three people, including a member of the CRS riot police, were

Not always united, Corsicans have sought independence from continental masters, notably from the Italian city-state of Genoa and from France after the defeat of Pascal Paoli, leader of independent Corsica. It might seem, therefore, that there is a certain inevitability about Corsican nationalism.

THE BURDEN OF INSULARITY

Insularity has constantly fed Corsican nationalism. The island lies not only relatively far from France, 175 miles from Marseille and 120 from Nice, but is nearer to Italy, 70 miles from Livorno (Leghorn), whence came the first and most long-lasting political influence on the island until the French troops under the Comte de Vaux managed to defeat the rebellious islanders at the battle of Ponte Nova in May 1769. This enabled the French king to implement the Convention of Versailles, by which sovereignty over the island was passed from Genoa to the French monarchy. Distance has remained an obstacle and therefore an issue between Corsicans and the French authorities. Travel time by sea is at least six hours from Nice, and flights are limited because there is no airport on the island capable of receiving the largest aircraft or able to cope with aircraft in any significant numbers. Indeed, the demand for improved transport has been a perpetual element in the history of Corsican nationalism. Recent measures dating from 1975 have included the reorganization of the sea links with a reduction in net fares, with the routes now administered by a special offshoot of the Société Nationale de Chemin de Fer (SNCF) and fares assessed at rates comparable to those on the French railways. Improvements have been made to the airports at Ajaccio, Bastia-Poretta, and the smaller airstrips at Calvi and Figari. But the cost of transport, and therefore of all goods moved to and from Corsica, remains a central issue in any discussions between local administrative institutions and the French government, just as it had been in earlier periods. However, in themselves transport costs and difficulties cannot explain the form and nature of Corsican nationalist demands. Transport is only one Corsican complaint against the governments of France.

The burden of insularity was exacerbated by a history of bloodshed. Opposition to the governance of Corsica by France and a sense of identity have been kept alive through centuries of conflict. Corsican nationalism in

killed at Ajaccio in connection with regionalist taking of hostages in a hotel (January 1980). It has been a common assumption that there have not been attacks on individuals. This is unfortunately not true, and a number of people have been injured during the last five years in regionalist activities, including a noted advocate and critic of the Corsican nationalists, M. Biaggi, injured September 9, 1977; M. Ange Albertini in March 1978; and M. Pierre Bertolini of the security service in Corse du Sud on December 8, 1978. There have been others.

the later twentieth century was able to look back to the brief experience of independence, a mythology whose greatest hero, Pascal Paoli, had been forced into exile by the French conquest of 1769. Legends of national heroes, dating back to the later Middle Ages, may not have signified a great deal to individual Corsicans, but they possessed a special relevance. Corsicans knew that there had been a period when they were independent and when they had fought for their independence. Corsica was one of the last territories to be gathered into the state of France, long after such provinces as Brittany and Languedoc. Nevertheless, Corsicans have not always been coordinated and vociferous in pushing forward their separateness and distinct traditions. They had apparently been fairly easily beguiled by the French assertion that culture came from France and that all civilized social and political life as well as economic development came from the French state. "C'est donc à la France qu'appartient l'honneur des premières améliorations exécutées en Corse. C'est la France seule qui a gouverné ce pays pour lui-même, pour le civiliser, non pour le préssurer ni le rendre comme avaient fait ses anciens dominateurs."[1] (Translation: It is then to France that the honor belongs of having brought about the first improvements in Corsica. It is France alone which has governed this land for its own sake, in order to civilize it not in order to oppress it nor to reduce it as former conquerors had done.)

It is, of course, true that France applied a vigorous administration to Corsica; plans for roads, justice, schools, and economic projects arrived within a year of the initial conquest and have continued in French projections since then. But two major accusations have dominated the recurrent Corsican complaints against this process since 1769: the French state has neither done all that it proposed or might have proposed, nor has that which has been achieved been performed in the appropriate spirit but rather in a spirit of colonial enterprise. Corsica, in short, has been reduced to the status of a colony within the metropolitan French nation-state.

Stress on the colonial relationship has not always been very marked. There have been moments when the Corsican has appeared to embody the political values of France rather more stoutly than many inhabitants of continental France. Napoleon established this as a respectable Corsican tradition, although he was by no means the first Corsican to place his life at the service of France and turn his back on the island. His achievement, from the Corsican point of view, was to cement the relationship, an achievement reinforced by his descendants in the midnineteenth century. When several thousand Corsicans died in World War I, when the island became the first metropolitan department to be liberated in 1943, substantially as a result of the Corsicans' own efforts, and when Corsica became the first French department to acclaim the overthrow of the last government of the Fourth Republic and the return to office of Charles de Gaulle in May 1958, the respectable preeminence of Corsica among the lands, regions, and provinces of France was reiterated. The words inscribed on an anti-Fascist plaque erected in Bastia in 1938, at the time of Mussolini's irredentist claims to Corsica, indicate this solidarity: "Nous jurons de vivre et de mourir français."* (Translation: We swear to live and die as Frenchman.)

Certainly, direct opposition to the French state was sporadic and ineffectual before the 1960s, although the allegations of colonial status and the intention to "tirer la Corse du marasme où elle s'enfonce de plus en plus"[2] were explicit, at least in the interwar years when the first autonomist movement was launched. (Translation: To pull Corsica out of the morass into which she sinks deeper and deeper.) The basis of this early movement was cultural, with demands for the teaching of what was described as the "dialect" in school, the reopening of the university and the creation of agricultural and hydrographic colleges, and the teaching of specifically Corsican history. In general, such a program neither progressed nor gained a wide and active support amongst the Corsicans. The mouthpiece of this movement was *A Muvra*, a publication that attacked French colonialism. The tradition of earlier Corsican nationalists was perpetuated in this publication and in the *Parti Corse Autonomiste*, founded in 1927. They held a series of congresses, presented as a reconvened States General of Corsica; as many as 600 attended in 1934. The Italian occupation of 1942 soon diverted attention from the autonomist demands. These were not revived at the moment of liberation in 1943, partly because the island was the first French metropolitan department to be freed and to be visited by General de Gaulle. The moment and the political will for autonomist demands were not ready. It required a more direct and dramatic assertion of colonialism to create a new movement.

Charles Lacretelle, writing at the beginning of the nineteenth century of the conquest and possession of the island by the French king, commented, "Ces insulaires montrerent l'indignation d'un peuple abusé par de vaines promesses."[3] (Translation: These islanders show the indignation of a people abused by vain promises.) This disillusion has persisted, and many Corsicans would not accept the view that French governments have removed the obstacles following from insularity. Corsica awaits special constitutional status.

French governments might claim that the penalties of insularity have indeed been recognized by the many particular and detailed arrangements granted to Corsica. Corsica is now a separate region (since 1970),

---

*The final word was defaced in 1975.

only briefly forming part of the region Provence-Côte d'Azur. The island, now consisting of two departments, Haute-Corse and Corse du Sud, has been the subject of a special interministerial commission and was accorded a management scheme in 1971 and several special "charters"— the most notable being the Charter of 1976. New arrangements have extended to such matters as transport subsidies, and exceptional and favorable rates of taxation on a number of commodities and in the application of the value-added tax. Numerous funds have aided the "Amenagement du Territoire" and have been made available for the development of the island and of its infrastructure. The French state supports Corsica by about 3,000 million francs, set against the 586 million francs raised on the island. But such economic advantages do not change the constitutional status and have not been completely accepted by all Corsicans as a sufficient proof of the "special" consideration they deem necessary. Nor is it generally accepted that such measures have out-weighed the disadvantages of the Corsican lot.

ECONOMIC GRIEVANCES

Corsican nationalism has recently become a political force despite concessions by the governments of France, particularly since 1946, because of the claim of continued colonialism on the island. The new colonialism has revealed itself most clearly in the fate of the Corsican population.

Despite the comparatively recent incorporation into the French state, the indigenous population has been in decline, and this decline and transformation has been most marked in the twentieth century. Reliable figures are impossible to find, and Corsican statistics, particularly those relating to population, are notoriously uncertain. The local branch of the National Institute of Statistics and Economic Study (INSEE), established in 1975, continues to draw attention to this problem of accuracy. Yet an overall drop in the number of people living on the island between the last decades of the nineteenth century and the last quarter of the twentieth century has been revealed. The population in the 1880s seems to have been in the region of 300,000. Current estimates suggest a figure of about 230,000. But perhaps more important than this general decline is the double tendency of a net emigration of Corsicans from their island and a consequent decreasing proportion of Corsicans among those in per-manent residence. Whereas in 1900 the bulk of the 300,000 or so inha-bitants were Corsican, the number who might be so described today has probably halved; some 75,000 of the approximate present population of

230,000 are not Corsican, leaving only some 155,000 Corsicans as against French, Italian, and other foreign nationalities.[4] The basis of contemporary anger lies in these features of the decline of the Corsican population in the two centuries of French rule. Hence, the debate about Corsican national identity returns again and again to the declining population and its dispersal among the cities of France and its former empire, the "diaspora" that has become an important element in the understanding of Corsican politics. The idea of being Corsican has remained strong and is reflected in the many associations of Corsicans in the diaspora.

The declining population has been matched by an economic decline. The island has remained virtually without major industrial development. The mountainous landscape is hardly appropriate to this, and prospects for employment are certainly no better than in any other largely rural area of France. Indeed unemployment would be much more serious were it not for the net emigration of Corsicans, especially young people. The declining population and poor productivity have combined to create an island of great natural beauty with abandoned villages and shrinking agricultural vitality. In the last 100 years, commercial production of crops, such as olives, olive oil, chestnuts, and timber, has virtually ceased. Land under cultivation had declined from about 40 percent of the surface area to some 15 percent at the beginning of the Fifth French Republic. Forest and scrub (*maki* or *maquis*) fires continue to destroy thousands of hectares every year.

Moreover, the measures adopted by the French state after 1946 suggested the extension of colonial status. The national economic recovery that began during the Fourth Republic made the weakness of Corsica more evident, and the question was then posed whether Corsicans benefited from French prosperity. The new nationalism emerged through concentration on the economic issues.

Official policy between 1960 and 1975 seemed to stress the unimportance of Corsica to France's economic development. A series of measures provoked varying degrees of protest and enabled the growing regionalist movement to proclaim the deliberate perpetuation of the colonial status in the pages of its publication, *Arritti*, and in organized demonstrations and public assemblies. The issues were predominantly economic. In 1960, it was proposed that the railway traversing the center of the island be closed. In 1962, the government expressed the intention of dumping atomic waste in a remote part of northern Corsica. Both measures were dropped after strong local protests. Similar demonstrations greeted government policy on the licensing of vehicles and the closure of asbestos mines at Canari, and the principal ports were blockaded in 1973 in further protest at transport costs and difficulties. More dramatic public outcry followed the revelation that the Italian company, Montedison, had been dumping waste material off the Corsican coast, the so-called Red Mud incident of 1972/73.

Although considerable public support and publicity was given such incidents, especially when street demonstrations were quelled by riot police, and leading regionalists were arrested on several occasions, they did not manage to establish a coherent and permanent nationalist movement. One government program in particular became an obvious target for the accusation of colonialism and the center of the evolution of Corsican nationalism in the later 1960s. The Regional Action Programme of 1947 had been followed by the creation of two agencies for the promotion of economic growth, one in the agricultural sector, Société pour la Mise en Valeur Agricole de la Corse (SOMIVAC), and another for tourism, Société pour l'Equipement Touristique de la Corse (SETCO). These were created in 1957 and appeared to confirm the recognition by the French government of the special needs of Corsica. The influx of "pieds noirs," the repatriated French coming from North Africa, particularly from Algeria after 1958, changed this picture.

SOMIVAC operated by making funds available for land improvement and for the provision of necessary agricultural infrastructures such as irrigation projects and roads, especially on the recently developed land on the eastern coastal plain of the island. The Society also provided loans for the purchase of holdings, including some newly created lots on the eastern plain. Many of the first category of projects were successfully completed, for example the building of water pumping stations and irrigation dams and of research stations that have led to the development of new crops for the island, notably artichokes, asparagus, and avocados. The second category of SOMIVAC projects aroused vigorous political opposition on the grounds that the principal beneficiaries were not Corsicans but pieds noirs. "C'est la mise en valeur de la Corse par les non-Corses"[6] was the gibe coming from *Arritti*, the autonomist paper. (Translation: It is the commercialization of Corsica by the non-Corsicans.) The official statement that the majority of recipients of actual plots of land or of subsidies for existing plots and mountain agriculture have been Corsicans or of Corsican origin was rejected.[7] The activities of SOMIVAC could not be unequivocally shown to have benefited the Corsicans in Corsica, and the bulk of the larger holdings have gone to "non-Corsicans."

The development of tourism was also not clearly beneficial. Much of the proposed hotel building of SETCO did not take place. While tourists arrived in steadily increasing numbers, although by no means on the scale experienced by the Balearic Islands, the creation of Corsican-owned hotels did not keep pace. Too many tourists continued to come as campers, and many new tourist developments have been in the hands of continental

French or even foreigners. Consumption of food and other goods by tourists has not been clearly in the interests of Corsicans and of local production and is open to the suspicion that the real beneficiaries are the continental producers and exporters. The ARC regionalist group therefore made the claim, "Tant que le tourisme sera conçu comme un simple produit de consommation, il sera perçu par les Corses comme une aggression et une colonisation."[8] (Translation: In so far as tourism is considered as a simple consumer product, it will be perceived by the Corsicans as aggression and as colonialization.)

The ARC, the title changed from Action Régionaliste Corse to Azzione per Rinascita Corsa in 1973, gained strength and importance through the issue of SOMIVAC policy and the pieds noirs. The overproduction of wine that led to fraud, bankruptcies, and a variety of malpractices was exposed and attacked by the ARC, especially since 1973. During this period, autonomism as presented by the ARC became the most prominent form of Corsican regionalism, while smaller groups with more positively nationalist aims and a record of greater violence, the Front Paysan Corse de Libération and Ghjustizia Paolina, were unable to claim such wide support. The ARC continued to publicize wine scandals and the outrage of extensive "chaptilisation" (forced sugaring of wine). This concern with the activities of SOMIVAC and with distortions in wine production led to the occupation of a farmstead belonging to a pied noir engaged in this production, at Aleria in August 1975. The resultant violence and deaths were a turning point in contemporary Corsican regionalism.

Increasing intervention by the French state had not resulted in an improved relationship, but rather had provoked considerable anger. Fiscal measures regularized in 1968, confirming exemptions from certain taxation (a principle first propounded in the Miot Decrees of 1811), and other aids did not stop the net emigration of Corsicans. The 10 percent growth rate achieved in Corsica in the decade 1960–70 and the confidence of the Schéma d'Amenagement of 1971 in the possibility of further development were viewed as secondary to the fact that Corsicans were still leaving the island because there was little improvement in employment prospects and because the mountain villages were still in decline. It was still possible for Corsicans to claim with conviction, if not with totally convincing evidence, that non-Corsicans were benefiting most from the progress that had been realized. The government view, on the other hand, was that the fiscal arrangements, the many plans and agencies, the division of the island into two separate departments in 1975 (planned in 1974), the Expansion Fund (created in 1968), and the Regional Council (strenghtening regional institutions, established in 1972) all constituted a special status for Corsica within the central state. But this was seen by the new Corsican nationalists to be an irrelevant view that did not meet their political arguments.

THE STRUGGLE FOR POLITICAL STATUS

Corsican nationalism was not fundamentally economic but was political. The French government had missed the point. It was a special constitutional status that the Corsicans wished in order that they might control their economic development. Colonialism was not an economic condition but a political one. The more cash that flowed into the island, the more important the answer to the questions, "Who benefits?" and "Who controls these funds?" Corsican nationalism in the period after 1945 was therefore not solely the result of economic decline nor a cry from a declining cultural group, but was the demand for an answer to political questions about power.

The force of these questions was in turn dependent upon a clear idea of who was Corsican, thereby making it possible to demonstrate that the Corsicans were not the beneficiaries and that they were not in control of these marvelous new devices for the future development of the island. Ironically, France had helped to define the Corsican identity through 200 years of administration. The cultural and social unity of Corsica was created in reaction to the French state. In the place of earlier centuries of disunity and strife within the island, the French administration had inadvertently created the idea of Corsicans as distinct from the continental French. The French official had destroyed the islanders' rural habits, forms of crude justice such as the vendetta, a degree of communal land usage, their church (this had not of course been the intention in 1768, but had come with the revolution and the subsequent church settlement), and their "culture," including the Corsican language or dialect. The French language came with the French educational system, French currency, and the French police officers and gendarmes. All served to make Corsicans more aware of France and, thereby, of Corsica.

This particularly affected the large numbers of Corsicans living "in exile," many in the former French Empire, but many in Paris, Nice, and Marseille. Away from the island, Corsicans found a nostalgic longing to create a Corsican cultural unity, which had hardly existed in the past when faction fought faction, when the villagers of the interior were sharply divided from the inhabitants of the larger coastal towns. The nationalist movement of the midtwentieth century rested on the support of Corsicans living in exile. Roland Rinaldi is one such Corsican. He worked in Paris, and his attitudes struck precisely the note of longing, the cry from the diaspora: "C'est pourquoi je pense avant tout, et toujours, à la Corse. Le seul environnement humain qui me convienne, c'est la frequentation de la communauté corse de Paris… avec ceux qui partagent mes preoccupations, parlent ma langue."[9] (Translation: It is why I think above all and always of Corsica. The only human society which agrees with me is to frequent the Corsican community of Paris… with those who share my preoccupations, speak my language.) The links with the island were reinforced by the annual pilgrimage. In summer, ferries and aircraft are full of returning Corsicans as well as continental French and German vacationers. M. Joseph Alfonsi, a shepherd of the village of Calasima, high in the mountains of the Niolo, noted in 1976 that in summer, "Il n'y a pas de touriste. Les gens qui viennent passer leurs vacances ici, sont originaires du village."[10] (Translation: There are no tourists. The people who come to spend their holidays here are originally from the village.) The same applies throughout Corsica. The distinctions between Corsicans and mainland French are not easily disappearing.

The differences were all the more marked by the presence of alien police and security forces including army units, especially training units of the Foreign Legion stationed in Corsica until 1976. Police posts and legionnaires have been favorite targets of opposition violence since the early 1970s, and the use of riot police (CRS) in handling demonstrations drew considerable criticism from the regionalists.

In this unfolding atmosphere of hostility between France and Corsica, the issues of language and education have played important parts. Although there was some emphasis on the linguistic issue in autonomist literature and claims before 1939, the emphasis has recently become much greater. The French state was slow to allow broadcasting time in Corsican and reluctant to accept Corsican under the terms of the Deixonne Law of 1951, by which certain regional dialects or languages were to be taught in local schools. Delays have occurred in the opening of the university of Corsica. (Paoli created a university to provide his administration with educated officials in 1755, but the French closed it in 1770.) Proposals have seen various remissions and setbacks during the last decade.

These cultural matters were not the cause of the resurgence of nationalism, but they constituted a relevant element in the movement. Corsicans asked why they were not given a separate university, why there was not more time devoted to local language broadcasting, and why Corsican was not taught in schools. They have been invited to do this by a few determined and enthusiastic Corsicans, intent on preserving local traditions on the point of disappearing at the hands of what they see as a colonial power. Gatherings of an educational kind became rapidly transformed into celebrations of Corsican culture, joyous meetings of discovering Corsican nationality. The process has had notable success through the "Scola Corsa" of Jean-baptiste Stromboni and the "Journées Corses" of Jean-Jacques Albertini, combining the study of Corsican language in prose and song, the history of the island, and the study and appreciation of its traditions and folklore with the analysis of contemporary economic and political problems. In recent years, Corsicans attending such educational summer activities at Corte have been able to move to the autonomist congresses held in the following days before finally departing to their studies or work on the mainland at the end of August. Cultural and linguistic issues have been important because they have united Corsicans on the island with those returning from exile on the continent. To be Corsican is not therefore a racial matter nor purely a matter of language or culture, but it is to be associated with the fate of the Corsican people at the hands of the French state. The idea of "le peuple corse" is neither solely a cultural nor racial idea, but is a political one.

But the crucial issue, since the eighteenth century, has been the form of the political association with France: Corsica is part of metropolitan France. Economic and social measures have not been followed by particular political arrangements. Consultation, the contemporary form of local association favored by the French state, in the Regional Council and in the practice of the Interministerial Missions for Corsica, is not acceptable to the nationalists. It might be argued that the Corsican, like the inhabitant of any other department or region of France, has the opportunity to express his view and to exercise his control over the body politic through the democratic electoral system of the "One and Indivisible French Republic." In this way he can demonstrate his approval of policies and personalities. He can apply constitutional pressure through the elected deputies, through the election of representatives to the councils and committees of the elaborate and extensive institutions of French local administration, and through the professional and other delegates attending the various committees of the regional administration. In some respects, the Corsican is especially favored. His region has only two departments, and the regional population is smaller than that of other regions.

But to the Corsican people and the advocates of their nationalism this is inadequate. The French democratic system has not been able to function for them in the same way as elsewhere. The French state has not freed Corsicans from abuses of the electoral system. The nationalist political argument has grown on the evidence of political abuse. Electoral fraud and the undue influence of traditional factions, or clans as is the conventional term, mean that democratic politics cannot be effectively applied. The autonomist accusation has concentrated on the failure of France to rescue Corsica from the worst feature of its history, the political hold of the clan. Thus the contemporary movements have stressed their "lutte intransigeante contre les Clans"[11] ("intransigent struggle against the clans") and their rejction of the clans as but another vehicle of French colonialism.

Much of recent Corsican history could be written as an account of the way in which local notables and the prominent families in the villages and valleys of Corsica gained a hold of the new administrative and economic institutions the French established. Particularly through the municipal office of mayor, the clans retained the loyalty and subservience of the local population. The dossiers of the French administration are filled with complaints about local officials and their handling of village affairs, and the island's prefects have for generations lamented the difficulty of controlling the activities of the municipalities on the island. The proliferation of institutions, even during the Fifth French Republic, has not changed the situation but has enabled the established interests to tighten their grasp of the economy and of the politics of the island by making yet more institutions available to them. Haggling over census returns is but one contemporary example. Several new institutions have been proposed since the violence of 1975, and the autonomists argue that this has increased the capacity for such influential activity on the part of local clans.

But the notion of clan is itself unclear. To some it conveys a social phenomenon quite common in many parts of southern Europe, a pre-eminence of local families grown out of the weakness of the state and the remoteness of the small centers of population, combined with the presence of a few large and relatively wealthy families. All these features were found in Corsica, and the social force of clans existed since time immemorial in a pronounced manner, persisting into modern times with the accretion of powers that accompanied the centralized state. Families have maintained and extended their impact in time-honored ways, office and marriage being the most traditional, and a number of names stand out from the eighteenth century to the present. The rollcall of names attending any of the meetings of the institutions of the administration reveals this. Some families have retained their importance for decades. The Rocca-Serra are among the most distinguished. The family has been powerful in the area of Porto-Vecchio and even in the institutions of the island. They have been members of the Conseil Général (we find them attending in the early nineteenth century), and in recent years Dr. Jean-Paul Rocca-Serra has served as a deputy, mayor of Porto-Vecchio, and on the Conseil Général. Other families have had a similar impact, including the Pierti and the Giacobbi since 1945. (M. F. Giacobbi has recently been one of Corsica's deputies.) To the autonomists, the clan has symbolized the entire political subjection of Corsicans to France.

Autonomism, as it has grown from the regional aspirations of some

Corsicans, has been essentially apolitical in Corsica. Apart from a brief excursion into local and national elections in the mid-1960s, the autonomists have spurned politics. Their early ventures produced very little support for their parliamentary candidates. For example, in the legislative elections at Bastia in March 1967, the "régionaliste" candidate, Dr. Max Simeoni (later to become one of the leading autonomists of the ARC and the UPC) obtained only 1,160 votes of the 31,527 votes polled in the first round and was thus at the bottom of the list of six candidates. But this seemed to endorse precisely the point the autonomists were making about the conduct of politics in Corsica. The island was not the home of bandits but that of clans who twisted politics to their advantage. The regionalist platform was "anti-fraude," and the 1967 elections were fought on this campaign, controlled by the Comité Anti-Fraude.

The effect was to establish the autonomists, and particularly the ARC, as a truly Corsican movement operating outside the normal range of political life on the island. Politics, especially electoral politics, was distorted by the corrupting influence of France and its colonialist hold over the clans who used all means of malpractice to retain their position and to subject the Corsicans. The autonomists could point to the many contested elections on the island through the Third, Fourth, and Fifth Republics. Electoral fraud was the central element in their political critique, and it meant that autonomism existed outside the politics of parties. The early history of the movement was thus directed toward the exposure of fraud in all its manifestations. It denounced the abuses of postal voting (abolished in 1975), the sadly familiar pattern of electoral malpractice that had been a feature of the island, with ballot boxes destroyed and startling divergences between votes cast and numbers on the electoral rolls, practices that go back to the earliest moments of "democratic" politics during the French Constitutional Monarchy of 1815. The autonomist cry was therefore oddly, or perhaps quite logically, reminiscent of Paoli's efforts to save Corsicans from practices and traditions to which they had become accustomed as a result of lack of government. For Paoli, the effort had been to reduce clan violence and vendetta and primitive forms of justice and retribution; for the regionalists, it was electoral irregularity and the abiding influence of the clans over all aspects of Corsican life. The argument was well summarized by Jean-François Revel in *L'Express*, "Les difficultés de la Corse étaient connues depuis fort longtemps. C'était même un 'classique' de l'histoire du colonialisme intérieur français. Retard et déséquilibres économiques, malaise linguistique et culturel, insertion factice dans la démocratie politique, en raison de la fraude électorale."[12] (Translation: The Corsican difficulties have been known for a long time. It is even a "classic" story of domestic French colonialism. Delay, economic imbalance, cultural and linguistic trouble, arbitrary intervention in political democracy through electoral fraud.)

The autonomist rejection of "le terrain electoral, decevant et compromettant" fell on a fertile soil. (Translation: the deceitful and compromising electoral landscape.) The Corsicans had consistently shown both a tendency to return those candidates representing the right or center-right of the national parties and to frequently support the government of the day. The island has also been noted for a relatively high proportion of abstentions.° This has remained consistent. The apparent conformity and the above average rate of abstentions are in part a reflection of the irrelevance of French national politics to Corsican problems. Even a local hero like de Gaulle did not manage to sustain a strong commitment on the part of Corsicans; his referendums continued to yield an encouraging level of support in Corsica, but the number of abstentions remained very high, with only 57.75 percent voting in 1969. No significantly new trend has appeared since de Gaulle's retirement and death. In the election for the membership of the European parliament in June 1979, only 35 percent cast votes in Corsica, and in March 1978 an average of almost 30 percent abstained in the legislative elections.

The regionalists have therefore rejected electoral participation and have adopted direct methods expressing their opposition. Demonstrations and vigorous publicity are well-established tactics. During the 1970s, they sought to draw the entire island into days of total inactivity, days during which the island was proclaimed "dead," the "journées de l'île morte," the "Isla Morta." By 1976 they were in a position to effectively immobilize Corsica. Fear of autonomist sanctions brought the island to a halt on May 17, 1976 in support of those autonomists on trial in Paris for their part in the raid on the Depeille farm at Aleria in 1975, particularly in support of the autonomist leader, Dr. Edmond Simeoni, the principal accused. This tactic has continued to be successfully, though sparingly, employed and is, in practice, an extension of the many well-organized demonstrations on the island since 1960. It has been possible to arrange because of the size and insularity of Corsica. It is, however, clear that the autonomists have a large amount of general support for their political arguments, if not for their more boisterous actions and violence.

There is some difficulty in establishing the precise strength of any of the regionalist organizations that have been created in Corsica. Some of the lack of precision arises from the fact that many young Corsicans studying or working on the continent return during the summer to support

---

°Only in 1946 was there a 60 percent poll in any national election or referendum in Corsica. In March 1979, the "right" took majority control of the regional council, against the national trend.

the congresses and activities devoted to the culture and the political future of their homeland. The summer "universities" and study days thus draw several hundred to participate in the various historical and cultural sessions. The large numbers that have flocked to the annual conferences held by the ARC, the most important autonomist group, have seemingly included a large proportion from this category. It is no accident that autonomist conferences have been held during the summer. Total numbers attending have been consistently impressive, with as many as 5,000 in 1975 and 1976. Since 1976, attendance has been less consistently high as the initiative has begun to slip away from this association and its successor, the Union du Peuple Corse (UPC).

Three factors have emerged concerning these groups. The first is the fluid and perhaps transitory nature of their support. The more dramatic acts have boosted public sympathy, witnessed in street demonstrations and meetings. The prominence of the Aleria raid in 1975 was thus the highpoint of autonomist popularity, sustained through the trial of those involved. The raid in 1976, which led to no deaths or trials but only the destruction of property (again belonging to a pied noir), was clearly aimed at publicity, but did not receive a similar level of support on the island. It is tempting to conclude that the degree of public sympathy has been in proportion to the severity of the reaction by the French authorities. Many Corsicans have expressed, by participation in public demonstrations for two decades, an understanding of the frustration that lies behind the autonomist movement and the suspicion that official reaction has been too heavy. In 1975, for instance, many well-armed CRS and gendarmes mobiles were employed at Aleria and at the riots in Bastia that followed. Trials have also attracted considerable public support.[13]

The second factor to emerge has been the predominantly young element among the active regionalists, whether as autonomists or as members of the other clandestine groups. Young Corsicans have been those most involved in the two crucial issues of recent years, unemployment and depopulation. The "Summer University" has habitually devoted sessions to rural depopulation and its consequences. These have readily turned into political debates about French policy and Corsican humiliation.

The third factor is less easy to establish. It would seem likely that there is a considerable overlap in membership between the various groups. There is no fundamental inconsistency in participating in the predominantly legal and peaceable activities of the ARC/UPC and simultaneously supporting one of the more violent groups, which have been officially declared illegal, such as the Peasant Front (FLNC) that combined a number of early violent groups. The trial of FLNC activists in 1979 brought explicit sympathy and support from UPC leaders. It is, however, impossible to ascertain numbers by the very nature of the problem. One fact remains: the French authorities have been exposed to a wide range of hostile activity with no easy means of knowing where and how the next incident will be produced.

A SOLUTION IN SIGHT?

The government has been exposed to this pressure because all regionalists have presented official policy as directly detrimental to Corsican interests as a whole or, at best, wrung out of the state tardily, reluctantly, and, in many cases, only partially. Corsicans have suffered from an official policy that has been constantly characterized by being "too little, too late." Despite the size of the financial subventions by the state and the necessary economic dependence of Corsica on France—an economic dependence never positively and unequivocally explained by any regionalist—the political initiative had passed to the autonomists in 1975. They could claim to show the extent of French pusillanimity and vacillation in the government's policy toward the island, and so they did. As a fact, concessions followed violence in 1975 and 1976.

Although the French state reacted firmly and rapidly, this very action seemed to demonstrate the truth of the regionalist case that Corsica had been long neglected and that too little had been done for the islanders. Increased grants flowed after 1975, and it was irrelevant that many had been planned before the Aleria raid. Special funds were created, and renewed attention was paid to all vital questions raised by the regionalists, notably sea transport, which was subsequently placed in the hands of the SNCF and treated on the same basis as rail transport in France. The educational question was given further attention by the renewed promise of a university, and in 1976–79 plans were laid for this as well as for colleges of education and agriculture. More broadcasting time in Corsican was agreed, and a cultural charter was promised (still awaited at the moment of writing). The fiscal balance sheet was much in Corsica's favor, but the political issues continued to attract nationalist attention.

Even Constitutional proposals appeared after 1975, though not always emanating from the government. A law proposed by the French Socialists in 1976 placed emphasis on the cultural issues and on the need for special democratic institutions, directly elected and representing local Corsican opinion. The Socialist proposal envisaged a derogation from the French Constitution to allow a large measure of autonomism for Corsica. The projected law was rejected by the autonomists on the same grounds as their rejection of the government administrative arrangements, namely that they failed to escape from the grip of the traditional politicians, that is, the clans. ARC denounced the Socialists, "qui en croyant soutenir les idéaux de la Gauche soutiennent, en fait, le clan Giacobbi (Socialist deputy). Par parenthèse, ils verront, les socialistes, ce que sera devenue leur projet de Statut Special quand il aura été passé à la moulinette de Giacobbi et Filippi. Avec la bénédiction tacite de Rocca-Serra..."[14] (Translation: who in believing that they supported the ideals of the Left, in fact supported the Giacobbi clan. By the way, the socialists will see what will become of their projected special statute when it has been passed through the mill of Giacobbi and Filippi. With the silent blessing of Rocca-Serra.) Their position has not altered materially since 1976. The precise explanation of how the autonomists envisaged this political goal was seen in their 1979 proposal for an organic law relating to Corsica, as a derogation from the constitution.

The UPC presents a case for a special constitutional status for Corsica—a statute for the island as an exception to article 72 of the French Constitution. By this proposed law, only foreign affairs, defense, and currency would remain the responsibility of the French government in Paris. Negotiated agreements between Paris and an autonomous Corsica would cover education, broadcasting, travel, taxation, justice, energy, social security, and postal and other communications. A provisional assembly would be followed by the election, by proportional represen-tation, of a legislative assembly and by the formation of an executive committee as well as a council representing the new administration. The autonomists have made clear that there can be little prospect of agreement between them and the present French government or its successors if these remain wedded to the conception of the central state supported by a number of locally representative bodies, like the present Regional Council, the Société d'amenagement Foncier et d'equipement (SAFER), and other institutions that concern themselves with the economic and social life of the present region of Corsica. The autonomist thesis is that such variants do not truly represent the Corsican nation, and that they cannot do so.

However, the significance of the autonomist UPC has declined somewhat since 1976. Some Corsicans have been impressed by the practical steps taken by the French governments since 1975, but others have drawn a different conclusion from the events of that year. For them violence and direct action have brought results and may continue to do so. The question is thus posed whether violence is inevitable in Corsica.

The tendency toward violence between the regionalists and the French state has been made more likely by the youth of many of those determined to change the present relationship. The "elders" of the old ARC, the brothers Simeoni, were themselves drawn into violence, more as a symbolic gesture perhaps than out of conviction. They seem now to have become depressed by this and to be under pressure from a new wave of regionalists. These new elements have attacked property—above all of those associated with the colonial state, banks and finance companies, foreigners, and members of the security forces. The targets have been principally buildings, installations, and cars, not individuals.° Some of the attacks in recent years have been exceptionally melodramatic: on the air base at Solenzara in March 1977 and that at the Ajaccio airport in 1976, for example; in 1979 the FLNC carried attacks to Paris. The identity of those carrying out the raids is rarely certain. Those who have been brought to trial are surprisingly diverse in their backgrounds, as were the 21 members of the FLNC tried in 1979. The likelihood of violence is encouraged by the availability of explosives and weapons as well as by the exceptionally favorable terrain. There are, however, other factors making violence more likely, and these are political rather than pragmatic.

Political relations between the French government and nationalist Corsicans have changed, and it is not clear where the initiative now lies. Autonomy is no longer the only acceptable constitutional solution for Corsican nationalists. The long rejected idea of separatism has become more prominent, especially for the FLNC. For others the future lies not in outright rejection and denunciation of French politics and the electoral system, but in seeking a real political accommodation with the existing political parties. In particular the Socialist Party is less tainted with the slur of centralism than are the "Gaullist" Rassemblement pour la République (RPR) and the Communists. They have the advantage of an early and precise statement of a policy for Corsica, the special statute proposed in 1976. Yet at present it is difficult to see how this could be developed. All four Corsican deputies are RPR (at the time of writing), and there is increasing evidence of a fissure between those regionalists concerned with finding a political accommodation and those who look to a more violent and forced break with France. There is even some sign that those Corsicans who wish to maintain the relationship with France are also turning to violence; bombing attacks on the FLNC have been increasing, particularly by the group calling itself "Francia." There is, therefore, little immediate hope of an end of the intermittent explosions, destruction, and violence on the island.

There have been a few suggestions that a European dimension may bring some relief to Corsica. However, the European elections in June 1979 lacked any local or regional dimension as conducted in France, and the French state has consistently taken a strong statist attitude in the European Community. Moreover, the French government has been

---

°At the time of writing, news is just coming of the taking of hostages and further violence in Ajaccio in January 1980.

keener to allow the "Overseas Territories" to benefit from Community funds than to spread the benefits to Corsica, which is part of metropolitan France. Corsica has not benefited significantly from membership. Lavish Community grants to the island might detract from the French government's stated view that Corsica has done well out of the association with France and that, in recent years, Corsicans are doing even better. The poor response to the European elections was not, therefore, especially surprising. It is possible that more coordinated action by the "Unrepresented Nations" in Brussels may alter a skeptical view of the Community.

Dr. Edmond Simeoni has perhaps grasped this alternative in his slow drift toward collectivism and "socialism" as means of redirecting the autonomist program. At the UPC congress in Ajaccio in August 1979, he stressed the international element in the struggle for liberty in Corsica: "La Corse est européenne." (Translation: Corsica is European.) He recalled the promises made in 1977 to seek an international solution to Corsican colonialism, an echo of the ARC appeal to the United Nations in 1975. His speech was followed by an emotional appeal—"L'Europe c'est vous, c'est nous"—coming from M. Coppieters of the Flemish *Volksunie*.[16] (Translation: Europe, it is you, it is us.) This was rapturously greeted by a crowd estimated by reputable sources at 5,000. But the European dimension to the political difficulties in Corsica has still to be revealed.

Meanwhile, the initiative seems to lie with the French government. Much of Corsican nationalism and regionalist activity has been a response to the actions of the authorities of the state in Corsica. Yet, although President M. Giscard d'Estaing recognized where the initiative lay in 1975, the nettle has not been grasped. "Il convient maintenant d'apporter des soutions complètes a des problèmes dont se préoccupent à juste titre, nos compatriotes corses, et dont le gouvernement avait entrepris de resoudre." (Translation: It is appropriate now to bring complete solutions to the problems which rightly preoccupy our Corsican compatriots, and which the government had undertaken to resolve.) Despite this assessment made in an open letter from the president of the republic to his then prime minister, M. Chirac, in September 1975, too many Corsicans still do not believe that "complete" solutions are being found.

APPENDIX A: PRINCIPAL REGIONALIST AND NATIONALIST GROUPS IN CORSICA

Autonomist Groups

- ARC Action Régionalistes Corse/Action pour la Renaissance de la Corse, 1967–76. Title changed in 1973.

- UPC. Union du Peuple Corse, established 1976.
- PPCA. Parti du Peuple Corse pour ï'Autonomie, formed in 1974 from Front Régionaliste Corse (1966), which became Parti du Peuple Corse, and Parti du Peuple Corse pour le Progrès, 1970.
- Parti Corse pour le Socialisme, 1973.
- Union de la Patrie, 1970.

Clandestine groups claiming responsibility for some of the violent incidents

- FPCL. Front Paysan Corse de Libération, established 1973. Banned January 29, 1974.
- Ghjustizia Paolina, established 1974.
- Front de Libération Nationale de la Corse, 1976. Largely an amalgamation of the two previous groups.
- Francia, 1976.

NOTES

1. Adolphe Blanqui, *La Corse: Rapport sur son Etat Economique et Moral en 1838* (Paris: Hachette, 1841), p. 5.

2. *A Muvra*, September 30, 1934.

3. *Histoire de France pendant le Dix-Huitième Siècle* vol. 4, (Paris: Plon, 1965) pp. 169–70.

4. These figures are taken from *Economie Corse*, the official INSEE publication, 1977 and 1978.

5. There is only one employer with more than 500 employees, and more than 70 percent employ fewer than 5. *Aspects de la Population Active en Corse* (1973). Similar figures were released by the Association pour la Promotion Industrielle de la Corse in Newsletter, Ajaccio, 1978. Janine Renucci, *Corse Traditionnelle et Corse Nouvelle* (Lyons: Gudin, 1974), p. 315.

6. *Arritti*, July 18, 1973.

7. See the official statistics published in the SOMIVAC publications and the summary in *Bilan Sommaire de l'Action de la SOMIVAC du 1957 à 1975* (Ajaccio, 1976). The Society claimed that 82 percent of individual beneficiaries were Corsicans or of Corsican origin.

8. Dr. Edmond Simeoni, "Nous ne Sommes pas le Tiers-monde," *Le Monde*, May 7, 1977.

9. "Compatriote non Eminent," *Kyrn* (December 1975).

10. "Quatre pas à Calasima," *Kyrn* (August/September 1976).

11. *Arritti*, February 23, 1968.

12. Jean-Françoise Revel, in *L'Express*, "Le problème de la Corse," 19 (September 1975): 4.

13. The trial of 21 Corsicans in June 1979 produced an appeal for public support from organizations including the Confédération Générale du Travail (CGT) and Force Ouvrière FO, the principal trade unions on the island, and the Fédération Départementale des Syndicates d'Exploitants Agricoles. *Le Monde*, June 27, 1979.

14. "Les Exploitateurs du Peuple Corse," *Arritti*, August 20, 1976.

15. Edmond Simeoni, "La Fraude Jugulée," *Arritti*, August 5, 1975.

16. *Le Monde*, August 21, 1979.

8

BRITTANY: "BREIZ ATAO"

David H. Fortier

This chapter is concerned with the dynamics of ethnic minority nationalism in Brittany: its origin and development from the formal inauguration of the movement in the nineteenth century to the resurgence of the "new ethnicity" following World War II.

Utilizing the model of socioeconomic change proposed by Hechter (1975) and referred to as "internal colonialism," France and Brittany are viewed as core and periphery.[1] The core, the centralized nation-state, is seen to dominate the underdeveloped periphery and to exploit it economically. As a consequence of malintegration between core and periphery, underdevelopment creates continuing stress in the regional social, economic, and political structure, providing a fertile breeding ground for mobilizing dissatisfaction through political action. Where regional inequalities coincide with cultural and linguistic differences, political protest often takes the shape of "nationalistic" demands, ranging from regional devolution to self-determination, in the name of a separate nation and culture. Cleavages along cultural (that is, ethnic) lines create a basis for the "new ethnicity" in which traditional cultural forms (such as the flag, anthem, language or dialect, and historic myths) are dramatized to take on new significance as symbols of regional solidarity and resistance against the centralized state. The social basis for ethnic politics is generated by the formation of groups committed to recruitment of membership from those who identify with the new ethnicity.

REGIONAL UNDERDEVELOPMENT

Any analysis of the genesis and development of Breton nationalism must therefore be seen against the backdrop of Brittany's status as a peripheral region. Geographic factors and historic circumstances have worked in tandem to check the region's economic growth and to curtail effective political integration with the centralized state while at the same time fostering the retention of distinctive cultural and linguistic traditions.

A major part of the problem of regional underdevelopment lies in Brittany's geographic isolation, which, coupled with limited natural resources, has served to inhibit industrialization and to perpetuate a marginal economy based on fishing and agriculture. Like a great thumb jutting into the Atlantic from the fist of France, the peninsula of Brittany has a ragged coastline with a number of natural harbors and access to rich fishing grounds. The interior, an undulating plateau or moorland with isolated forest areas, is marked by a central spine of rocky headlands that remain remote and uninhabited. For centuries cultivation remained fixed within a zone of arable land seldom more than six kilometers from either coast.

Until the late nineteenth century when the second agricultural revolution brought radical changes in technology, the Breton peasant economy was stabilized basically on a self-subsistent level. Farming of mixed crops was carried on with primitive tools and hand labor; small-scale fishing was supplementary. Agricultural productivity was limited by soil deficiencies and the scarcity of arable land. Any surplus produced served only to perpetuate a feudal order in which the landowner-nobility were scarcely better off than the tenant-peasant. Under such conditions a system of share-tenancy (*métayage*) became the dominant form of land holding. The latter half of the nineteenth century found the region a rural backwater remote in space and in time from the economic changes that had begun 50 years earlier to transform the peasantry in France. Only in the last two decades of the nineteenth century did Brittany see the beginning of a radical transformation of its economy and regional culture. The results of these changes were to have a precipitating effect on the rise of nationalistic organizations and the shaping of a nationalistic ideology.

The second agricultural revolution, emerging alone with the Industrial Revolution, drew from a common pool of scientific experimentation and knowledge. Major innovations in the field of agriculture included techniques of crop rotation, the use of chemical fertilizers, new crop types, and improved farm machinery. Although these innovations had been slowly transforming agriculture in other regions of France as far back as the late eighteenth century, they were slow to reach Brittany. The factors of physical isolation and cultural conservatism certainly operated as major barriers; it was not until about 1880 that the transformation began, primarily through the medium of newly established farmers' syndicates.

The agrarian syndicalist movement, which did so much to break down peasant conservatism, was sponsored not by peasants but by innovators from the landed aristocracy and bourgeoisie. Inspired by the Social Catholic ideology of the times, explicit in such writings as those of sociologist Frederic Le Play, the sponsors of agrarian reform saw in the formation of syndicates a method of reaching the ears and mind of the peasant and a means of effecting socioeconomic change in rural society. Encouraged by a bill passed by Parliament in 1884 legalizing such groups, large landowners in Brittany began setting up local syndicates, later to be united in a powerful regional structure and federated in 1886 as the Union Centrale des Syndicats des Agriculteurs de France (UCSAF). Although agricultural syndicates were open to all strata of rural society, from large landlords to share-tenants and farm laborers, leadership and control remained in the hands of a paternalistic landed aristocracy.

The agrarian syndicalist movement was given further impetus by countermoves to establish rival organizations. Republican leaders, again not peasants but town-dwellers with a sense of mission, set up their own versions of syndicates. Called cooperatives (*mutuelles*), the emphasis was economic rather than social or moral and, among other things, provided farm credit and insurance.

A radical phase of the syndicalist movement emerged in the last years of the nineteenth century. Dissatisfied with the conservative doctrines of the Social Catholics, militant priests organized a splinter group known as the Christian Democrats. In Brittany, the new faction was led by Felix Trochur, a young Breton priest who preached activism and emancipation and who was instrumental in establishing a network of syndicates along with insurance and credit societies.

Despite the divergences in motivation and viewpoint, the factions within the agrarian syndicalist movement were united in a common goal: to increase the productivity of the peasant and, by marketing surplus commodities, to make small-scale farming a profitable enterprise. In the last two decades of the nineteenth century the desired changes were effected in most of rural Brittany. The use of new equipment, new cultivation methods, and chemical fertilizers made possible both an extension and intensification of cultivation. An innovation in plow design spurred a trend toward massive land clearing, opening up the interior moorland, once used only for sheep pasturage. The introduction of new forage crops now permitted the raising of horses, cows, and pigs. Rye, the traditional grain staple, was replaced by wheat and new types of vegetables that found a ready local market.

Although mixed farming tended to remain the basis of Breton

agriculture, a shift to market gardening occurred in areas along the coast where milder microclimates favored early vegetables. The building of a railway line in 1880, linking coastal Brittany to Paris, further accelerated the trend toward cash-cropping and, in a number of areas, canneries were established to handle surplus commodities. By the turn of the century, agriculture had been transformed into an economic enterprise that aimed at maximum production and maximal profits in a competitive market system on both regional and national levels. Whether the peasant sold milk and butter or surplus wheat locally or produced peas and artichokes for sale in Paris, his involvement in the world of the marketplace entailed a major shift to a new way of life in which the self-subsistent quasifeudal isolation of the past was replaced by an emergent awareness of his integration within a regional and national politicoeconomic system.

The railway line that opened up Brittany to national and world markets spurred the development of another sector of the regional economy, the fishing industry. Prior to the construction of the railway line in 1880, fishing was scaled to the needs of the local market. With the development of fast transportation, fish hauls could be shipped to meet the demands of the Paris market. Fishing rapidly became commercialized; fleets increased in size and became highly specialized, particularly in deep sea fishing for cod and tuna and off-shore fishing for sardines. In turn, the development of shipbuilding and the construction of local canneries changed fishing villages into small-scale commercial ports.

THE RAMIFICATIONS OF REGIONAL CHANGE

Thus, at the turn of the century, major technoeconomic changes in rural and maritime Brittany had brought to an isolated, self-sufficient, but poverty-ridden population the promise of "modernization" with its attendant benefits. But the results of these changes within the next two decades of the twentieth century were largely negative. Demographic expansion checked the gains from increased agricultural productivity, and entry into a competitive world market rendered the Breton fishing economy highly vulnerable to price fluctuations. The eventual decline in the economy, coupled with a growing realization of Brittany's peripheral position with regard to the center of economic and political control in Paris, created a favorable climate for incipient nationalism.

Increased productivity, one of the prime effects of neotechnical agriculture, served not only to tie the peasant to the local market, but substantially enlarged his food supply and improved his diet. The result was an expansion in family size, creating a significant surge in population growth out of proportion to available arable land. The drift from rural areas to local towns and cities was accelerated, but, because urban areas were limited in size and number with small-scale industries that could only absorb limited labor, the result was simply to increase the number of unemployed. The alternative was massive migration from the region: between 1891–1911 the exodus increased to 206,000 compared with 126,000 from 1872–1891.[2] The inability of the Breton economy to keep pace with population growth was becoming increasingly evident.

The decline of the highly specialized fishing industry further added to a sense of crisis. In the fast expanding competitive market of commercial fishing, Brittany soon fell behind. The important sardine industry was first struck. An oversupply in conjunction with heavy competition from foreign trawler fleets brought a collapse in prices. Conflict was generated internally: fishermen disputed with canneries over prices, factory workers were at odds with bosses, and fisherman undercut fisherman.[3] At about the same time, deep-sea fishing was declining for the same reasons. Competition from foreign mechanized fleets and the invasion of European markets by cheaper products each year reduced the number of ships leaving Breton ports. By the beginning of World War I, fleets had dwindled, ports were at a standstill, and unemployment was widespread. The war itself effectively brought to an end what had been for more than three decades Brittany's major enterprise.

THE EMERGENCE OF BRETON NATIONALISM

Against this background of increasing socioeconomic dislocation at the turn of the century, a growing awareness of regional disadvantage was accompanied by considerable political disaffection with the centralized bureaucracy in Paris. What Bretons perceived to be a crisis peculiar to the region's special problems was not apparently recognized as such by the national government. Its inaction, interpreted as disinterest, created a climate of strong regionalist antipathy; one solution appeared to be some form of regional autonomy. Crystalizing around this issue, the movement of protest took on a nationalist coloring with the establishment of the Union Régionaliste Bretonne (URB), called by one historian "the first avowedly Breton regionalist society."

> With this society's appearance in 1898 the Breton movement embarked irreversibly on the path of self-conscious political action. Thereafter, for both Breton patriots and their French adversaries alike, it became a permanent part of Brittany's history.[4]

Prior to this latter crystalization of Breton national feeling, a latent nationalism had existed since the French Revolution. Under Jacobin rule, the political rights of regional autonomy were revoked and the Breton language suppressed. Through the nineteenth century, a small group of patriotic liberals struggled to keep alive a consciousness of an indigenous Breton culture and language. Writers and historians scoured the past for evidence of a separate national heritage. In the romantic tradition of the early nineteenth century, a collection of folk tales, *Barzaz-Briez* (The Bards of Brittany), signified a literary tradition distinct from that of the French. Breton historians emphasized the centuries of political independence that ended in 1532 when, as a result of the marriage of Anne (Duchess de Bretagne) to the king of France, the duchy was annexed to the expanding state, retaining, however, its own sovereign assembly until 1789. Historians kept alive the memory of Genera Cadoudal, who led the Bretons against Napoleon in 1804 and was subsequently defeated, tried, and executed. Thus historic events became translated into myths of protest against the tyranny of the state.

Although intellectuals were the most active in the attempt to retain a sense of Breton identity, the effects of their scholarly efforts were probably limited. The appeal seemed directed more at the small aristocratic, land-owning class whose conversion to French culture and language had become conspicuous by the early nineteenth century.

It was a different matter among members of the peasant class whose identity as Bretons was apparently not in question. In the late nineteenth century, increased farm income was channeled into conspicuous consumption. Especially in the western half of the peninsula (Basse-Bretagne), costly and intricately designed costumes of a distinct Breton style appeared, along with ornate carved furniture. Each district elaborated its special costumes, traditional music, and dances. At the turn of the century when peasantry as a way of life was dying out in other areas of France, it was reaching new peaks in Brittany.

From these various themes and symbols of Breton culture, the URB fashioned an ideology that wove together the concept of cultural revival and a program of economic and political reform. It called for the teaching of Breton in the school system, a recognition of former Breton rights by an increase in regional representation at the parliamentary level, greater effort and expenditure to develop natural resources, and the alleviation of the economic crisis in ports and farms. Although an intransigent central government chose to ignore the demands, the URB was instrumental in establishing a precedent, indeed a model, for future nationalist associations. From this point on, the goal of establishing an improved economic order was linked with the re-creation of a past identity viewed as a kind of golden age of political freedom, with cultural and linguistic autonomy.

NATIONALIST ORGANIZATIONS BEFORE WORLD WAR I

In the period of economic crisis prior to World War I, the nationalist movement expanded rapidly with a proliferation of associations and the appearance of a number of periodicals attempting to foster a distinctive "Breton consciousness." A Catholic association founded in 1905 by a liberal priest, Abbé Perrot, dedicated to the revival of the language and traditional culture, symbolically took for its name the Breton term Bleun-Brug (Heath Flower). Although professing not to be concerned with political goals, Abbé Perrot took a firm regionalist position with respect to a restoration of former rights as the only means of pressuring for economic and social reform. Bleun-Brug was particularly effective in supporting and stimulating interest in traditional Breton music, songs, dances, and costumes, organizing regional festivals and sponsoring language classes for young people. At the same time, the intellectual elite at the forefront of the movement was attempting to reach all segments of the public through periodicals, newspapers, and reviews. More than a dozen periodicals, some exclusively in Breton, appeared during the prewar era, a few polemical in nature but all dedicated to reviving a sense of ethnicity and to coupling economic reform with political and cultural freedom. To all nationalists, the Breton language became the symbol of the new ideology. Petitions to permit the teaching of the language were sent yearly to Paris between 1905–11, but they were greeted by silence.

The movement entered a separatist phase in 1911 with the establishment of the first Breton nationalist party (Strollad Broadel Breiz). Two aspects differentiated the organization from the URB. The new party was led by a small group of young liberal writers and journalists who espoused political activism in contrast with the URB's conservative and pacifist program. Furthermore, the basic tenet of the party platform was the complete severance of ties with France and the creation of a sovereign nation. It was a stride beyond the URB's cautious plea for restoration of regional rights. To further circulate this demand, an official party organ, *Breiz Dishual* (Free Brittany), was founded; its rallying cry was "Brittany for the Bretons." Within its pages appeared one of the strongest denunciations of the French government yet heard. Speaking of French "oppression" since Brittany's annexation in 1532, it cited the gradual attrition of liberties and the loss of the language, customs, and civil and religious traditions that constituted the former national patrimony; it spoke of the refusal to assimilate to French culture in terms of the ability of "the Breton soul" to survive and resist all efforts to crush and annihilate it. Likening Brittany to enslaved Ireland and Poland, the party called for independence and nationhood, with the use of its own flag, its own language, and its own national hymn.[5]

Although the militancy of the nationalist party was eclipsed a few years later by the outbreak of the war, the pattern of political action in the name of nationalism was set as a model to be resurrected in a new guise at a later date.

THE RISE OF FACTIONALISM

While the disruption of four years of war brought an end to specific organizations and the diverse publications supporting Breton nationalist goals, some evidence of the movement's viability was revealed at the Peace Conference in 1919. Phrasing the aspirations of Breton separatists in terms of the Wilsonian principle of self-determination, a petition was presented to President Woodrow Wilson and the conference members called for national sovereignty in the name of Brittany's former independence. The petition was signed by 800 *notables*: deputies, senators, general councilors, and the five Breton bishops.

The following years saw the inauguration of a series of new periodicals and reviews dedicated to a revival of the nationalist movement. One journal, *Breiz Atao* (Brittany Forever), was considered the most influential.[6] Like a phoenix rising from the ashes, it embodied the resurrection of the polemic, the spirit, and the fervor of the prewar publications. In French and Breton, it addressed itself specifically to the leading economic problems of the postwar decade, linking the only hope for economic development with political independence from France. Pointing to the recently gained freedom of the Czechs, Bulgars, and Poles, it stated that "the incapacity of the French state machine, the inactivity of the French people faced with the profound crisis of our epoch, force us to look to ourselves to find a solution for our economic problems."[7] Chief among the issues pinpointed by *Breiz Atao* were the increased exodus from the farms, the neglected ports, and urban unemployment. Calling attention to the disparity between taxes paid out and government spending for the region, economic salvation was viewed in terms of autonomy: utilization of regional revenues for self-development, the creation of industry, rehabilitation of the ports, and revitalization of a farming economy undermined by unfavorable market conditions.

Through the 1920s *Breiz Atao* remained the principal voice of the nationalist movement. Although at first a quarto review, it was later to become the official organ of a formal party organization. Supporters of the movement held annual congresses to discuss policy and its implementation; at the Congress held in 1927 the decision to form a nationalist party was announced. Le Parti Autonomiste Breton (PAB) was officially founded a few months later.

Internal dissension soon arose over the issue of separatism and nationhood versus federalism. The concept of a European federation was gaining adherents among other national minority groups. Some Breton nationalists saw distinct advantages to be gained not only in the structure of federation, but also in allying the new party with similar political organizations representing minority groups in other areas of Europe. Eventually those favoring federalism over separation emerged in control of the new party, with *Breiz Atao* the official party journal. Factionalism continued, however, and, combined with financial difficulties, effectively undermined party organization. In 1931 the separatists regained leadership of the movement, reforming in the name of a new party, the Parti National Breton (PNB).

Although their goals were designed to be realized through legitimate political channels, neither the PAB nor the PNB gained enough popular support to carry through a successful electoral campaign. Schism within the ranks of the nationalist leaders, even after the emergence of the PNB, continued to weaken the effectiveness of the nationalist movement as a totality.

The need to awaken the public of Brittany, and of France as well, to the urgency of the Breton problem set the course of PNB throughout the Great Depression of the 1930s. The party launched a vigorous propaganda campaign through *Breiz Atao*, combined with nonviolent demonstrations at government-sponsored ceremonies and during visits by French government officials.

Coincident with the emergence of PNB's program of a "politics of force" was the opening phase of a new "politics for violence." Modeled after the Irish Sin Fein, a secret association formed, calling itself Gwenn Ha Du (White and Black) after the colors of the Breton flag. Echoing the PNB's program of achieving economic, cultural, and linguistic reforms through independence, it began a series of violent demonstrations against the central government. One of the initial acts, in 1932, was the blowing up of a statue in Rennes, which commemorated the union of Brittany with France, at the very moment the French premier was attending the celebration of the 400th anniversary of that union in another Breton city. During the next few years, there were numerous acts of terrorism such as the bombing of administrative buildings in various towns and cities of the region. Less militant separatists, although overtly disavowing the Gwenn Ha Du, realized its value. One writer, while admitting it was a terrorist organization, claimed it had nevertheless struck a forceful blow for the cause and had served to whip up the energies of the otherwise apathetic Breton.[8]

The demonstrations also had the effect of reinforcing the French government's negative attitude toward the Breton nationalist movement and its demands, at the same time alerting Paris to the need for a confrontation with the activists.

Though the separatists remained divided over the degree of extremism necessary to achieve their goals, there was implicit agreement that political action had to be taken outside of legitimate channels. Opposed to this new point were the regionalists whose pacifism, conservatism, and belief in moderate legitimate courses of action branded them as the reactionaries of the movement. Some of these associations were among the pioneers of the movement: the Catholic Bleun-Blug, the URB, Association Bretonne; others like the Gorsedd of Bards, although supporting Breton claims, had been essentially apolitical. In 1936 these associations combined in a Front Breton to formulate a program for political, economic, and cultural reforms under a regional scheme. Forty-one candidates at the general elections agreed to accept the program, and 15 were elected.

While the regionalist view achieved some temporary political representation, these successes were not followed by any action on the part of the government to meet even moderate demands. In response, the separatists accelerated their antigovernment propaganda and demonstrations. Finally, in 1939, the government officially dissolved the PNB and banned its newspaper. Two of its leaders who had escaped to Germany were condemned to death in absentia; others were imprisoned.

The exiled leaders in Germany appealed to that government to support their demands for independence and apparently were assured by high officials that a Breton state would be set up at the end of the war.[9]

After the invasion of France and its subsequent defeat in 1940, Breton nationalists looked to the German conquerors for support. The separatist faction reemerged—from exile and prison—and a new organization, Conseil National Breton, was formed to implement the program leading to eventual autonomy. The Parti National Breton was resurrected and the official party newspaper given a symbolic title, L'Heure Bretonne (Brittany's Hour). But their demands for complete autonomy and their violent anti-Vichy stand brought about several adverse reactions. The Vichy government pressured the German administration to take active measures against the Breton nationalists. Although no repressive action was taken, German support of extremist nationalist goals weakened, and a shift was made instead to the more moderate demands of the regionalists. Accordingly, in 1941, the Breton language and history were admitted as subjects within the schools, radio broadcasts in Breton were authorized, and a Celtic institute was set up to coordinate the cultural societies dedicated to research on the Breton intellectual and artistic heritage. The regionalists were also instrumental in setting up a Comité Consultatif de Bretagne modeled after the prerevolutionary Parlement de Bretagne, but it failed to obtain an official status.

The concessions granted to the regionalists, while minimal, served to antagonize the French and widen the breach between the Bretons and French, eventually leading to open conflict. The Vichy government regarded the newly found gains as evidence of an anti-French secessionist plot. Some members of the *maquis*, the French resistance movement, apparently linking nationalist gains with pro-German collaborators, began, in 1943, a campaign of assassination against Bretons who belonged to any nationalist group, whether political or cultural in emphasis.

The climax of the anti-Breton campaign came with the murder of the founder of Bleun-Brug, Abbé Perrot, the pioneer and symbol of the nationalist movement. The effect was to shift many "neutral" Bretons into open opposition to the French Resistance. A radical splinter group from the PNB organized a military unit, the Formation Jean-Marie Perrot, to oppose the maquis. It aligned itself with the Germans and accepted German arms and uniforms. The internecine conflict continued, a symbolic demonstration of the widening gap that separated Breton goals and French determination to oppose them.

The French view that the Perrot unit typified Breton pro-German and anti-French activities led directly, in the postwar period, to the severe suppression of all aspects of nationalism. After the liberation, the concessions allowed by the Germans were withdrawn and the language banned; arrest warrants were issued for anyone connected with any Breton society or association, irrespective of political orientation. Sentences of banishment, confiscation of property, and loss of civil rights were passed. A number of Bretons were imprisoned, some leaders escaped to Ireland, and 15 were executed in 1946.

The result of this punitive action was to strengthen the base of the movement rather than to weaken it. From this base, a fresh growth of nationalist associations soon emerged, expressing at first cultural rather than political or economic goals. Brittany's failure to recover from the postwar economic slump soon directed attention to the need for action, and economic demands came once more to the fore of nationalist programs.

THE POSTWAR PERIOD

The decade following the liberation was marked by general economic stagnation in both rural and urban sectors of Brittany. A wartime shift from commercial cash-cropping to a base of mixed farming and self-subsistence had now to be reversed. But past experience with unstable prices tended to produce a conservative reaction—diversified farming once revived was sustained as a hedge against market fluctuations and rising food prices, even at the risk of income loss and a lowered standard of living.[10] The exodus from farms to towns and cities began again. Urban areas, however, had suffered widespread and, in some cases, total destruction during the invasion, and reconstruction was lagging. An already atrophied industrial sector was unable to provide necessary employment for the growing population. In 1947–50, major strikes and demonstrations broke out among shipyard workers in two of Brittany's major ports, St. Nazaire and Brest.

Beginning in 1948, while other areas of France entered a period of growth and expansion, regions such as Brittany and, particularly, its more isolated western area (Finistère) continued in a state of stagnation and decline. Between 1954 and 1962, the number of farmers fell by 25 percent and that of fishermen by 20 percent. The scarcity of jobs caused by population surplus and social mobility intensified migration: 2,500 young people were leaving Sud-Finistère annually. The signs of demographic imbalance were evident after 1950, and the declining ratio of young people in the total population compared unfavorably with the national average.[11]

Those who remained—a new generation of farmers—were instrumental in breaking away from the pattern of mixed farming. The period from 1950 to the late 1960s saw a transformation paralleling the second agricultural revolution of the late nineteenth century: a shift to commercial specialized crops but with improved technology. Just as the new plow marked a major innovation in the past, the tractor now became the craze. Rapid mechanization was stimulated both by the government's stress on expansion and productivity and the availability of credit from farm syndicates. But, as Wright points out, mechanization was not always the solution to the peasant problem and often had uneconomic consequences: one was a heavy burden of peasant indebtedness, and another was the unprofitable attempt to mechanize too small a farm.[12]

And, too, the modernization of agriculture was more than a matter of change in technology. On the distribution side, the marketing system had changed little in 50 years. An archaic transportation system and the long distance to the Paris market in combination with competitive pricing from more favored regions often created a situation of feast or famine. The government's slowness to take more than minimal action to regulate the anarchy of market pricing finally produced a violent reaction from Breton commercial farmers.

Beginning with the "artichoke revolution" of 1960 and continuing into 1961, farmers began a series of mass demonstrations in market garden areas, climaxing in the *jacquerie* of June 1961. At that point, some 4,000 farmers on tractors, protesting a sharp drop in commodity prices, jammed the highway leading to the market town of Morlaix. The leaders were young syndicalists whose later arrests triggered almost two weeks of rural insurrection.

THE RENAISSANCE OF THE NATIONALIST MOVEMENT

The worsening economic crisis again brought to the forefront the latent forces of the nationalist movement. Fragmented groups, their organizations officially dissolved in the postwar reprisals, began to draw together after 1950 under the unofficial designation of Comité d'Etudes et de Liaison des Intérêts Breton (CELIB). Its principal goal was to facilitate regional economic development and expansion through merging various economic, occupatonal, and cultural groups in a united front, a regional pressure group that would draw up and present programs of economic reform to the government. Although its aims were primarily economic, the structure of CELIB included a cultural commission concerned with winning official recognition.

Avowedly apolitical, it was nevertheless a reformation of prewar conservative regionalist groups and as such was opposed by the more politically active separatists, who viewed the solution of economic problems as possible only within the context of political action and cultural autonomy. A schism also developed within the CELIB between those who wished to remain politically neutral and those who favored seeking left-wing support.

Despite its official recognition as an advisory group by the government in 1961, some eight years later it had still been unable to achieve any of its goals in parliament. As the failure of the CELIB became evident, the initial reservation of antiregionalist critics seemed justified. Countermoves to create alternative programs brought a proliferation of nationalist associations, which, while sharing common goals, differed in emphasis and means of achievement. Two types emerged in most cases, reflecting continuity with patterns or in some cases actual organizations established in the prewar period: those with a strong politcoeconomic bias and the cultural organizations that stressed language reform and the revival of Breton dance, music, and the arts. Those inclined toward political action included, in the order of their founding: Le Mouvement pour l'Organisation de la Bretagne (MOB), Union Démocratique Bretonne (UDB), Front pour la Libération de Bretagne (FLB), Sav Breizh, and Strollad Ar Vro (SAV).

An early opponent of the CELIB policy of qualified regionalism, the MOB was founded in 1957 in the tradition of the prewar federalists. Its program outlined the evolution of Brittany toward internal federalism within the French state. But, because of de Gaulle's intransigence, it later shifted its line in favor of independence from France and incorporation within a European federal state.[13]

Led by a militant intellectual, Yann Fouere, a platform of political, economic, and cultural demands was announced with the familiar emotional overtones of prewar appeals: "The spirit of the Breton political movement is decapitated—we must give it a head, a spirit, a goal, a flame, a hope, a will." The appeal to young militants was a strong one, and it was chiefly this group that responded. Caerleon, patriot and historian of the nationalist movement, states that the MOB became categorized in time as extremist and failed to capture widespread popular support.[14] By 1972 it was virtually moribund.

To represent the more conservative element, the UDB was formed in 1963, calling for a special regional assembly with effective autonomy in economic and cultural affairs. Though regionalist in aims, its policy of direct political action through sponsorship of Bretonnant candidates for election clearly marked a return to the prewar policy of the Parti Nationaliste Bretonne.

The FLB represented the extremist faction. Essentially embracing the policy of terrorism that characterized the prewar Gwenn Ha Du, it sought to dramatize the issues of regional neglect and inequality through a campaign of violence and harrassment, including the bombing of police stations, prefectures, and tax offices selected as symbolic of centralized authority and domination. Beginning in 1966, bombing incidents accelerated until in 1968 at least 25 were reported. The government response was increased police surveillance, culminating in 1969 with more than 50 arrests of suspected members and a temporary halt of terrorist activity.

In June, 1978 the bombing of a part of the Chateau de Versailles devoted to Napoleonic paintings and treasures was perhaps the most dramatically symbolic of more than two dozen bomb attacks claimed by the FLB between September, 1976 and that date. The two twenty-eight year old men arrested for the Versailles attack were said to have boasted, during the subsequent trial, that loyal Bretons they had struck against the symbol of imperialist French culture. (Daily Telegraph, London [Paris correspondent release], 12/1/78).

The ideology of the FLB was both sophisticated and compelling. The concept of Brittany as another Algeria was a major keynote. The demand for "decolonization" of the region was put into the context of the post-1945 worldwide movement to free former colonies. In taking action toward this goal, the FLB claimed in a 1968 manifesto to have borrowed the schemes and methods that had proven effective in anticolonial struggles in other parts of the world.

The effectiveness of this image of an oppressed people battling against tyrannical domination was only magnified by the wholesale arrest and long incarceration of the suspects without trial. Public sympathy was prevailingly on the side of the FLB; although the acts of violence were deplored, it was pointed out that no lives had been lost—the strikes were symbolically against government property only. Even supporters of non-violent protest were quick to point out that the government's continued neglect of Brittany was breeding the violence. René Pleven, conservative politician and writer, makes the point that, "The public powers can stop attempts of the agitators most effectively by announcing a plan of sweeping action. Obvious economic difficulties of the region aid the agitators to find cooperation in the population."[15] Reece, in a detailed report and analysis of FLB organization and activities, notes that the diversity of class backgrounds of arrested militants indicated that nationalist views had a wide spectrum of support in the peninsula, including factory workers, farmers, intellectuals, military officers, business managers, and priests, and that more than two-thirds of the 36 alleged members whose ages were reported were less than 29 years old.[16]

The fact that the nationalist movement springs predominantly from disaffection of the younger generation was demonstrated in the 1968 riots in Paris. Sav Breizh was a short-lived group that had its genesis in the nationwide so-called "cultural revolution" of May-June 1968. During the fighting in the Paris streets, young Bretons, emigrés, and students carried their black and white flag alongside representatives of other French minority groups, the Occitans (of Languedoc) and Corsicans among others. The Breton program, socialist in leaning, consisted of the familiar blend of tradition and innovation; it demanded self-government with the aim of alleviating underdevelopment, protecting the traditional culture, and restoring language. But current issues were also stressed; included were opposition to the common market, a moratorium on farmers' and workers' debts, agricultural cooperatives, and an affirmation of solidarity with all other oppressed minority groups, including the Blacks of North America and the Indians in South America.[17]

The most recent group to emerge, the SAV, coalesced in 1972 from the more conservative members of earlier nationalist groups. But, while originally right-wing in orientation, the membership has steadily supported policies associated with the socialist movement and the increasingly leftist VDB, and it has been suggested that a merger with Union Démocratique de Bretagne (UDB) is a possibility for the near future.

Certainly this would unify two rival nationalist groups and reinforce the existence of a single Breton political party.

But legitimate political channels are viewed by a minority of radicals as having failed too often in the past. Renewed terrorist activity in 1973 and the bombing and total destruction of the main television transmission tower for Brittany in 1974 were evidence that the FLB was still regarded as the powerful arm of the nationalist movement. The argument that the miniscule amount of time national television allotted to Breton language programs was a threat to the preservation and propagation of the indigenous language was understandable to many.

During my field work in Brest in 1973 and 1975, it was evident that Breton youth and young adults were becoming a powerful force in the renaissance of Breton consciousness. Prominent in the assertion of the new ethnicity was the use of sleeve and sweater patches displaying the Breton flag or symbols of identification with Celtic heritage. Traditional folk-dancing events (*Fest-Noz*) were often held several times a week and were overwhelmingly attended. Breton music, traditional and modernized, along with music of Ireland and Scotland, dominated jukeboxes in a growing number of cafes and bars dedicated to fostering a new Breton consciousness and its links with the broader Celtic world. Breton recordings, virtually unavailable before 1965, were escalating between 1973–75. Breton language classes were offered in evening courses at several lycées as well as at the University of Brest. Some classes were held in sections of more than 100 students, primarily young adults. Although firm figures were not available, membership in such a popular organization as UDB was asserted to consist predominantly of men and women between 18 and 30 years of age.

In conversations and interviews with informants, there was an expression of open hostility and resentment against the French government and people. Whereas the government was popularly identified as the major offender, local animosity was often directed toward the French who, as tourists and summer residents, were seen as condescending and demeaning. In the presence of French visitors, local residents deliberately used whatever Breton they knew, or, if educated, spoke in English, however poorly. Breton students often preferred to hitchhike in Wales or Ireland when traveling during the summer and welcomed in return visitors from other Celtic regions. "Cultural exchanges," particularly of singing and musical groups, were forging strong links among Celts. As one young local informant put it, "First a Breton, then a Celt; never a Frenchman."

In conclusion, a new consciousness, even pride, in being Breton seems finally to be taking root in the new generation. Although membership in formal political organizations may be low proportionate to the regional population, the acceptance of the new ethnicity appears to be the clearest expression of the swelling flood of protest against years of recurrent cycles of regional economic crisis and decline. Brittany, viewed as a peripheral region, is very much a part of the same Celtic "fringe" Hechter speaks about in his work on internal colonialism in Great Britain.[18] Similarly, economic malintegration in France, between the core (the centralized bureaucracy) and the underdeveloped periphery, jeopardizes the stability of the social and political order. Further, when social and economic inequalities are perceived in ethnic terms and translated into the nationalism of political action—barriers are set up that truly threaten the integrity of the nation-state.

NOTES

1. Michael Hechter, *Internal Colonialism: The Celtic Fringe in British National Development 1536–1966* (Berkeley and Los Angeles: University of California Press, 1975).

2. Jean Delumeau ed., *Histoire de la Bretagne* (Toulouse: Privat, 1969), p. 466.

3. Ibid., p. 466.

4. Jack E. Reece, *The Bretons Against France* (Chapel Hill: University of North Carolina Press, 1977), p. 24.

5. René Barbin, *Le Mouvement Breton: Autonisme et Fédéralisme*, (Rennes: Imprimerie Bretonne, 1937), pp. 114–15.

6. Ibid, pp. 127 ff.

7. Ul Bolitho, "France's Ireland," *Outlook* 54: 248.

8. Barbin, *Le Mouvement Breton*, pp. 141–45.

9. P. B. Ellis, *Wales, A Nation Again: The Nationalist Struggle for Freedom* (London: Library 33, 1968), p. 188.

10. Edgar Morin, *The Red and the White: Report from a French Village* (New York: Random House, 1970), p. 52.

11. Ibid, pp. 49 ff.

12. Gordon Wright, *Rural Revolution in France: The Peasantry in the Twentieth Century* (Stanford: Stanford University Press, 1964), p. 145.

13. Ellis, *Wales, A Nation Again*, p. 192.

14. Ronan Caerleon, *La Révolution Breton Permanente* (Paris: La Table Ronde, 1969), pp. 50 ff.

15. Ibid, p. 171.

16. Reece, *The Bretons Against France*, pp. 207 ff.

17. Caerleon, *La Révolution Breton*, pp. 204 ff.

18. Hechter, *Internal Colonialism*.

9

ETHNIC CONFLICT AND MODERNIZATION IN THE SOUTH TYROL

Flavia Pristinger

At the first elections of the European parliament, the ethnic party of the South Tyrol, the People's Party (SVP), which for more than 30 years has been the political representative of almost all of the German-speaking people of the region, chose to side with the principal party of the Italian state, the Christian Democrats (DC); the SVP thus refused to join with the autonomous movements, especially those of the Alpine regions, that were committed to a common slate. Because the minority of the South Tyrol is known for its unusual cultural and socioeconomic vitality and for its successful campaign for autonomy, this choice merits examination. What were the reasons for it, and what is its significance?

Beyond indicating the obvious motivation of the SVP to have its own candidate elected, the decision of the representatives of the South Tyrol points, without a doubt, to a political choice—adherence to the group of moderate forces in the political geography of Europe.

The party seems intent upon representing itself on the European scene in a decidedly more political and less ethnic light. Its logic is that of a smaller political party interested in forming alliances that would maintain the present political, economical, and social equilibrium in Europe. By examining the political history of the South Tyrolean minority over the last 30 years, one realizes why it should have such priorities today. Its concerns with autonomy have already been satisfied, and those concerns therefore no longer constitute a source of conflict or of mobilization for the minority. The people of the South Tyrol are now interested in stabilizing their acquired status as the dominant group in the area, with respect not only to the small Ladin minority but also, paradoxically, to the Italian linguistic group.

The people of the South Tyrol today are a dynamic and privileged minority in comparison with other ethnic and linguistic groups in Italy, and they are an advanced example of a solution to European ethnic conflicts: they are capable of controlling and advancing the growth of their group while guarding its ethnic character, and they possess the proper political, legislative, and financial instruments for administering autonomously the economic and social development of their territory.

The minority of the South Tyrol has reached this crossroads after a long and contradictory development, the basic of elements of which should be outlined. In the course of its development, the minority, like most ethnic minorities, has faced a long period of being ignored on economic and social levels, of cultural isolation and privation, and of periods of bitter tension in its dealings with the country that ruled it.

THE ORIGINS OF THE CONFLICT

The annexation of the South Tyrol to Italy (1919) marked the traumatic beginning of a new period in its history, separating it from Tyrol and Austria, whose culture it had for many centuries shared.[1] This annexation presented delicate problems of national identity and of the relationship between the Italian state and the internal entity that would soon become its most rebellious ethnic minority.

The annexation did not damage the equilibrium or the coexistence of the different ethnic-linguistic groups in the area. These included the German-speaking group, which was much more consistent and deeply tied to the patriotic history of Tyrol and which had a strong cultural identity; the Ladins, an old population speaking a neo-Latin language, concentrated in the highest valleys of the Dolomite region; and the Italians, who came for the most part from the populous valleys of the Trentino.[2] Both minority groups (in 1910 the Italians in the South Tyrol comprised 3 percent of the population and the Ladins a little less than 4 percent) were in some measure subject to assimilation by the dominant German element, more so in the case of the Italians, who were not protected as were the Ladins by a barrier of geographic isolation.

On the other hand, the overall backward productive structure of the South Tyrol in the first decades of this century, which was characterized by a primarily rural economy, a low incidence of industrial activity, and a modest tradition of commercial exchanges, explains the absence of any form of social division of work among the three groups and the uniformity of social stratification among them.[3]

Following the annexation, the formation of a new national identity in the South Tyrol was destined to encounter its most difficult obstacle in the "ethnic compactness" of the German-speaking community, which had been not weakened but, in fact, strengthened by the breaking of its ties with its former rulers.

It is known that the problem of national identity in ethnic minorities can be confronted politically in two ways: by a policy of assimilation directed at eliminating the distinctive cultural characteristics of the minority by absorbing them in the dominant culture or by a policy called "unity within diversity" (political unity, cultural diversity) that seeks to legitimize national authorities and win obedience for them without eliminating minority cultures. The second policy is based on a different political balance achieved by giving each ethnic group representation proportionate to its numerical size at the various levels and in the various sectors of organization of the state.[4] Since the annexation, the minority of South Tyrol has experienced both these policies of integration, for the failure of the policy of assimilation forced the Italian state to choose the policy of "unity within diversity," a choice that has been seriously applied only in recent times.

The problem that arose for Italy after the annexation was that of assuring that the minority would respect the central political institutions; that is, it had to resolve the crisis of legitimacy caused by the inclusion of a new territory and a new population within the confines of the nation.[5] If a "physiological" solution to the crisis were possible (the traditional South Tyrolean respect for authority, nurtured by centuries of Austrian domination and strict Catholicism would have certainly helped further such a solution),[6] its implementation was prevented by the brutal policy of Fascist denationalization, which postponed the beginning of any solution to this problem until after the war.

In the few years between annexation and the advent of Fascism, there was a relatively tolerable climate for the development of a minority identity because of the absence of authoritarian initiatives or efforts toward assimilation with the dominant community. Although the Italian government did not allow a special form of autonomy for the new minority, it limited its intervention to bureaucratic and administrative influences.[7] On the economic plane, integration was attempted only in certain sectors of industry and commerce.[8]

Significant for the future was the change in political representation that came about with the unification of the two principal political parties of the South Tyrol. The People's Party of Tyrol (the popular party of Tyrol), which represented the farmers and the conservative and clerical elements, joined with the Deutschfreiheitliche Partei (the liberal German party), which represented the urban interests of the commercial middle class and the professionals. This unification created in 1919 the "Deutscher Verband" (German alliance), the precursor of the ethnic party (Sammelpartei) that became the voice of the "substructure" of the politics of the South Tyrol after the war. A testament to its vast population among the people of the South Tyrol (it was popular despite its short existence; the Fascists suspended its operation in 1926) are the results of the elections of 1921 in which its four candidates were elected as the only representatives of the minority on a platform of defending its ethnic quality. Requests for self-rule, for the preservation of the German character of the area, and for exemption from military service for the people of the South Tyrol were its main objectives.[9]

The corruption produced by more than 20 years of Fascist rule in the South Tyrol is at the root of the discrimination suffered by the people of the South Tyrol until recent years and of their long contention with the Italian state, which has been especially heated since 1955. The policy of denationalization under Fascist rule was very pronounced, both at the structural level (interference with the ethnic composition of the population, with the productive structure of the area, and with the local labor market) and at the politicocultural level (restrictive measures concerning the means of expression and maintenance of the German character of the region such as language, the press, schools, unions, and so on).

On an economic and social plane, the grave disequilibrium brought by Fascist rule greatly affected local life. An industrialization plan of vast proportions culminated in the creation of an industrial zone in Bolzano in about 1935, which radically modified the traditional composition of the region. Exploiting the ample reserves of hydroelectric energy in the South Tyrol made possible in just a few years the construction of large factories for metallurgy, chemistry, and so on.[10] Thus an imbalance was created between this new dynamic reality and the traditional sectors of local industry.[11] To support this process of industrialization, a massive Italian immigration was promulgated; this influx had the consequence of disturbing the traditional ratio between the different ethnic and linguistic groups of the region and of introducing sharp inequalities in socioeconomic status.

Three migratory waves during the Fascist era raised the number of Italian-speaking residents of the South Tyrol from about 7,000 (3 percent) before the annexation to 104,750 (35 percent) in 1943. The first, which ended around 1925, was composed mainly of staff workers in the state bureaucracy and military; the second, of a much greater scope, provided workers necessary for the industrialization; the third was determined by the effects of the accord on the "options," to be discussed. The principal destination for the immigrants was Bolzano, the capital, the population of which grew in the years 1921–27 by a median annual increase of 25.8 per

1,000 inhabitants; in the period 1937–39, this rate shot to 93.1. In Bolzano, and later in other major cities, the Italians became the majority.[12] The Italian immigrants came to dominate the cities, and the Germans the rural areas; this development is reflected in the distribution of the German and Italian populations according to levels of altitude. In 1939, the percentage of Italians residing in areas where the altitude is from 200 to 300 meters was 58 percent, whereas the Germans comprised 15 percent.[13] At the end of the Fascist era, the separation between Italian city and German countryside constituted its most burdensome legacy.

But it was not only in the industrial sector that Fascist economic policies brought grave and long-lasting consequences. In particular, there was a progressive deterioration of local agriculture, which was forced to compete with the national market. This resulted in damaging effects such as abandonment of important types of cultivation, drastic reductions of livestock, and a crisis in the grape-growing sector, which before the annexation had been one of the most important sectors in the local economy. Furthermore, the stability of the social structure of the South Tyrol was undermined by the abolition of the tradition of the "closed farms," carried out with the purpose of disintegrating the farmer class of the region.[14] The people's strong attachment to the land and to tradition, however, limited the scope and effectiveness of this measure. Between 1929 and 1954 (the year in which the institution of the "closed farms" was fomally restored), the "closed" properties were reduced by 6.2 percent to about 12,000.

But the most damaging effects for the minority of the South Tyrol resulted from the "options," a tragic consequence of the Nazi-Fascist alliance.[15] Confronted with the alternatives of renouncing their German ethnic identity or of being transferred to the Germany of Hitler, 83 percent of the German and Ladin populace, about 240,000 people, chose to emigrate. Nonetheless, only 30 percent actually left the country between 1939 and 1943, the year in which these "options" were suspended because of the war; of this 30 percent, the majority came from nonagricultural sectors of the society. Those who emigrated were for the most part dependent workers. Divided by profession, the emigrants respresented 67 percent of the South Tyrolean industrial workers and artisans, 40 percent of the workers in tourism, 83 percent of those in transportation, and 9 percent of those in agriculture. This loss of active forces therefore struck the minority of the South Tyrol in the most vital economic sectors, which were concentrated in the urban centers; between 1939 and 1943 these centers suffered a net population loss of more than 40 percent. The reduction in the local job force further stimulated Italian immigration, which reached its peak during those years.[16]

One can easily see how the sum of these factors, which shattered the traditional dominant position of the German-speaking group, came to shape the future of the interethnic relations in the South Tyrol. In the long run, the system of ethnic division of labor instituted by Fascism weighed even more heavily than the simple numerical changes in the population. The exclusion of the minority of the South Tyrol from the modern factors of production and its total dependence on the outmoded agricultural sector brought growing imbalance to the conditions of life and limited the possibility of progress for the various groups in the region.

The process of economic and social isolation was accompanied by a progressive cultural deprivation that was brought about by a series of restrictive measures aimed at effecting a rapid de-Germanization of the South Tyrol. These measures included the abolition of German schools, the introduction of Italian as the only language for teaching and as the official language of public and judicial administration, the exclusion of German-speaking citizens from civil service jobs, the progressive Italian-ization of geographical names and family names, and the almost total supression of German-language publications.[17]

Two particular consequences of this policy merit discussion. First is the emergence within the German-speaking community of elements that are typical of a "subculture" phenomenon.[18] The community of the South Tyrol became increasingly isolated and assumed an attitude of self-defense; this attitude, which became apparent soon after the annexation, increased under the pressure of the Fascist attack on the ethnic integrity of the minority. This withdrawal from the outside world, the tendency of the minority to look within itself and to lean toward the past,[19] became the most outstanding characteristic of the community of the South Tyrol, and even after the Fascist era, it remains one of the principal obstacles to cultural exchange with the other ethnic components of the province. The isolation of the minority makes for a strong sense of identity among the people of the South Tyrol, for feelings of ethnic solidarity, and for intense participation in the life of the group.

A second important consequence of the policy of de-Germanization was the resurgence among the German-speaking population of strictly nationalistic sentiments that were alien to the tradition of the South Tyrol, even with its strong regional patriotism.[20] It was in this new climate that the political leadership that led the battle for autonomy was formed.[21]

THE BATTLE FOR AUTONOMY

The development of the ethnic question of the South Tyrol from the postwar period to today has been notably complex because of the interaction of many institutional socioeconomic, political, and cultural factors.

The political-institutional vicissitudes of the South Tyrol are marked by two different statutory treatments of the problem: the "special statute of the Trentino-Alto Adige region," enacted immediately after World War II but only partially put into practice, and the "package" (incorporated in the new statute for autonomy), which is today almost fully in effect. The passage from the first of these to the second can be seen as the result of a process of increasing mobilization by the minority of the South Tyrol that has succeeded in forcing the Italian state to respect and protect its ethnic identity.

This process was driven forward by the SVP, the ethnic party of South Tyrol, whose fortune has been solidly joined to that of the battle for autonomy. The party has enjoyed a fundamental role in administering and mediating the conflict with the Italian state, a role that has legitimized it as the only instrument of representation and of political direction for the minority so far.[22]

In effect, the birth of the party, which took place officially in May 1945, can be viewed in a certain sense as an institutional response to the political "question" expressed by the community of the South Tyrol immediately after the war, a question determined by the unifying interest of the community in defending the ethnic integrity of the group.[23]

This objective became the central issue in the program of the party, which aimed above all, "... 1) to restore, after 25 years of Fascist and Nazi oppression, the cultural, linguistic and economic rights of the people of South Tyrol, based on the fundamental principles of democracy."[24] Elsewhere, the SVP affirmed the goal "... of grouping together in this party all who belong to this language and culture, thus the entire group of the people of South Tyrol... who can be contrasted to the other ethnic group... only in its totality, and not to the individual parties"; the party also stated that such a program was undertaken "in the necessity of defending against attacks these fundamental rights of all and [that] it is also possible that the program might cease the moment this necessity no longer exists."[25] In fact, the objective of an "ethnic defense" has remained at the center of the program and the propaganda of the party, even since autonomy has been gained.

At the formation of the party, the most notable persons of the community of the South Tyrol participated, assuming leadership. These were notables who had not been too compromised by Nazism and non "optants," many of whom came from the ranks of the Deutscher Verband, whose tradition of unity the nascent SVP explicitly proposed to emulate.

Its popularity grew rapidly and became diffuse; within a few months of its conception, the new party could count as members 70,000 of the

220,000 people belonging to the ethnic group.[26] The first electoral success of the party was a plebiscite vote in the elections of 1948 in favor of the SVP; this was the first of many successes, which have been hurt only in recent years by the opposition of antagonistic slates.

Among the factors that strongly contributed to the party's becoming legitimate and consolidated, an especially important one was the support it received from the local Catholic church, traditionally very influential, which urged all the people of the South Tyrol to join the new party.[27]

Internally, however, the party suffered divisions that resulted from its composite nature; there was a considerable difference of view in particular between the membership of predominantly conservative farmers and the bourgeoisie who provided liberal leadership. This conflict, always latent but always overcome in the name of ethnic solidarity, has become subdued since the change at the top of the SVP toward the end of the 1950s; until then it was controlled, in effect, by the uncertain developments of the central question of autonomy.

The immediate postwar period brought, above all, the shattering of the hopes of the people of the South Tyrol for a possible re-annexation to the mother country of Austria.[28]

Nevertheless, the memory of the discriminations suffered under Fascism was too strong, and therefore the issuance of the "Statute of Autonomy for Trentino-Alto Adage Region" evoked, on the whole, a positive reaction and satisfaction. (Its ratification, in fulfillment of the De Gasperi-Gruber accord, occurred with the constitutional law of February 2, 1948.) How distant and arduous the attainment of autonomy would really be the political leaders of the minority could not then suspect. In an official letter, they affirmed, "...with heartfelt pleasure that the agreement De Gasperi-Gruber, which occurred in Paris in September 1946, inasmuch as it concerns the fundamental problem of autonomy, is now near to reality," and "in the application of the Statute an atmosphere of reciprocal faith and understanding will be created among the linguistic groups of our province which is necessary to attain a fruitful collaboration for the development of the region and for the common interest of the country."[29] In fact, however, the acceptance of this statute on the part of the South Tyrolean group did not occur without reservations, especially concerning the coupling of the autonomy provided for in the De Gasperi-Gruber accord with a similar concession for the neighboring province of Trento. This coupling established the region in which the German-speaking people of South Tyrol were a minority as the area under consideration for autonomy instead of the province, where they constituted a majority; in the years since, the coupling has shown itself basically capable of altering the objectives and the importance of the statute.

The accpetance of the coupling, which was the result of a realistic evaluation on the part of the SVP, constituted, nonetheless, the premise for the beginning of a long and contradictory collaboration with the Christian Democrats (DC); this collaboration lasted more than 30 years and was based on a partition of power between the two parties and a tacit accord to divide the zones of influence at the regional, provincial, and local levels.

The decision to make this alliance, which was already in effect at the elections of 1948 (the reciprocal support for the respective candidates allowed the SVP to gain five parliamentary representatives), was justified by the SVP to the South-Tyrolean minority as being the result of a deep ideological affinity and common interests (in particular the complete establishment of autonomy) between the two parties.[30]

In reality, the climate of faith and optimism that seemed to reign in the South Tyrol in the first few years after the issuing of the statute was not destined to last long. The attitude of cooperation that the Italian government demonstrated in those years, by issuing some significant provisos in fulfillment of the De Gasperi-Gruber accord, gave way to increasing disengagement concerning the effective implementation of the statute. (Among these provisos was the revision of the "options," to allow the exoptants to regain Italian citizenship, the stipulation of a preferential agreement for the exchange of goods with the Vorarlberg Tyrol, and the recognition of degrees earned abroad by the people of the South Tyrol.) To this was added the self-contradictory tendencies of the DC of Trentino, on the one hand concerned with the real local and party desire for autonomy and, on the other, subordinated to the political objectives of the higher echelons of the party.

With these premises, the struggle for autonomy by the people of the South Tyrol began, and it did not conclude until the end of the 1960s with the institution of the "package." In tracing briefly the major stages of the increasingly radical conflict between the German-speaking minority of South Tyrol and the dominant Italian element, one can perceive roughly four phases.

The first phase was characterized by the progressive loss of faith in the Italian state by the people of the South Tyrol, caused by the state's failure to effect the practical norms of the statute and by its institution of a series of restrictive measures.[31] The measures that most exasperated the German-speaking community were those adopted for the state-financed sector of the building industry, which artificially increased Italian immigration in order to modify the ratio of the ethnic work force in favor of the Italian group. These measures renewed among the people of the South Tyrol the fear of assimilation, which had abated after the fall of Fascism, and led, with the shout of alarm of "Todesmarsch," to an intense campaign of mobilization in the minority.[32] Administered by the SVP, this reached its peak at the end of the 1950s and favorably prepared the way for terrorism. Until then, in fact, the opposition of the people of the South Tyrol was limited to protests and pressures exerted by a substantially moderate political class, always anticipating the conciliatory intervention of the state. (This is the attitude that emerges, for example, from the memorandum presented in 1954 by the parliaments of the South Tyrol to the Italian government "on the situation of the Latin and German ethnic groups in the South Tyrol.") In fact, the collaboration of SVP and DC continued at both regional and provincial levels and at the central level (in the form of support for the DC governments). Thus, the SVP contributed paradoxically to strengthening a party that came to manifest a more and more antiautonomy position.

The second phase began in 1955, the year the Austrian treaty, which once again gave freedom of action in foreign policy to the fatherland of the people of the South Tyrol, was signed. The appeal made by the South Tyrol to international tribunals (Austria, UN), that is, to foreign instruments of defense and pressure, reveals an increasing deterioration in its relationship with the Italian state. The beginning of this quarrel with Austria, which backed the formal request for autonomy of the province of Bolzano, imparted to the controversy an agitated and excited atmosphere. It exacerbated the opposition between the South Tyrolean minority and the central government, which was firm in wishing to treat the question of the South Tyrol as an "internal" problem and, therefore, was also firm in considering the intervention of Austria an unwanted interference. The minority, strengthened by the backing it had obtained, began openly to aim at a substantial revision of the basis for autonomy. Separatist tendencies among the people of the South Tyrol became stronger, culminating in the request for "Los von Trient."[33] This led to the presentation in parliament of a "plan for South Tyrol concerning a Statute for autonomy for the Region of South Tyrol." (Known as the "Tinzl-Sand proposal," it was presented in parliament in 1958 and provided for a large extension of the powers of the local administrations.)

Without delving into the developments of the diplomatic vicissitudes of the relationship between Italy and Austria, it must be noted, nonetheless, that the internationalization of the question of the South Tyrol constituted an important success for the minority and, in particular, for the SVP, and it contributed in a definitive manner to giving impulse and vigor to the South Tyrolean claims.

At the end of the 1950s, strong dissatisfaction had built up within the German-speaking community because of the evident failure of the politics of collaboration practiced by the SVP and also because of the steady worsening of socioeconomic conditions for the minority.

This dissatisfaction tended, in general, to be expressed in two directions: at the Italian "enemy," attacked with an increasing hostility that reflected the growing vigor of the separatist tendencies of the "Los von Trient," and at the minority's own political class, which was accused of impotence and of excessive moderation in defending the interests of the group. The first tendency brought an end to the collaboration of the SPV and the DC, which concluded with the withdrawal of the German-speaking exponents from the Guinta Regionale (Regional Council) in 1959 and with the revocation of minority support for the central government. The second tendency led to a substantial change in the leadership of the party, which was an important turning point in the history and in the policies of the SVP. The new generation of leaders affirmed itself at the congress of 1957; its leader was Silvius Magnago, who is still the "charismatic" leader of the minority of the South Tyrol today. Lacking a "democratic" past or any parliamentary experience, the new leadership manifested "... a tendency toward dangerous simplifications that drove it toward a drastic opposition to all that was foreign."[34] Thus, with the advent of the new leadership, the party assumed a far more uncompromising stance. (Contributing to this was the fact that in the 1950s, after a first phase of denying party admission to Nazi elements, numerous exoptants— many of whom were of doubtful democratic persuasion—had succeeded in infiltrating the SVP and gaining—although still a minority—increasing influence.) This was accompanied by a more zealous mobilization of the German-speaking group toward the objectives of the "Volkstumskampf." The famous mass manifestation of Castelfirmiano (1957), in which 35,000 South Tyroleans rallied under the shout of "Los von Trient," represents undoubtedly one of its most vital moments.

In the years that followed, there was also a progressive transformation of the organizational structure of the party. With the establishment of new executive (Präsidium) and consultative organs and with the institution of a series of measures intended to develop the territorial functions of the party, the SVP had changed from a party of "notables" into a highly centralized bureaucratic organization by 1964.

The third phase of the fight for autonomy was marked by a period of terrorism. The imminence of failure by the international tribunals following the hardening of positions by the two interested governments brought to a head the internal tensions in the South Tyrol, which were spurred on also by the fiery nationalistic campaign of the SVP.° The first terrorist attack, which destroyed the statue of Mussolini that the South Tyroleans called the Aluminum Duce, was followed by various other

---

°The failure came in January 1962, and the communique issued at the end of the encounter spoke explicitly of "irreconcilability" in the points of view of the two delegations.

attacks, which usually concided with negotiations between the foreign ministers or with the meetings of experts.

Traceable in part to the same ideology that inspired the politics of the SVP, the terrorist movement was a radical development that resulted from an extremist interpretation of the slogans "Todesmarsch" and "Los von Trient."

> Next to the politically and juridically legitimate power of the SVP, the terrorist movement was thus a second force that in part derived spontaneously from the society of South Tyrol and in part was implemented by Austrian and German subversive and nationalistic groups that considered South Tyrol a provisional operating zone for their programs.[35]

In fact, for many years the German-speaking population sided with the attackers because of the large-scale attention, even at the international level, that their campaign focused on the question of the South Tyrol. The terrorist groups fell, however, into increasing isolation, which was caused by many factors. These included the lack of political motivation given to the attacks, especially when they begin to take human lives; the moderating action carried on with increasing vigor by the local church; and the prevailing, with the passing of time, of extreme neo-Nazism over the initial objectives of the terrorists of the South Tyrol.

The Italians had various reactions to the terrorists. On the one hand, there was harsh repression by the police, which gave rise to the accusation that they sought to strike at the SVP in addition to the terrorists and to reduce the complex problem to a simple question of public order; on the other hand, there quickly arose the tendency in the press and in public opinion to attribute the tragic terrorism to the fervent nationalism promulgated by the political leaders of the South Tyrol. Despite the different attitudes toward the terrorist movement, it is undeniable that in one aspect it was effective: only after the terrorism did the Italian government seem to appreciate the gravity of the situation and to recognize that a quick solution to the problem of autonomy for the South Tyrol was necessary. The succeeding developments in the situation confirmed that

> ... minorities gain protection, liberty, and rights when the social costs of keeping them in subordination outweigh the advantages, when the dominating element finds it more advantageous to integrate the minorities by methods of participation, rather than by isolating them or assimilating them altogether.[36]

With the formation of a commission to study the problems of the South Tyrol and to present concrete proposals for solutions, the last phase of the struggle for autonomy began. (The "Commission of 19," composed of representatives from almost all the parties, presented its final report in April 1964.) For the first time, the discussion was moved from the international to the internal level, thereby giving a direct voice to the minority of the South Tyrol (without Austrian intervention) and allowing debate at both juridical and political levels. The proposals contained in the final report of the commission came to form the central part of the "package," the whole of the measures agreed to by the Italian and Austrian governments and by the SVP;° from this the new statute for autonomy was derived.

The measures, which constituted a radical reform of the "Special Statute for the Trentino-Alto Adige," consisted of a massive transfer of legislative and administrative powers to the province of Bolzano and of a series of modifications to the former statute; these changes emphasized the new role of the province, to the detriment of the region. The measures also provided, among other things, for a partial release of the school system of the South Tyrol from the national norms, the application of "ethnic ratios" for admission to public jobs, an ample bilingual program, and financial autonomy.

This massive transfer of power from the state (and, therefore, from the Italian group) to the German-speaking minority in a few years substantially modified the status of the interethnic relationships in the South Tyrol and thus initiated a new problem.[37]

The effects of the new autonomy statute that directly affect daily life have created a widespread discontentment among the Italians. The application of the "ethnic ratios,"° which in some cases has caused disorder in public utility services, has in particular augmented the tension. In general, it now seems that the administration of the great autonomous powers tends to a separate development of the ethnic and linguistic groups. This tendency has manifested itself up to now primarily in problems in the educational field and in the bilingual problem. Given this situation, the prospects for a "modern" identity for the South Tyrol, which would be tied to a unified development of the local society and which would protect the precious diversity of the three ethnic groups, appears destined to fail because of the division that has been imposed as a means of social and political conservation.

°At the extraordinary congress of the SVP on November 12, 1969, only 52.8 percent of the delegates voted for approving the "package."

°This mechanism controls not only selection for public jobs but also, for example, allotment of public housing. For years, strong pressure has been exerted on the SVP to link the system of proportions to the population census instead of to the composition of the elected assembly as is now the case. This request aims, among other things, to eliminate the incogruencies derived from electing Germans from the lists of Italian national parties that present candidates of various ethnic and linguistic extractions.

THE SOCIOECONOMIC CONTEXT

In analyzing the dynamics of ethnic conflict, the often fundamental importance of socioeconomic factors must be taken into account. Often, for example, analysts do not consider that, at the base of many ethnic questions, lie the marginalizing effects of an economic development that corrodes the "grounds" of minority cultures and contributes to their extinction. In particular in a European context, in which traditional ethnic groups are predominant, the dissolution of a rural society caused by the mechanism of capitalist development constitutes the greatest danger to its existence. On one hand, the large scale expulsion of workers from agricultural occupations often results in a reduction of the ethnic group through emigration or relocation to the cities; on the other, the crisis of values and traditions in the rural community, which reflects its secularization, weakens the ethnic identification and cohesion felt by the group.

An analysis of this type reveals the limitations of the traditional view of minorities as socially homogeneous groups, and it underscores the necessity of thoroughly examining their internal structures. Determined by the contradictions inherent in the process of development, internal differences in fact do arise, and these social inequalities cannot always be reconciled by the logic of ethnic solidarity and group cohesion. If analyzing the structural dimension in which ethnic questions are developed constitutes an essential premise for a more precise examination of the process of minority emancipation also in a political institutional sense, this is especially appropriate in the case of the South Tyrol. A reconstruction of the more important socioeconomic transformations in the South Tyrol, made possible by the availability of sufficient official data, increases insight into the conflict between the South Tyroleans and the Italian state and into the interethnic relations. In light of the socioeconomic history, there emerge little-known, yet fundamental, aspects of the conflict: the tenacious resistance of the German-speaking minority to the process of ethnic disintegration caused by economic development and the search for, and affirmation of, a model for development that is compatible with ethnic traditions and values.[38]

It is first necessary to examine the "ethnic reproduction" of the South Tyrol. The evolution of the size of the ethnic group, has been determined by the natural and migratory movements of the population.

Although it changed markedly during the Fascist period, the relative size of the ethnic groups has been much more stable since the war. Nevertheless, it is important to note that the increase in population—on the whole, the result of a high birthrate—corresponds to different rates of increase in the three groups (See Table 9.1) Until 1961 the German-speaking minority (also the Ladins) tended to contract because of a

TABLE 9.1

Ethnic Composition of the Population of the
South Tyrol: 1953, 1961, 1971
(in percent)

	Germans	Italians	Ladins	Total
1953	62.7	33.6	3.7	341,521
1961	62.3	34.3	3.4	373,582
1971	62.9	33.3	3.7	414,041
Percent Variation 1953–1961	+ 8.6	+12.0	− 0.8	+ 9.4
Percent Variation 1961–1971	+11.9	+ 7.4	+22.7	+10.8

Source: The facts relating to 1953 come from an appraisal by A. Leidlmair, Bevolkerung und Wirtschaft in Südtirol (Innsbruck: Wagner, 1958).

deterioration of its socioeconomic well-being. Since 1961, however, there has been a net increase in the German-speaking population and a sharp drop in the Italian population. This tendency is confirmed by the fact that, in the years 1961–71, the villages of the South Tyrol situated at an altitude above 500 meters—villages in which the majority of the population is German-speaking or Ladin—demonstrated a uniform level of growth, while the population decreased noticeably in the villages in the valleys, where the greatest part of the Italian group is concentrated. A second important fact concerns the rates of employment in the ethnic groups. On the whole, it decreased constantly in the period 1951–71, especially in the last 10 years, when it dropped from 42.8 percent to 37.2 percent; in recent years, however, there has been a revival.[39]

According to the results of a study based on variables including migratory movements, reduction of workers in agriculture, and modifications in the structure of the population by altitude, the reduction almost exclusively affected the villages situated above 500 meters, which in 1961 were the home of 75 percent of the agricultural workers.[40] A great demographic increment and a parallel fall in the official employment rate are therefore phenomena that, until the late 1960s, primarily affected the South Tyrolean minority. To the different geographical concentrations of the three linguistic groups, there correspond different occupational structures: the German-speaking group is characterized even now by a strong incidence of agricultural occupations, practiced even at high altitudes throughout the province; the Italian group, located primarily in cities, is predominantly devoted to industrial occupations and public jobs.

It is precisely the evolution of the occupational structure that furnishes an important indication of the changes that have occurred in the South Tyrol since the war. (See Table 9.2.)

TABLE 9.2

Occupational Structure in the South Tyrol according to the Sector of Economic Activity: 1951, 1961, 1971
(in percent)

	1951	1961	1971
Agriculture	42.6	30.6	20.3
Industry	23.3	28.1	30.6
Public Administration	10.5	9.2	7.8
Other Sectors	23.6	32.1	41.3

Source: ISTAT

As a whole, the movements of the labor force from one sector of the economy to another reveal a situation analogous to that prevailing during the same period at the national and international levels: a net decline in the agricultural component, a large increase in the tertiary component, and an increase, modest in this case, in the industrial component.

To appreciate the consequences of this evolution on the internal structure of the minority of the South Tyrol, one must compare the present situation with that of the early 1950s: the percent of Germans and Ladins in agriculture was 67; in public administration, 5; and in other sectors, 28; the percent of Italians in agriculture was 3; in public administration, 35; and in other sectors, 62.[41]

These data reveal the heavy specialization of production by the three groups, which was determined by the policies of Fascism. The German-speaking people worked for the most part in the agricultural sector, while the Italians dominated industry and other sectors. In those years, however, this type of ethnic division of labor did not seem to constitute a cause for tensions and was not even discussed; nevertheless, the South Tyrolean minority began to feel the need for new developments.

There are two reasons for the relative acceptance (at least in the first phase) by the German-speaking minority of this specialized agricultural role; one is tied to its past history, the other to recent developments. The minority had nurtured, through the centuries, characteristics and traditions typical of a relatively self-sufficient rural community; its isolation was reinforced by the mainly mountainous territory. The advent of Fascism accentuated the tendency toward isolation by reinforcing the conviction that the survival of the ethnic character of the group was tied to the conservation of a rural system of life. In particular, Fascism transformed what had historically been the disinclination of the population of the South Tyrol to undertake industrial occupations not at least tied to agriculture into real resistance to the phenomenon of industrialization,[42] which for them had become synonymous with Italian immigration and the instruments of assimilation.

Progressively, nonetheless, the state of relative functional-productive integration among the ethnic groups ended in crisis because of the specific modalities of the economic development of the South Tyrol, which caused increasing inequalities in the material conditions of life for the three groups. The tendency toward slackness and the consequent impoverishment of the economy of the South Tyrol, which took place at the end of the 1950s, was afterward accentuated by the effects of the ethnic conflict, such as the terrorism at the beginning of the 1960s. This economic decline struck the German-speaking population (also the Ladins) in a particularly grave manner and gave rise to strong feelings among them of "relative deprivation" in comparison with the Italians; this worsened the interethnic conflict.

The demand for a more equitable distribution of the economic resources of the province, voiced with increasing awareness by the minority of the South Tyrol, was born of real and somewhat dramatic motivations. Starting in the 1950s, the German-speaking community faced head-on the crisis of the traditional agricultural sector, which provided the material basis for its survival. In the years from 1951 to 1971, the population employed in agricultural occupations decreased by 50 percent and a huge number of small farms ceased to produce (almost 2,000 failed in the 1960s alone). Simultaneously, the income produced by the agricultural sector was constantly reduced, increasing the gap between the agricultural and nonagricultural sectors.[43] This phenomenon must be seen as part of the vast process of rationalization of the agricultural structures that took place throughout Europe, striking with particularly harsh consequences the marginal agricultural areas of low productivity such as the predominantly mountainous territory of the South Tyrol.[44] This caused an ever-increasing disequilibrium between the medium-large capitalist farms of the lowlands, operating in the fruit-growing sector, and the large majority of small farms in the mountains, which were less and less capable of producing a sufficient income for all the members of the farm family. (The lines of the agrarian policies of the European Common Market are traced in the Mansholt Plan of 1968.)

The social consequences of these phenomena were already very grave at the beginning of the 1960s, given the rate of unemployment and underemployment in the countryside of the South Tyrol, which was in those years overtaken by a true demographic "explosion." Rendering the situation even more dramatic was the inadequacy of occupational outlets for the unemployed agricultural population, which forced many to emigrate. (In 1971, the "absentees for reasons of work" in the South Tyrol were about 11,250, of which more than 80 percent were of German and

Ladin tongue.) Without a doubt, the strong resistance to industrialization after the Fascist experience by the German-speaking community contributed greatly to this state of affairs. This stance established the economic policies of the leadership of the South Tyrol, who for a long time strongly restricted any possibility for expansion of the industrial occupations. They preferred instead to give massive aid to the agricultural sector and to promote new openings for work, even if seasonal or part-time, in the tertiary sector and, above all, in tourism, in which the people of the South Tyrol have "invested" with increasing success their rich patrimony of habits, costumes, and traditions.

But this policy soon revealed its limitations. The abnormal expansion of the tertiary sector, which by 1971 came to represent more than 50 percent of total employment, had shown itself through the years to be not only fragile (founded as it was upon an unstable business like tourism and on an inefficient commercial structure) but also, in the long run, incapable of solving the employment problem of the German-speaking minority. The worsening of the situation and the consequent sharpening of internal social tensions necessitated cautious rethinking and revision of economic policy. At the beginning of the 1960s, there had already been noticeable agitation among the entrepreneurs and the labor unions of the South Tyrol, who had strongly criticized the leadership of the SVP for having policies totally extraneous to the problems and the interests of production and labor.[45] The protest against the "unilateral" economic policy of the SVP, which was so absorbed in the process of gaining autonomy that it overlooked the more vital survival needs of the ethnic group, later came to have important effect.

Yet, even among the higher political echelons of the minority, there slowly arose the realization that development of the industrial sector was necessary. The means of putting such development into effect, however, soon became the object of a heated debate that affected the entire German-speaking community. A "romantic" model of industrialization was affirmed as a result of this debate, mainly preoccupied with guarding the agrarian character and the touristic and recreational functions of the South Tyrol by means of various restrictions concerning the dimensions and the sites of industrial plans, their compatibility with tourism, and so on. The tendency toward a certain revival in industrial employment starting at the end of the 1960s appears to have been a result of this new policy. There followed the creation of numerous small- and medium-sized industries situated, unusually enough, in the rural areas of the province, indicatng that it was primarily the German-speaking people of the South Tyrol who were to benefit.[46] It is also important to note that the beginning of this new process of industrialization, administered by the leadership of the minority, coincided with the advent of a solution to the ethnic conflict.

There were many factors that favored the development of new industry in the traditionally marginal area of the South Tyrol: its favorable geographical position from the perspective of increasing capitalistic integration at the European level; the presence of an abundant, cheap, bilingual, mobile, and mostly nonunionized labor force; and the facilities conceded by the local administration.

The years leading up to the present have substantially confirmed that the leaders of the South Tyrol have adopted a model of economic development for the region that continues to assign a major role to agriculture, the support for which aids the development of tourism (which is connected to agricultural activities); industrial development, which is administered with great caution and moderation, has been assigned the secondary function of being a simple safety valve for unemployment. Thus, for the future of the South Tyrol, those sectors that value the customs and traditions of the German-speaking minority more highly and will therefore safeguard its ethnic identity assume a central importance. The leadership has shown that it believes that the guarantee of such safeguards lies in conservation of the existing social and ethnic equilibriums and, above all, in the existing political equilibrium of the South Tyrol.

In short, then, it is possible to see in the evolution of the structure of production in the South Tyrol during the last 30 years a basic tendency toward the overcoming of the rigid system of ethnic division of labor imposed by Fascism. In particular, one can identify in the local agricultural crisis and in the subsequent deterioration of material conditions necessary for the "ethnic reproduction" of the German-speaking minority the decisive element that results in competition for a new, more equitable division of resources among the different groups. The minority is thus in danger, for if "... the evolution of society brings a decrease in the request for services furnished by a specialized minority, and if ethnic characteristics are tied to this functional specialization, the minority risks becoming extinct."[47]

It is the perception of this risk—although not in such drastic terms—by the German-speaking people of the South Tyrol, who are aware of their increasing economic and social isolation, that causes them to aim at renovating the socioeconomic structure as a new guarantee of survival.

To what degree and through what means this objective has been reached can be evaluated by comparing the figures for the participation of the ethnic groups in economic activities in 1961 with those for 1971. (See Table 9.3.)

Although the work force has been drastically reapportioned by the massive process of expulsion previously mentioned, more than 90 percent of the workers in agriculture are still German speakers. At the same time,

TABLE 9.3

**Ethnic Composition of the Working Population of the
South Tyrol according to Economic Sector: 1961 and 1971**

(in percent)

	Germans		Italians		Ladins		Total	
	1961	1971	1961	1971	1961	1971	1961	1971
Agriculture	91.0	91.8	4.7	4.6	4.2	3.6	49,001	31,207
Industry	46.3	54.7	49.6	40.9	4.0	4.3	44,966	47,060
Public Administration	23.4	25.8	75.3	72.5	1.2	1.7	14,799	12,060
Other Sectors	59.9	60.0	37.4	36.5	2.7	3.3	51,337	63,643

Source: ISTAT

however, the German-speaking group has considerably bettered its position in the nonagricultural sectors, reducing the gaps between it and the Italians; on the contrary, although there was a modest increase of Italians in the tertiary occupations, their numbers decreased in industry, a traditionally Italian preserve.

The consequence of the period on the occupational structure of the people of the South Tyrol and on other groups can be seen in Table 9.4. These figures confirm unequivocally the change that has occurred, and they indicate its importance and direction.

One more development must be examined: the significant quantitative transformation that has taken place in the class structure of the minority.[48] It is important to acknowledge the limitations and difficulties of an empirical study of social classes that utilizes statistical data. Table 9.5, which follows criteria of statistical aggregation tested in analyzing class composition at a national level,[49] is based on data taken from occupational statistics. Nonetheless, the comparison, possible only for the years 1961 and 1971, is significant.

A growth of the bourgeoisie (entrepreneurs, professionals, administrators, and government officials) in this period took place in all three groups, but it did so most consistently in the German group, which was directly involved in its industrial revival in the second half of the decade, and in the Ladin group, thanks to the expansion of the tourist trade. Simultaneously, these two groups experienced a reduction in the small independent bourgeoisie (self-employed workers, such as "direct" farmers, small merchants, and artisans, and the people who work for them) that was tied to the agricultural crisis and to the associated decrease in the number of small farmers. (In 1970, the concerns run directly by the farmer represented about 90 percent of the total number of agricultural concerns in the South Tyrol.)

A strong increase in the number of blue-collar workers is also a common characteristic of all three linguistic groups. However, while these workers constitute almost a third of those employed within the Italian group, precedents that excluded them from public jobs have rendered them of inferior importance in the other groups.

The percentages of those classified as the working class in 1971 were almost equal in the different groups. This relative equilibrium seems to be the result of a balancing that took place in the 1960s between the German and Italian working classes: the latter underwent a large decrease (almost 7,000 people or 21 percent), while the German working class increased after the recent process of diffuse industrialization.

In a comprehensive evaluation of this evolution, the most significant fact that emerges is, without a doubt, the profound socioprofessional restructuring of the German-speaking group, which takes place in the

TABLE 9.4
Occupational Structure of the Linguistic Groups of the South Tyrol: 1961 and 1971
(in percent)

	Germans		Italians		Ladins	
	1961	1971	1961	1971	1961	1971
Agriculture	44.8	19.9	4.2	2.7	37.9	20.6
Industry	20.9	26.9	40.6	36.6	33.5	29.3
Public Administration	3.5	3.3	20.3	16.6	3.3	3.7
Other Sectors	30.8	39.9	34.9	34.1	25.3	46.4
Total	99,626	95,705	54,959	52,605	5,426	5,511

Source: ISTAT.

TABLE 9.5

Appraisal of the Working Population of the South Tyrol according to Social Class and Linguistic Group: 1961 and 1971
(in percent)

	Germans		Italians		Ladins	
	1961	1971	1961	1971	1961	1971
Bourgeoisie	1.6	3.1	3.3	4.3	0.9	3.8
Small Independent Bourgeoisie	42.4	33.9	13.6	14.7	46.2	37.0
Clerks (white-collar workers)	8.2	14.7	24.2	32.3	6.4	12.7
Working Class	47.8	48.3	58.9	48.7	46.5	46.5
Total Employed	100.0	100.0	100.0	100.0	100.0	100.0

Source: ISTAT.

context of strong social mobility in the last 15 years. Clearly indicating the extent of this change is the increase in the number of those pursuing secondary education. (See Table 9.6.)

TABLE 9.6

The German-Speaking Population of the South Tyrol according to Degree Earned: 1961 and 1971
(by percent of population older than 5 years in each group)

	1961	1971
College Degree	0.8	0.9
High School Degree	2.4	3.7
Junior High School Degree	7.5	14.8
Grammar School Degree	76.7	65.2

Source: ISTAT.

It is then in this global process, accentuated in the 1970s, that one can perceive the real renewal of the minority of the South Tyrol after a deep impoverishment that lasted for more than half a century.

SOCIAL STRUCTURE AND POLITICAL SYSTEM

The process of social reorganization of the minority of the South Tyrol took place, considering the breadth of the disruptive measures effected by Fascism, with surprising swiftness. The capability of the minority for structuring itself in different fields (cultural, productive, labor, political) and for creating capillary structures of association-organization to unify it by exercising considerable power of mobilization must be seen as indicative of an unquestionable vitality. It is a strongly sectorial society, yet it is simultaneously integrated, thanks to its political culture, which stimulates an intense civic participation.[50]

It is important to note that this process of reorganization resulted in a society that preserved the characteristics that the South Tyrol displayed before annexation, especially a rigid system of classes (Stände).[51] Endowed with great stability, this society preserves the traditional ethnic life in which religion and local patriotism play a primary role. In the past, it had gone through the organizational stimuli of Catholic sectorialism, which manifested itself with success in the Austrian and German context of the nineteenth century, finding in the South Tyrol a particularly fertile terrain in the rural environment of the small- and medium-sized farms.

Thus, after World War II, did there arise a more complex web of organizations: a system of agricultural cooperatives of production and consumption (dairies, wine cellar cooperatives, unions for collective buying, and so on) and the rural savings banks (Raiffeisen), important structures of agricultural credit diffused throughout the entire province, with a solid and efficient organization and a strong hierarchical frame.

A fundamental role in the process of reordering the agricultural world of the South Tyrol was played by what can be considered one of its fundamental associative structures: The Südtiroler Bauernbund (the farmer alliance of the South Tyrol), a broad-based professional union that enjoys great prestige and influence in the South Tyrol.

The process of organizing the minority outside of the agricultural field, in fields that were more harshly struck by Fascism, was more complex. In particular, there were difficulties in organizing the working class, which was fragmented in the artisan shops spread throughout the territory and strongly reduced following the "options" emigration. Nonetheless, relevant efforts were made in this sector by the Katholischer Verein der Werktätigen (KVW), which was constituted in 1948 as an autonomous Catholic organization affiliated with the national union federation, the Christian Association of Italian Workers (ACLI). (This affiliation is the basis of a certain mistrust of the KVW on the part of the people of the South Tyrol. The same can be said for the labor union SGB, affiliated with the Italian Confederation of Union Workers.) With the passing of the years, the KVW sphere of action has become larger; it has grown from union assistance to political activities, and from helping the workers of the South Tyrol who had emigrated abroad to providing a whole series of services within the province. At the end of the 1960s, the KVW had 27,000 members, subdivided into 283 local groups.[52] It has considerable political influence, which it prefers to exercise indirectly; it avoids inserting its own people in key positions in the party and in the administration of the province in order to concentrate on a massive presence at the local level and, therefore, control of the farmer base. Like the church, the KVW, not wanting to be too involved in the ethnic conflict, believed that it should mediate primarily at the local level.

As early as immediately after the war, there was, in addition to the KVW, the labor union Südtiroler Gewerkschaftsbund (SGB-CISL), which was able to attract only modest membership among the German-speaking and Ladin workers, as is demonstrated by the low percentage (about 10 percent) of the work force affiliated with labor unions at the end of the 1960s. In 1946, however, the ethnic labor union was born: the Autonomer Südtiroler Gewerkschaftsbund (ASGB). This union combined the appeal of Christian affiliation with that of ethnic solidarity and thereby became legitimized by the SVP as "the South Tyrolean labor union." The ASGB organized German and Ladin workers according to rigid ethnic criteria in order to separate them from the Italian workers and from the influence of the national labor unions. This role of the ethnic labor union was demonstrated by the course of action it followed from the very beginning and by its various methods of intervention, which included diffuse antistrike propaganda, masked by ambiguous appeals to the principles of social Christian doctrine and by a hostile policy of opposition to the Italian workers and labor unions, and by a constant policy of distortion in ethnic terms of the supposed Italian opposition to the demands of the workers of the South Tyrol, a tactic designed to foment competition for jobs among the workers of the different linguistic groups. (Significant to this effect is the letter from the files of ASGB, "Echo der Arbeit.") With the passing of the years, however, these policies began to have negative effects, resulting in the increasing isolation of the ASGB, despite the support of the SVP and other minority organizations. In the 1970s, there was a great membership increase in national labor unions among the German-speaking and Ladin workers, which significantly reflects the process of new unionization taking place in the areas of recent industrialization.[53]

The cultural structures of the South Tyrolean minority and the activities the minority undertakes merit analysis. These structures fulfil the fundamental function of sustaining and strengthening ethnic identity and solidarity through the conservation and transmission of the values and traditions of the group.

Extramural universities, bands, grassroots theater groups, chorus and cultural clubs, and various expressions of the local farmer folklore are some of the most prominent means of perpetuating local customs and traditions, popular songs, church music, and so on; in addition, there are the "Schützen," a voluntary group of fire fighters with folkloristic and military characteristics. Some figures give an idea of the consistency of the cultural structures. At the end of the 1960s, there were in the South Tyrol 176 bands with about 5,000 members, 135 grassroots theater groups, and 70 cultural clubs tied to the Association of the Extramural University (URANIA).[54] These groups, mostly founded in the 1950s, serve a capillary function; like the system of cooperatives, they provide for a subdivision into local groups (Ort), zones (Gebiet), and districts (Bezirk), united at the top in the "Dachorganisation," which coordinates and controls at the provincial level the activities of all the groups.

A necessary point of reference for all the cultural initiatives undertaken in the South Tyrol is the Südtiroler Kulturinstitut, founded in 1954. Endowed with ample funds from the administration of the province and from generous contributions from German-speaking countries, it plays a central role in promoting and controlling cultural decisions through its more than 73 centers located throughout the province.[55]

Beginning in the second half of the 1960s, there was a virtual monopoly on culture and information (written information is, in fact, controlled by the SVP) in the South Tyrol, which became the object of frequent disputes between the intellectuals and the students of the minority, who were always critical of what they called, in spite of its seemingly dynamic traits, a "versteinerte Gesellschaft," a "petrified" society.[56] In effect, the culturally monolithic aspects of the South Tyrol were more and more the expression of a forced cultural homogeneity, irrevocably tied to the past by a well-consolidated policy that suppressed any comparison with the new or the foreign; this policy made a largely ideological use of tradition for legitimizing and establishing the leadership and the political system in force.[57] There took shape the concept of a collective historical past, which emphasized particular ideas and periods of the history of Tyrol—those that exalted, by evoking an intense and emotional collective identification, the solidarity of the group—while even famous episodes that were expressions of internal division (for example the struggle of the farmers) were practically forgotten.[58]

All this contributed to a uniformity in the cultural and other attitudes and behaviors of the German-speaking group, and it led to a marked tendency toward conformism, toward accepting and transmitting without criticism the myths and conventions of the past. This tendency has been reinforced by the cultural isolation of the minority, determined first by its refusal to compare itself with the dominant Italian culture and second by its marginal position in regard to the German cultural sphere. Indicative of the first, for example, is the recent hardening of separatist principles in the educational field, which aims at impeding the development of even limited common learning experiences between German and Italian schools; indicative of the second is the subordinate position of the South Tyrol in regard to the universities of the German world.

The arguments advanced to justify the continuation of closed attitudes regarding the Italian culture and community often center on the necessity of defending the German language of the minority. This is without a doubt a real problem, for the language of an ethnic-linguistic minority constitutes the most essential element of identity and solidarity for the group. Nonetheless, despite the concerns over language, it is precisely in the area of language that signs of progress can be seen. The damages produced in this area (just as with the public schools) by the Fascist program of Italianization have, albeit slowly and with difficulties, been largely remedied. On the one hand, the few social milieu in which the German language survived even during the Fascist period—in the family and in religion—have confirmed its stability. On the other hand, recent scientific research on the status of the German language in the South Tyrol concludes that

... in the past thirty years it has recuperated in numerous ways. All the changes... usage within social environments have been in favor of the German language.... A further expansion of the German language was reached when (concurrent with application of the new statute of autonomy) even the Italians in some sectors were forced to use German, if not exclusively, at least along with the Italian language.[59]

The fact that today, with the exception of the military, there no longer exist in the South Tyrol social environments that are the exclusive domain of the Italian language must be seen as an indication of the revival of the minority culture.

It is also important to specify that the linguistic form that is best preserved among the German speakers of the South Tyrol is a strictly local dialect that, according to linguists, has a particular vitality compared with German.° Its stability proves that dialects are particularly effective in the peripheral areas, where communication with the larger linguistic community is weaker, because they lead to the creation and promotion of a local-regional identity and a sense of protection against the penetration of "foreign" elements. (It is to this end that the local dialect—although, according to some, it no longer fits the linguistic needs of the present—continues to be defended by the cultural and political leaders of the minority against a single German language.)

A final aspect of the ethnic and cultural society of the South Tyrol is the solidity of its ties with the vital Catholic matrix, which is among the most traditional and rural; these ties reflect the perpetuation, in the German-speaking environment, of the historical ideology of "Glaube und Heimat" (Faith and Country). It must be mentioned that the vast influence that the Catholic church enjoys, thanks in part to its solicitous response in defending the ethnic group during the Fascist period, has a solid base. There is a huge readership of the local Catholic periodical (in many cases, especially in the mountainous zones, the only periodical besides the daily newspaper, *Dolomiten*), and there is strong church control of the schools, of editorials, and of professional associations (teachers, entrepreneurs, and so on), as well as a direct influence, through its own exponents, on all the cultural organisms.[60] Since immediately after the war, the political goals of the local church have always favored the political unity of the minority. This support of the policies of the "*Sammel-partei*" (catch-all party) has not prevented an influence of moderation in the ethnic conflict, and this helps to explain the vast powers of inter-

---

°The German language is present in the South Tyrol on three principal levels: strictly local dialect, the regional spoken language (which is more influenced by the Italian), and the standard language, Hochsprache (which remains an artificial language, whose use is restricted to the scholastic and formative field).

vention that the church in the South Tyrol has today. (Among the "historical figures" of the South Tyrol in the last 30 years, many are ecclesiastical: Bishop Geisler, the Canon Gamper, and von Ferrari. The intervention—at first, very explicit—of the church of the South Tyrol in the ethnic-political question became progressively more cautious and moderate after the outburst of terrorism.)

The society of the South Tyrol thus seems to have a hierarchical and authoritarian structure that is rationalized to the extreme. Actually though, the complexity of this structure contrasts only in appearance with the monolithic quality of the external face of the minority. To the apparent multiplicity of the organizational-associational aims of the minority, there corresponds actually just one underlying function: to strengthen the ethnic identity and cohesion of the group. It is easy at this point to arrive at the conclusion, based on the last 30 years of political history of the minority, that ethnic cohesion in the case of the South Tyrol takes the form of political cohesion, becoming therefore a central source of support for the power of the ethnic party. This realization gives rise to a number of considerations. First, the peculiar nature of the relationship between the society of the South Tyrol and its political structure is such that political participation is exhausted entirely in the "civil" dimension, that is, through massive participation in voluntary associations and sectorial interest groups. The result is that the party must cover all the functions of a system of representation. In order to legitimately exercise this role, the party is forced to structure itself as a "mirror" of the society and of its organized interests, to develop to the fullest its sociological representativeness. This takes place by means of a complicated balancing act aimed at assuring a proportional representation in the party of the various classes and social categories: Bauernbund, KVW, ethnic labor unions, ethnic-cultural organizations, and so on.

Certainly the battle for autonomy waged successfully by the SVP has been a major factor in determining the heavy integraiton between the party and civil society. While the struggle took place, the political unity of the minority was justified by the ethnic party as necessary to the massive mobilization of the group. Since the end of the battle and the lifting of the "state of ethnic emergency," the political unity of the group has functioned as an efficient resource of legitimization and consensus, and the identity between ethnic solidarity and political solidarity has been sustained by the SVP through the massive use of all its direct and indirect propaganda methods. The situation is not unlike blackmail, and even today it heavily influences the political activities of the people of the South Tyrol. Proof of this is the intimidation encountered by any criticism of the political policies of the SVP and, above all, by the difficulties encountered by those promoting a pluralization of the party system in the South Tyrol.

In the last decade, three small opposition parties have emerged in the German-speaking community. Their presence, even if it signifies a break in the political monopoly of the ethnic party, has not in fact succeeded in damaging the party position nor in affecting in any significant way its decisions. It is interesting to note that this process of differentiation in the party structure of the South Tyrol developed in conjunction with the beginning of a concrete solution to the ethnic conflict and with greater progress in the interethnic relationships. Until then, opposition and attempts at separatism had been short lived. For example, there was the "Aufbau," which at the beginning of the 1960s was an expression of real uneasiness and discontentment in the community; there was also the Tiroler Heimatpartei, which was born after the demise of the "Aufbau" in 1964 as an opposition party to the right of the SVP, but which became extinct in only a few years. (At the elections for the Regional Council in 1964, the Tiroler Heimatpartei (party of the Tyrol fatherland) gained more than 5,000 votes and a seat.) At the basis of these failures, beyond the ability shown by the SVP in absorbing all dissension (in part by compromising its exponents, in part by supporting the most heartfelt claims), is the fact that the political climate was for the most part unfavorable to any anti-unitarian appeal in those years of intense mobilization for autonomy.

The first stable form of opposition surfaced after the second half of the 1960s in the form of the Soziale Fortschrittspartei Südtirols or Party of South Tyrol for social progress (SFP). Founded in 1966 by the provincial council member Jenny, after his expulsion from the SVP, this party is of a social-democratic persuasion. Now in decline, the party is important more for its original significance as a challenge to the power system of the SVP and as a break in the political unity of the South Tyrol than for the modest results it has been able to obtain. Of particular interest was its proposal of a long-term global plan for providing positive outlets for the needs of expansion that exist in the South Tyrol, especially those expressed by the new emerging strata: workers, clerks, technicians, and young college graduates. There did not correspond to the desire for change, however, an adequate capacity for translating into modern political policies the aspirations for reform, which were limited to a short-lived daily polemic against the policies of the SVP. Significant in this respect is the almost total absence of the SFP from the labor union movement of the South Tyrol, even if this is justified by its having had strong reservations about a union with an ethnic base (ASGB) that is subordinated to the political power. This helps to explain the scantness of approval, even electoral approval, obtained by the SFP among the working class of the South Tyrol.

The direction given by the social-progressionists to the problem of the relationship with the Italian political parties is new. Their inclination to different types of contacts has been realized over the years through collaboration with parties of common Italian orientation. This caused the SFP, on the occasion of the national political elections, to express a clear choice in favor of the Italian Socialist Party, a sort of an Italian version of the ideological and political links with the Austrian socialists and West German social-democrats that the party had cultivated.

Uncommonly uncompromising, however, was the position of the social-progressionists regarding the definitive solution to the problem of autonomy. Their proposal to create an autonomous region of the South Tyrol is presented as the only one capable of definitively eradicating the "psychosis of assimilation" that had become rooted in the minority of the South Tyrol during the Fascist period and, thus, of liberating from prejudices and ambiguity the relationships among the ethnic groups. Such a conviction caused the SFP to react negatively to the "package." The results of the SFP at the electoral level have not been particularly significant (at the elections for Regional Council they gained 2.3 percent of the vote in 1968 and only 0.7 percent in 1978), partly because of the frequent crises (of unclear origin) that have afflicted its internal organization.

Two new opposition parties appeared at the beginning of the 1970s: the Partei der Unabhängigen or Party of the Independents (PDU) and the Sozialdemokratische Partei Südtirols (SPS). Both have repulsed on more than one occasion attempts at assimilation into the SVP, which they reproach for having betrayed the original goals of the "Samelpartei" (catch-all party) in favor of particular and influential organized interest groups. The PDU, which is composed of discontented elements of various socioeconomic groups such as land owners who fear being dispossessed by the unrestrained building trade, has never developed a meaningful opposition and its electoral results have also been modest. More influential has been the SPS, which, at least in the beginning, registered reasonable electoral success (5.1 percent in 1973 and 2.2 percent in 1978.). Ideologically, it is national-populist and tries to attract, above all, the less affluent strata of the rural environment. In addition, it has catered to the labor union movement of the South Tyrol (with which it enjoys a certain influence), and it has committed itself to promoting a resurgence of the ethnic labor union, for which it demands greater autonomy from the dominant party. Among the minor parties, it has shown itself to be the most interested in unifying the opposition forces to tackle the SVP. Its attempts at promoting a common slate at the recent elections, however, were unsuccessful. This is a symptom of the inability of the minor parties to go beyond limited debate against the overwhelming power of the SVP, which, undoubtedly, in the practical administration of the new and vast jurisdictions conferred on it by the new statute of autonomy, has found its most solid source of legitimacy and reaffirmation of its supremacy.

The inability of the "German" opposition to produce an alternative policy for the minority of the South Tyrol, a policy capable of opposing or at least modifying the predominantly conservative demands of the SVP, is at the base of an important political phenomenon that has manifested itself in recent years: the appearance, in an active role, of left-wing Italian parties in the political arena of the German-speaking group. The presence of German-speaking candidates on their slates, which reflects an attempt by these parties to present themselves as interethnic political entities, has resulted in electoral success of a political significance that goes beyond the number of votes obtained. It provides policy-oriented choices to the very small part of the electorate of the South Tyrol that is more progressive. In addition, it signals the presence of symptoms of erosion of the ethnic rigidness of political attitudes, which can be seen as indicative of a certain political modernization. This phenomenon is also confirmed, on the conservative side, by the way the SVP has won some votes from the more traditional sections of the Italian-speaking group. The association of this "catch-all" party, which in recent years has become increasingly more organic, with the economic and political model of the Baviera di Strauss and its emphasis on being an authoritarian, anticommunist, Christian Democrat party show that it wants to present an appeal capable of overcoming ethnic barriers.

This appeal to order and to conservation, which in the last electoral campaigns replaced the need for defending ethnic identity as the central issue, inevitably created a climate of artificial political-ideological polarization, especially strong among the German-speaking group° but felt throughout the entire local political scene. As noted, new tensions already weigh on that scene, resulting from rigid administration of the new autonomy in an apartheidlike fashion.

These choices carry grave implications and significance for the future of the South Tyrol. Behind them it is possible to see the efforts of the ethnic party to establish a new basis of legitimacy as the champion of order and social peace, since the solution of the ethnic conflict weakened the principal reasons for political cohesion within the German-speaking community.

°Loud and particularly significant was the "appeal for the liberty of opinions in the South Tyrol," signed by 83 notable exponents of the cultural, political, and economic world of the German-speaking population, on the eve of the congress of the SVP in 1978. It stated, among other things, that "the monopoly on information and cultural activities which exists in the South Tyrol has promoted and promotes intolerance, defamation... a degree of impunity unique among the democratic countries of Europe," and deplored the climate of cold war that crushes anyone who is not on one or the other side of the barricades and, in particular, "whoever does not let himself be tied to the train of anticommunism." Under these conditions, "there no longer exists any autonomous cultural role."

The future development of the minority in the South Tyrol depends on how this supremacy, which does not seem to be contested, endures. Also dependent on the welfare of the ethnic party is the position of the South Tyrol in the European scene. The alternatives facing the minority are a definite choice in favor of the more conservative elements and, therefore, in favor of a destiny as a small nation—a museum of traditions and antihistorical nostalgia—or the choice of a courageous search for new ways of developing its identity in a manner tied to the social and democratic progress of Europe.

NOTES

1. On the motives and circumstances that caused Wilson and Italian and international public opinion to consent to this abrogation of ethnic principles, see M. Toscano, *Storia Diplomatica della Questione dell'Alto Adige* (Bari: Laterza, 1967) and M. Castelli, *La Questione Altoatesina* (Milano: Capriolo and Massimino, 1961). It must be remembered that the South Tyrol (the Italian name of Alto Adige goes back to the era of Napoleon) coincides with the province of Bolzano.

2. The changes of the ethnic-linguistic boundaries of the South Tyrol have been reconstructed, on the basis of a rich documentation, by O. Stolz, *Die Ausbreitung des Deutschtums in Südtirol im Lichte der Urkunden* vol. 4 (München: R. Oldenbourg, 1927). See also E. Kuhebacher, "Die Geschichtliche Entwicklung der Deutsch-Italienisch Sprachgrenze," *Der Scheern* 46 (1972): pp. 16–20.

3. On the socioeconomic structure of the South Tyrol before the annexation, see in particular A. Leidlmair, *Bevolkerung und Wirtschaft in Südtirol* (Innsbruck: Wagner, 1958); C. Pan, *Die Südtiroler Wirtschafts—und Sozialstruktur von 1910–1961* (Wien: Braumüller, 1963); O. Stolz, *Geschichte des Zollwesens, Verkehrs und Handels in Tirol und Vorarlberg von den Anfangen bis ins XX Jahrhundert*, (Innsbruck: Wagner, 1953).

4. See M. Weiner, "Political Integration and Political Development," in *Political Modernization: A Reader in Comparative Political Change*, ed. C. E. Welch, Jr. (Belmont: Wadsworth, 1967).

5. On the process of creating an identity and legitimacy, see K. W. Deutsch, "Social Mobilization and Political Development," *American Political Science Review* 55 (1961): pp. 400–12; on the solution of the crisis of identity, S. Verba, "Comparative Political Culture," in *Political Culture and Political Development*, ed. L. Pye and S. Verba (Princeton: Princeton University Press, 1965), pp. 30–43.

6. See A. Langer, "Zum Selbstverständnis der Südtiroler," *Die Brücke*, 8–9 (1968): pp. 34–42; C. Gatterer, *Im Kampf gegen Rom*, (Wien: Europa Verlag, 1968).

7. See B. Schloh, "Italiens Politik in Südtirol 1919 bis 1949," in *Südtirol, Eine Frage des Europäischen Gewissens*, ed. F. Huter (München: Oldenbourg, 1965): pp. 50–69.

8. The annexation to Italy did not alter the situation of economic decline of the area of the South Tyrol, which was destined to become more acute. See A. Langer and B. Lovera, *Analisi delle Classi e delle Contraddizioni Sociali nel Südtirolo* (Trento: Ruffino, 1972).

9. See O. Stolz, *Geschichte des Landes Tirol*, (Wien: Tyrolia, 1955); P. Herre, *Die Südtiroler Frage*, (München: Beck, 1927).

10. Industrial employment increased 7 percent between 1910 and 1939. Today the four major industrial plants alone employ nearly 5,000 workers. See C. Pan, *Die Südtiroler Frage*.

11. On the character and consistency of the industry of the South Tyrol before 1918,

see V. K. Honiger, *Ursprung und Entwicklung der Industrie im Tiroler Etschland,* (Trento: Ruffino, 1956).

12. On the changes in the ethnic composition of the population of Bolzano, see F. Demarchi, *Sociologia di una Regione Alpine,* (Bologna: Il Mulino, 1968).

13. See A. Leidlmair, "Bevolkerung und Wirtschaft 1919–1945," in *Südtirol, Eine Frage des Europäischen Gewissens,* ed. F. Huter (München: Oldenbourg, 1965), pp. 112–30.

14. This ancient institution of the Tyrol, still present today in the South Tyrol, sanctions the indivisibility of the property of the small farmers (of medium size), which passes by heredity to the firstborn son: a constraint that is particularly justified in the mountain properties due to their low productivity. A reduction in their size would in fact greatly affect the living conditions of the farm family and produce, in the long run, a depopulation of the mountains. On the institutions of the "closed farm" and the connected problem of the depopulation of the mountains see, also for its adequate bibliography, A. Leidlmair, *Bevolkerung und Wirtschaft in Südtirol.*

15. Regarding the content and the partial execution of the Berlin accord of 1939, see M. deBlock, *Südtirol* (Groninger: Wolters, 1954); C. Battisti, *Opzioni, Riopzioni e Separatismo in Alto Adige* (Firenze: Instituto di studi per l'Alto Adige, 1954); B. Zallinger-Thurn, *Il Problema Altoatesino sotto il Profilo Nazionale, Politico ed Europeo* (Bologna: Cappelli, 1953).

16. This fact, elaborated by the "Arbeitsgemeinschaft der Optanten," is reported in A. Leidlmair, *Bevolkerung und Wirtschaft in Südtirol.*

17. On the measures taken by the Fascist government to Italianize the South Tyrol, see in particular M. deBlock, *Südtirol*; O. Stolz, *Geschichte del Landes Tirol.*

18. On the form of "subculture" in relation to the phenomenon of political participation, see A. Pizzorno, "Introduzione allo Studio della Partecipazione Politica," *Quaderni di Sociologia* 3–4 (1966).

19. On the subcultural, ecological, and sociological characteristics that determine the degree of closure of the society toward the outside, see G. Sivini, *Ceti Sociali e Origini Etniche* (Padova: Marsilio, 1970).

20. The diverse origins of nationalism and ethnocentrism are analyzed by A. D. Smith, "Ethnocentrism, Nationalism and Social Change, *International Journal of Comparative Sociology* 1 (1972).

21. To this effect see J. Perkmann, "Nationalismus in Südtirol," *Die Brücke* 16 (1969).

22. Although we are dealing with a system based on a "dominant" party (which must, that is, take into account the existence of minority parties), there are nonetheless analogies with some aspects of a one-party system: relative to social origins (the obvious bifurcation— ethnic, racial, religious, among socioeconomic groups—that cannot be solved by secession or territorial separation), relevant to the phase of development in the societies in which they manifest themselves (generally in an initial phase), relevant to their ideology (which establishes "…a popular base, defines the enemy, and proclaims the need for fighting the enemy and precedes a definite final victory.") See S.P. Huntington, "Social and Institutional Dynamics of One-Party Systems," in *Authoritarian Politics in Modern Society,* ed. S. P. Huntington and C. H. Moore (New York: Basic Books, 1970), pp. 5–17.

23. On the "environmental pressures" that contribute to the structure of a political party, see S. J. Eldersveld, *Political Parties: A Behavioural Analysis* (Chicago: Rand McNally, 1964).

24. See *Der Volksbote,* May 13, 1945.

25. From a document cited in K. Gruber, *Versuch einer Analyse des Südtiroler Parteiwesens unter Berucksichtigung Historischer Vorgegebenheiten,* (Wien: Molden, 1971).

26. See F. Huter, *Südtirol, Eine Frage.*

27. Regarding the crucial role played by the local church in defending the ethnic group

during the Fascist period, see C. Gatterer, *Im Kampf gegen Rom* (Wien: Europa Verlag, 1968).

28. On this delicate phase, rich with diplomatic initiatives, see K. Ritschel, *Diplomatie um Südtirol*, (Stuttgart: Seewald, 1966); M. Toscano, *Storia Deiplomatia.*

29. See P. Altari and E. Vallini, *La Questione dell'Alto Adige* (Firenze: Parenti, 1961).

30. See the "Wahlvereinbarung der SVP mit der DC Trentina," *Dolomiten*, March 23, 1948.

31. To this effect, see C. Gatterer, *Im Kampf gegen Rom.*

32. The canon, of which M. Gamper wrote in *Dolomiten*, October 28, 1953, referring to the resumption of Italian immigration into the South Tyrol in the years following the war: "It is a funeral march that in which we find ourselves since 1945, if salvation does not arrive at the last moment...."

33. Launched in 1957, the password "Los von Trient" (Leave Trent) synthesized the separatist aspirations of the people of the South Tyrol. See, for example, the conclusions of the extraordinary Congress of the SVP on May 8, 1960 (*Dolomiten*, May 9, 1960).

34. See C. Gatterer, *Im Kampf gegen Rom*, p. 984.

35. J. Perkmann, "Nationalismus in Südtirol." p. 6.

36. See A. Boileau, R. Strassoldo, and E. Sussi, *Temi di Sociologia delle Relazioni Etniche* (Gorizia: Instituto Sozicile Italiano Generale, 1975), p. 25.

37. A proposal for a precise and critical analysis of the contradictions and conflicts that emerged in the first years following the application of the new autonomy is the subject of the journal *Debatte Politisch-Theoretische Zeitschrift für Opposition in Südtirol, für den Sozialismus* 1 (1978).

38. This synthesizes the interpretive scheme of my work: F. Pristinger, *La Minoranza Dominante nel Südtirolo: Divisione Etnica del Lavoro e Processi di Modernizzazione dall'Annessione Agli anni Settanta*, (Bologna: Patron, 1978).

39. See *Alto Adige 1981: Documento Programmatico Preliminare al Piano di Sviluppo Provinciale* (Bolzano: Instituto Economica, 1973).

40. Ibid.

41. The percentages given are the result of estimates made by C. Pan, *Die Südtiroler Frage.*

42. On the presumed "spontaneous aversion" of the people of the South Tyrol toward any form of industrialization, see F. Dorrenhaus, *Das Deutsche Land an der Etsch*, (Innsbruck: Relinka, 1933).

43. In 1971, the medium income per employee in the agricultural sector in the South Tyrol was equal to 60 percent of the medium income of the province. See *Alto Adige 1981*.

44. On the precarious living conditions of the small farmers of the mountain region of the South Tyrol, see J. Perkmann, "Poverty Class," *Die Brücke* 8–9 (1968): pp. 34–42.

45. This protest movement, known as "Aufbau" from the title of the program, also involves prestigious elements of the SVP; see C. Gatterer, *Im Kampf gegen Rom.*

46. M. Kersting, *Industrie und Industriepolitik in Südtirol* (Innsbruck: Wagner, 1973).

47. A. Boileau, et al, *Temi di Sociologia*, p. 71.

48. On the relationship between ethnic stratification and class structure, see W. Marston, "Social Class as a Factor in Ethnic and Racial Segregation," *International Journal of Comparative Sociology* 20 (1968): pp. 280–96.

49. The most famous, which has caused a widespread theoretical and political debate, is by P. Sylvos Labini, *Saggio Sulle Classi Sociali* (Bari: Laterza, 1974). Critical responses are collected in *Capitalismo e Classi Sociali in Italia*, ed. M. Paci (Bologna: il Mulino, 1978).

50. On the aspects and modalities of this type of participation, see A. Pizzorno, "Introduzione allo Studio."

51. Indications on the configuration and the historical dynamics of the "Stände" in the context of Tyrol can be derived from O. Stolz, *Geschichte des Landes Tirol*; F. Huter, *Südtirol, Eine Frage*.

52. Harald Johannes, *Die Sozialarbeit des KVW* (Innsbruck: Wagner'sche Universitätsbuchhandlung in Kommission, 1969).

53. A good reconstruction of the union battles in the South Tyrol in the last 30 years is in J. Perkmann, *Arbeitskämpfe in Südtirol*, attached to *Die Arbeiterstimme* (1978).

54. A detailed map of the most important "Vereine" (clubs) present in the South Tyrol is in the special issue of *Schlern* 20 (1967): pp. 1–40.

55. See S. Salvi, *Le Lingue Tagliate*, (Milano: Rizzoli, 1975.)

56. See J. Schmid, "Die Versteinerte Gesellschaft," *Die Brucke* 16 (1969): pp. 22–40.

57. On the phenomenon of "ideological traditionalism," referring to the position of traditional elites in preindustrial societies, see G. Germani, *Sociologia della Modernizzazione* (Bari: Laterza, 1971).

58. See the in-depth analysis of J. Schmid, "Über den Tirolismus," *Die Brücke* 5 (1968): pp. 18–26.

59. A lucid analysis of the sociolinguistic situation and a useful contribution to understanding the problems and the prospectives of the bilingual phenomenon in the South Tyrol is in K. Egger, *Zweisprachigkeit in Südtirol* (Bozen: Athesia, 1977), pp. 16–32.

60. Regarding the control of the church over the German-language press, see S. Stuffer, "Die Macht der Athesia," *Die Brücke* 3 (1968): pp. 12–22.

10

ETHNIC TENSIONS IN SWITZERLAND: THE JURA CONFLICT

Kurt Mayer

Switzerland is often cited as a model of linguistic pluralism, a society that has managed to weld four different language groups—German, French, Italian, and Romansh—into a stable and harmonious unity. It was an accident of history that the Swiss Confederation became a multilingual state in 1798, before differences of language had come to be considered ideological barriers to nationhood. (From 1291 to 1798, German had been the only official language of the Swiss league.) The maintenance of linguistic peace in Switzerland in the face of intensifying European nationalism during the nineteenth and twentieth centuries has been possible only because of the balancing effects of structural conditions, the equilibrating qualities of demographic forces, and the conscious adoption of judicious political solutions.[1]

Having developed historically as a voluntary federation of particularistic political communities, modern Switzerland is characterized by great diversity of economic, political, and cultural conditions. With few exceptions, however, the divisions of the society overlap in such a complex fashion that the cleavages are constantly attenuated or neutralized by shared loyalties. This explains why Swiss history has been remarkably free of linguistic conflicts; religious and economic conflicts have always been more salient. But one glaring exception to the general linguistic harmony has occurred in a peripheral region, the Bernese Jura. In this area, linguistic and religious differences do not cut across one another but, rather, coincide, thereby reinforcing each other. The result has been sharp ethnic conflict, which has led recently to the separation of the northern part of the Jura from the canton Berne and the creation of the new Swiss canton, Jura.

HISTORICAL ORIGINS

The origins of the Jura problem date back to the Congress of Vienna in 1815. However, to understand the causes of the conflict it is necessary to go back even further.[2] In 999, King Rudolf III of Burgundy, affected by the end-of-the-world fears current at the close of the first Christian millennium, made a substantial gift of territories located in the Jura mountains to the bishop of Basel. This donation established a feudal clerical principality, the bishopric of Basel, which was a constituent part, a fief, of the Holy Roman Empire of the German Nation. Most of the succession of bishops who governed the area were German-speaking nobles, and the official language of their courts was German, even though the majority of their subjects were French-speaking. In those days, language differences were not a political issue and it was not unusual for rulers to speak a language different from that of their subjects. Originally, the bishops resided in the city of Basel; but, when this city adopted the Reformation in 1529, the episcopal court moved to Porrentruy, where it remained until 1792.

The historical development of the southern parts of the bishopric differed in certain important respects from its northern part, and the results of these differences continue to influence the political conflict in Jura in the late twentieth century. In the fourteenth and fifteenth centuries, the southern valleys of the Jura mountains entered into a series of defensive alliances and combourgeoisies (Burgrechte) with the adjoining Swiss Confederation, particularly with the powerful city of Berne, their immediate Swiss neighbor. Consequently, these southern areas enjoyed a measure of autonomy. Militarily they were included in the Swiss defensive system and considered part of the Swiss zone of neutrality, which protected them from the ravages of the Thirty Years' War, in the course of which the northern territories of the bishopric, being considered "imperial soil" (Reichsboden), suffered repeated invasions and occupations by the belligerents. Moreover, during the Reformation, these allied areas of the southern Jura followed Berne in its conversion to the new creed of Protestantism, while the northern parts of the bishopric remained faithful to the Roman church. Despite this religious split and the defensive alliances and combourgeoisies in the south, however, the sovereignty of the Prince-Bishops still extended over the entire territory of the Jura and was recognized by the European powers, including the Swiss Confederation.

The rule of the Prince-Bishops ended in 1792, when French revolutionary troops occupied the northern parts of the bishopric and the current Prince-Bishop fled to Vienna. After a brief interval of independence as the Rauracian Republic, the northern area was annexed by France in 1793 and became the Departement du Mont Terrible. The southern parts remained untouched for four more years, thanks to their protective alliances with Switzerland. But in the winter of 1797–98, French troops overran and occupied all of Switzerland, and the southern parts of the Jura now shared the fate of the north. In 1800, the entire territory of the former bishopric was annexed by France and incorporated into the Alsatian Departement du Haut Rhin.

This state of affairs continued until the defeat of Napoleon in 1814, when a temporary governor was appointed by the victorious allies. The northern parts of the area were provisionally occupied by Austrian troops and the southern parts by Swiss troops, while the Congress of Vienna deliberated about the disposal of the former bishopric, which it considered "masterless territory." Judging by the contents of a number of different petitions submitted to the Congress, the opinions of the inhabitants varied widely.[3] A number of local officials in the French-speaking, Catholic areas of the north desired a revival of the former bishopric, either as an independent state or as a Swiss canton. Some intellectuals in the former capital of Porrentruy wanted a return to France. The small German-speaking Catholic part of the north, the Laufen district, also wanted the revival of the ecclesiastical state, or, barring that, a unification with the neighboring Protestant canton of Basel. In the French-speaking and predominantly Protestant areas of the south, some people wanted incorporation by Berne and others wished to become a separate Swiss canton. These petitions were not submitted by elected representatives of the people, but rather by officials appointed by the temporary governor and by notables who spoke mainly for themselves.

The decisions of the Congress of Vienna were little influenced by these contradictory petitions, for it was guided entirely by major political and strategic considerations aimed at surrounding France with a ring of buffer states strong enough to resist any further imperialistic adventures. Only two alternatives were feasible: the creation of a separate Swiss canton, Jura, or annexation by the canton of Berne. From the beginning, Metternich proposed the latter solution because it would strengthen a large Swiss canton in which the prerevolutionary aristocratic regime had returned to power. The Jura was offered to Berne as compensation for the loss of former rich subject territories, Vaud and Aargau. Although these territories had become independent cantons and equal members of the Swiss Confederation, Berne obstinately demanded their return and at first rejected the offer of the Jura as a poor bargain. In the end, it changed its mind when it became evident that it could not recover Vaud and Aargau. Thus Metternich prevailed, and, in 1815, the Jura was formally and legally annexed by the canton of Berne, except for two outlying villages that were attached to the cantons of Basel and Neuchatel. In the Act of Annexation, signed by seven delegates from Berne and seven delegates from the Jura, the Protestant Bernese government solemnly undertook to protect the Roman Catholic Church in the Jura and to grant its new citizens the same political rights as those enjoyed in the old parts of the canton. But Berne flatly refused to grant the demands by the Jurassian delegates for recognition of the French language, and it would not concede to the Jura any special minority representation in the legislative or executive branches of the canton. In retrospect, it seems ironic that these linguistic and political concessions were subsequently obtained from Berne without great difficulty, while the solemn commitment to protect the Roman Catholic Church was repeatedly and drastically violated. These violations caused a deep-seated resentment that plays a role in the conflict; for the most part, however, the dispute has been fought on purely linguistic rather than religious grounds.

The attachment of the Jura to the canton Berne has been called a forced marriage that in time turned into a marriage of convenience but never became a love affair. This description applies more to the north than to the south, but it is true that relations between the newly acquired Jura and the old parts of Berne were never easy and were often stormy. In 1815, the 60,000 inhabitants of the Jura regions, now generally called the Bernese Jura, amounted to one-sixth of the total population of the canton; in 1970, they represented one-seventh or 140,000 out of a total of 983,000. Mainly French-speaking (72 percent in 1970) and predominantly Roman Catholic (63 percent in 1970), and having different customs and a Gallic temperament, the Jurassians have always considered themselves a minority, and most of them have felt little affinity for the more stolid, stoutly Protestant, German-speaking inhabitants of the old parts of the canton. The cultural differences were accentuated by the peripheral geographical location of the Jura and its physical distance from the capital city of the canton. The northernmost part extends like a peninsula into France (its landscape is Burgundian in character), and it is separated from Berne and from the rest of Switzerland by mountain ranges. Road and rail connections are limited, and contacts between the Jura and the capital city of Berne have always been tenuous.

To be sure, relations between the old and the new parts of the canton Berne were not always stormy; they had their ups and downs, peaceful periods alternating with rebellions. Altogether, however, separatist movements have arisen no fewer than six times in the Jura. During the nineteenth century, these movements were caused twice by political grievances and twice by religious conflicts. In the twentieth century, liguistic grievances have been the immediate cause both times, but the lingering after-effects of the earlier religious struggles have had a potent underlying effect on the outcome of the latest, most decisive conflict, as shall be discussed. The four nineteenth century separatist movements were confined mainly to the north; the south was either uninvolved or found itself in opposition to the north. In the linguistic conflicts of this century, north and south were unanimous at first, but both times the south later broke ranks.

The call for separation of the Jura from Berne was raised for the first time in 1830 by some anticlerical Jurassians from the Catholic north, who were in the vanguard of the liberal movement of that year. When the German-speaking areas of the canton promptly joined in the popular uprising against the aristocratic regime, though, this first separatist effort was quickly abandoned. The Bernese patricians abdicated in the bloodless revolution, a liberal constitution was adopted that recognized French as a second official language in the Jura, and the Jurassian separatist leaders accepted important posts in the liberal administration.

Only a few years later, the anticlerical zeal of the liberal government led to the first serious power struggle with the Roman Catholic Church. In 1834, the Bernese government joined six other liberal canonal govern-ments in adopting a declaration of principles that proposed to nation-alize the church, democratize its organizations, and subordinate it to the state. In 1836, the Bernese legislature ratified this agreement, dis-regarding a petition signed by 8,000 Catholic Jurassians against it. There-upon, the population of several towns in the north rose in open rebellion, clamoring loudly for separation. The Bernese government promptly deposed the prefects of three northern districts, who had attempted to mediate, and sent 12 battalions of troops to occupy the Catholic areas. The Jurassians asked for help from France, which in its capacity as one of the guarantor powers of the annexation treaty of 1815, reacted sharply with an ultimatum to Berne, threatening war. The government backed down and rescinded the ratification of the offending principles. Peace and order were restored, and the second separatist movement dissolved.

Three years later, another conflict came to a head, causing separatist feelings to well up strongly once again. During the period of French rule, the French civil law, the Code Napoleon, had become the law of the land in the Jura. In 1815, the Jurassians had resisted the abolition of the clear and logical provisions of the French code and objected to the substitution of cumbersome ancient local laws and the equally antiquated Bernese legal system. Because of this opposition, only some Bernese statutes had been declared applicable in the entire Jura; others applied only in the south, and parts of the French code remained valid in the north. The result was confusion, and in 1839 the parliamentary delegation from the Jura unanimously demanded that the entire French code be restored to the whole Jura. The refusal of the legislature to grant this request led to renewed separatist agitation in the north, which was met by sharp repressive measures against the leaders, who were accused of treason. The leading Jurassian politician, Stockmar, who had headed the liberal movement and had been a member of the liberal government, fled to France, and other leaders were jailed.

Almost all of the legal and political grievances of the Jura were satisfactorily resolved seven years later when the liberal government was overturned by a new radical movement. Stockmar was able to return from exile to take a seat in the new radical government. He also played a major role in drafting a new cantonal constitution, adopted in 1846, which recognized French and German as fully equal languages throughout the canton. The new constitution allowed the entire Jura to retain the Code Napoleon, which remained valid until all of Switzerland adopted a unified modern civil code in 1912. Some tax inequities of long standing were also removed at the time, and the relations between the new and the old parts of the canton entered a comparatively peaceful phase, despite sharp political swings back and forth between radical and conservative majorities. The Jura participated actively in these passionate party struggles, but for once, changing political fortunes were identical in German- and French-speaking Berne, and the Jurassians were not chronically in the minority. From 1846 on, it was an unwritten rule to reserve two of the nine seats on the cantonal executive council for Jurassians, and, with rare exceptions, a Jurassian was regularly elected to one of the canton's two seats on the federal Council of States, Switzerland's senate. Thus, around the middle of the nineteenth century, it appeared that the integration of the Jura was making progress, and cooperation between the French and German parts of the canton seemed assured.

This process was interrupted again two decades later when the Jura became deeply involved in a second violent conflict between the Roman Catholic Church and the liberal state, a conflict known as the "Kulturkampf," a struggle that was fought with particular vehemence in Germany and in a number of Swiss cantons. The trouble began in 1864 when Pope Pius IX published a "syllabus" denouncing all liberal ideals and political programs as fundamentally in error. The ensuing conflict was escalated when the Vatican Council of 1870 proclaimed the dogma of papal infallibility. A number of dissenters defected from the Roman Catholic Church and organized a new denomination known as Old Catholics, and the anticlericals perceived this development as an opportunity to subjugate the Roman church and bring it under the control of the state. Berne joined four other cantons in the diocese of Basel in an attempt to depose the bishop. It ordered the Catholic priests to suspend all further commun-ication with him; when 69 priests in the Jura disregarded this prohibition, the Bernese government deposed them and expelled them from the country. It also reduced the 74 Roman Catholic parishes in the Jura to 28 and handed them over to Old Catholic clergy. In 1874, the Bernese legislature passed a law providing that all clergy were to be elected by the population of the parish, that eligibility had to be established by a state examination, and that the government reserved the right to confirm elections. In a referendum, the law was adopted by an overwhelming majority by the canton as a whole, but, in the Catholic areas of the Jura, negative votes outnumbered affirmative ones by three to one. The Protestant regions of the southern Jura returned no less than 95 percent affirmative votes.

When the Catholic communities of the north actively resisted the law and supported their exiled clergy, the Bernese government once again ordered military occupation. At this point, the Swiss federal parliament intervened and declared the expulsion of the priests from their native canton unconstitutional. The priests were now able to return from France, but they were not allowed to officiate. They held services clandestinely in the woods and barns, while the Old Catholic clergy installed by the government preached in empty churches. The fierce struggle, which lasted for five years (1873–1878) and caused great bitterness, gave rise to the fourth separatist movement. Eventually, a face-saving compromise was reached that permitted the government to give up its unavailing struggle against the Roman Catholic Church. But it was a long time before the last vestiges of the "Kulturkampf" disappeared. In 1921, Berne again resumed contractual relations with the diocese of Basel—de facto, it had ceased 40 years earlier to interfere with the bishop's exercise of his ecclesiastical functions in the Jura. Today no formal religious grievances remain, but the hostile feelings aroused by the religious persecutions of the nineteenth century still reverberate. The chickens came home to roost 100 years later when the Catholic north voted to separate from Berne, while the Pro-testant south elected to stay.

For a while, the settlement of the religious conflict seemed to have ushered in another era of comparatively friendly and calm relations between the old and the new parts of the canton. To be sure, the Catholic Conservative Party, which was the largest party in the north, stood in opposition to the radical party that controlled the cantonal government. But it was able to form a very effective coalition with a Protestant conservative opposition party in the German-speaking part of the canton. At the same time, the governing radical party was closely tied to radicals in Jura, where they were a minority. This crisscrossing of a Jurassian minority with an old-Bernese majority and of a Jurassian majority with an old-

Bernese minority provided a considerable degree of political integration for the Jura. However, proportional representation was introduced in 1919; at the same time, the farmers split away from the radical party, and the new farmers' party became the hegemonial party in the German-speaking area, dominating the Bernese government as it still does today. The farmers' party has few adherents in the northern Jura, while the Christian Democrats, successors to the Catholic Conservatives, are strong only in the northern Jura. The Christian-Democrats were never coopted into the Bernese government coalition. This exclusion, which is unusual in Swiss coalition politics, proved to be very shortsighted, for it undermined the political relations between the Jura and old Berne. This is clearly demonstrated by the results of many referenda. Prior to 1919, the Jura voting districts had participated equally in the changing majorities and minorities of all voting districts of the canton, but, after that year, the three French-speaking, Catholic districts in the north always voted differently from the large majority of the German-speaking districts. They were often joined by some or all of the three French-speaking districts of the Protestant south. Thus, after 1919, the Jura had become a chronic political minority.[4]

Although the religious struggles had subsided after the end of the "Kulturkampf," the language problem began to develop into a sensitive issue around the turn of the century, creating new frictions. This problem was the result of fairly extensive migrations brought about by the industrialization of the country. The migratory streams flowed both ways: many French-speaking Jurassians were attracted to the growing nearby city of Biel in the German-speaking area, which was developing into a major center of the renowned Swiss watch industry. While Jurassians were flocking to Biel and other cities, both in Switzerland and abroad, a reverse migration of considerable proportions was also taking place. Factories being established in the Jura, mostly in the south, by German-Swiss industrialists attracted workers and executives from the German-speaking parts of the canton. Moreover, quite a few of the farms relinquished by Jurassians moving to towns and cities were bought by German-speaking farmers from the old parts of the canton, which had a surplus farm population. Thus the proportion of German-speakers living in the French Jura as a whole had, by 1880, risen to nearly 24 percent and, in two of the three southern districts, to more than 36 percent. A number of German-speaking schools had been established. These were viewed with misgivings by the French-speaking Jurassians, and their mistrust increased sharply when the German Empire began to engage in a large-scale pan-German propaganda effort during the years preceding World War I. This propaganda emanated mainly from the adjoining Alsace, which had been annexed by Germany in 1870. It was met by a determined reaction to the actual or supposed threat of Germanization, which united all French-speaking Jurassians, north and south, Catholic and Protestant. With the outbreak of the war, the linguistic grievance suddenly flared up into another separatist movement, the fifth since annexation 100 years earlier. At first, the Jurassians were almost unanimous in their desire for separation, but, after a while, the Protestants of the southern districts began to reconsider, fearing that they would be dominated by a Catholic majority in a new canton. Moreover, the Bernese government had met the objections to the German-language schools and closed most of them. In the end, the agitation, which had lasted from 1915 to 1919, subsided almost as abruptly as it had begun.

After World War I, there followed a quiescent period; the perennial quarrels seemed to have been composed, and relations with Berne seemed to be on an even keel. The outward calm proved deceptive, however, for the estrangement actually continued. The marginal geographic position, the religious cleavage, and the linguistic minority position had not really changed, and the reversal in the political party landscape after 1919 had added to the Jurassian malaise. A minor incident sufficed to ignite the flames of separatist passion more intensely than ever before. In 1947, a routine shuffle of portfolios took place in the cantonal government. One of the two Jurassian members was assigned the Department of Public Works by his colleagues in the executive council, but his appointment was blocked by the legislative assembly on the ground that, in this important post, a French-speaker would have trouble making necessary contacts with German-speaking rural communities. The assignment was therefore given to a German-speaking member of the council. This insensitive blunder caused a storm of protest in the entire Jura. A "Committee of Moutier" was immediately formed that included prominent people from the whole of Jura. This committee presented a long list of grievances and reform demands to the Bernese government. First and foremost among the reforms demanded was recognition that the canton Berne was composed of two distinct peoples, the Bernese and the Jurassians. The committee also demanded the establishment of a second parliamentary chamber in which Jurassians would have half of the seats. Further, the two customary Jurassian seats in the executive council were to be guaranteed by the Jurassian voters in a separate election district. Other demands included educational autonomy for the Jura, suppression of the few remaining German-language schools, expansion of courses given in French at Berne University, educational facilities in French for the children of Jurassian civil servants living in the German-speaking capital city, complete equality of French and German in the cantonal constitution, and decentralization of the cantonal civil service.

After some hesitation, the government proposed a 19-point program embodying many, though not all, of these demands. Accordingly, a number of changes in the cantonal constitution were adopted in 1950 by an impressive referendum vote of 69,000 to 7,000. The modified constitution expressly recognized the existence of two peoples in the canton. It recognized the Jurassian flag as official flag of the Jura, to be flown alongside the Bernese flag in the area. It not only granted full equality of French and German as official languages, but also required that only French could be used in the six French-speaking districts of the Jura. In addition, it guaranteed the two Jurassian seats in the cantonal government. However, the demands for a separate election district and for a second chamber were not met.

Although the concessions were considerable, they failed to satisfy the separatists. They resigned from the Moutier Committee, which was consequently forced to dissolve. The dissolution decisively weakened the proponents of regional autonomy within the canton of Berne, and the Jurassians split into two diametrically opposed forces. By 1947, a new separatist movement had already been founded. It called itself "Rassemblement Jurassien" (RJ) and it drew its main support from the Catholic north. In 1952, the "Union des Patriotes Jurassiens" (UPJ) was founded (it is now called "Force Democratique"), and it vigorously opposed separation; its support was centered mainly in the Protestant south. Ever since, these two organizations have been locked in a bitter struggle characteried not only by verbal attacks but also by occasional physical violence.

THE LINGUISTIC ARGUMENT

It has been necessary to review the history of the Jura, its recurrent conflicts with Berne, and its internal divisions and dissensions at some length in order to understand the course of this most recent conflict. The overt battle is now being fought exclusively over ethnic-linguistic issues, yet the reverberations of the nineteenth century religious conflicts have played a potent, albeit concealed, role in the ensuing plebiscites. The foremost leaders of the RJ, intellectuals Roland Beguelin and Roger Schaffter, base their demands for a separate canton on the argument that the Jurassians constitute a separate ethnic group that differs from old Berne in its different historical experience (the episcopal state) and in its French language and culture. History is cited to support the claim that in 1815 the rights of the inhabitants of a formerly sovereign state were disregarded by placing it, against its will, under the tutelage of German-speaking Berne. Here they have been forced to play the role of a minority whose culture has been oppressed, because this minority can be legally crushed by majority vote in the German-speaking areas—by "democratic totalitarianism." The RJ therefore demanded that the entire Jura be liberated from the yoke of Berne. As a result, the weekly newspaper of the RJ bears the name "Jura Libre."

The historical argument, however, is subordinate to the linguistic one, and it is the French character of the Jura that is continuously stressed in the separatist propaganda. This ethnic-linguistic mystique is based on an emotional ideology cultivated in France by a group of activists under the slogan "Ethnie Francaise."[5] Beguelin and several other RJ leaders participate regularly in the activities of this group, activities which are aimed at forging close ties among all francophone communities both in Europe and overseas. In turn, the "Ethnie Francaise d'Europe" forms a part of the "Union Federaliste des Communautes Ethniques Europeens," which looks forward to a federated Europe based not on the traditional nation-states, but rather on a regrouping of peoples according to languages and cultures.

It is with such intensely self-conscious ethnic conceptions, which are entirely atypical of Swiss traditions and are, therefore, met with no sympathy even in the other French-speaking cantons, that the RJ has tried to rally the entire French-speaking population of the Jura to the cause of separatism. The RJ forms a movement that cuts across all political parties; and, although it does not nominate candidates at elections, it supports its sympathizers and opposes known antiseparatists. The RJ is also strictly nondenominational. Beguelin, its executive secretary and foremost leader, is a Protestant born in the south, and there are other Protestants in both the north and the south who are fervent separatists, just as there are Catholics who are adamantly opposed. Indeed, the leader of the antiseparatist "Force Démocratique" in the south, Genevieve Aubry, is a Catholic born in the north. Nevertheless, the cause of separatism has prevailed only in those areas of the Jura that are both French-speaking and Roman Catholic. Each of these factors is a necessary condition, but by itself each is insufficient. Only where they have appeared in combination has the cause of separatism triumphed.

This was shown clearly in a series of plebiscites held in 1959, 1974, and 1975. In the winter of 1957–58, the RJ launched a popular initiative demanding a decree for a special referendum polling only the voters in the Jura about their wishes for a separate canton. Although the question on the ballot on July 5, 1959 was not separation itself, it was construed by both supporters and foes as a test of the separation issue. The vote in the old parts of the canton was overwhelmingly negative, with 63,787 opposed and only 7,967 affirmative. The question was also defeated in the Jura itself, by a vote of 16,354 to 15,163. The Jura then consisted of seven administrative districts. Four of these were in the north: Porrentruy,

Franches Montagnes, Delemont, and Laufen. All four of these districts had a predominantly Catholic population, and the first three were French-speaking, but Laufen had always been entirely German-speaking. The three southern districts, Moutier, Courtelary, and La Neuveville, were all French-speaking and had a predominantly Protestant population. In the three French-speaking Catholic districts of the north, the 1959 vote was 11,108 affirmative to 4,109 negative. In Laufen, the German-speaking Catholic district, the vote was 1,450 negative to 533 in favor, and, in the three southern, French-speaking, Protestant districts, the vote was 10,004 opposed to 3,522 in favor. Thus, even if the German-speaking Laufen district were disregarded, the six French-speaking districts taken together had rejected the proposal for a special Jura referendum by a very narrow majority of 14,904 to 14,630.

The 1959 plebiscite did not settle the issue. On the contrary, it exacerbated the conflict, which then entered its most acute phase. The Bernese government and the antiseparatist UPJ, which had vigorously fought the initiative, both took the position that the separation issue had been settled once and for all because a majority of the Jurassian voters had opposed it. The RJ refused to accept this verdict, arguing that the Jura had been outvoted by the old parts of the canton and that the small negative majority in the French-speaking Jura districts had been caused by the German-speaking immigrants from the old parts of the canton. This latter argument was rather dubious, however, for by 1960 the German-speaking minority in the French-speaking Jura as a whole had declined to 15 percent, and, in the three southern districts that had rejected the proposal by a majority of nearly three to one, it had dropped to 21 percent.

The RJ now proceeded to organize its movement more tightly, founding women's auxiliaries and a very aggressive youth group, which was soon matched by an equally aggressive antiseparatist youth group. The RJ also began to extend its propaganda campaign abroad, trying to exert pressure on Swiss public opinion by arousing sympathies in France. Such efforts met a very cool reception in France, which stood to lose much more elsewhere if it adopted the "ethnie" ideology than it could possibly gain in the Jura. But these activities served to arouse lively indignation in Switzerland. On the other hand, it is true that the Bernese government handled the situation with little imagination. For seven years after 1959, it adamantly refused to discuss the separation question any further.

The hardening of the opposed position led to an increasing series of incidents that included not only demonstrations and counterdemonstations but also two waves of terrorist attacks, in 1962 and in 1965–1966, in which plastic bombs and dynamite were used to blow up buildings belonging to antiseparatists, military barracks, a bank, and a railway line. These acts, which copied methods used in the South Tyrol and in Quebec at the time, were committed by a small group of three terrorists not connected with the RJ. The RJ disapproved of the terrorism and repeatedly warned its adherents not to resort to violence, but it was nevertheless widely blamed by Swiss public opinion as morally responsible for the excesses. The RJ youth group also carried its activities beyond the Jura. In 1967, it created disturbances at the federal government's New Year's reception of foreign diplomats; in 1968, it disturbed a session of the federal parliament; in 1972 and 1973, it temporarily occupied the Swiss embassies in Paris and Brussels; and it repeatedly organized demonstrations in Strasbourg, where the Council of Europe meets.

THE MAKING OF THE CANTON JURA

Meanwhile, the Bernese elections of 1966 had brought about some personal changes in the cantonal government, and two new members, one of them from the northern Jura, were instrumental in budging the government from its fruitless policy of trying to ignore the Jura problem. Finally, in 1969, the government proposed amendments to the cantonal constitution that provided for two alternative procedures: (a) the drafting of a Jura statute providing greater autonomy for the region within the canton Berne, and (b) upon demand, the population of each of the seven Jura districts was to be allowed to vote by itself about separation. A second plebiscite could then be demanded by any administrative district to decide whether to join a new canton. Finally, a third plebiscite would allow individual communities along the new frontiers of the canton to decide whether they wished to join. In March 1970, these constitutional amendments were accepted in a referendum by both the Jura and by the old parts of the canton.

The RJ demanded that ethnically German inhabitants from the old parts of the canton not be allowed to vote in the forthcoming plebiscites, while French-speaking Jurassians who had migrated elsewhere should be permitted to participate. These demands could not be met because article 43 of the federal constitution expressly provides that all Swiss citizens are entitled to vote in their own communities and nowhere else.

In accordance with the 1970 constitutional amendments, the Bernese parliament labored to produce a draft of an autonomy statute for the Jura, but by then it was too late and the project was stillborn. Recognizing this, the government scheduled the first plebiscite on separation for June 23, 1974. The question asked was, "Do you want a canton Jura?" The results are shown in Table 10.1, to which data on religion from the 1970 census have been added.

It is evident from these district results that both language and

TABLE 10.1

Canton Jura Plebiscite Results June 23, 1974

| | | | Percentage of Swiss Citizens | |
Administrative District	Yes	No	Roman Catholic	Protestant
North				
Delemont	11,070	2,948	80	20
Porrentruy	9,603	4,656	85	15
Franche Montagnes	3,573	1,058	85	15
Laufen	1,433	4,119	82	16
South				
Courtelary	3,123	10,260	20	78
Moutier	7,069	9,330	38	61
La Neuveville	931	1,776	14	84
Total Jura	36,802	34,057	58	41

Source: Compiled by the author

TABLE 10.2

Voting by Religion and Language
Canton Jura, 1974 Plebiscite

Independent Variable	R^2 (Coefficient of Determination)	Significant at level of
Catholic Religion	0.76636	0.001
French-speaking	0.25819	0.001
Catholic Religion plus French-speaking	0.78792 (+0.02156)	0.001

Source: J.R.G. Jenkins, "Linguistic and Religious Determinations of Jura Separatism: A Report" (unpublished report by Glantegid Associates Ltd., Waterloo, Canada, 1975)

Note: Leaving out the German-speaking district of Laufen, the 122 election districts of the six francophone areas were submitted to a regression analysis, employing three variables: the percentage of affirmative votes in the 1974 balloting, the percentage of Swiss citizens who were Roman Catholics in 1970, and the percentage of French-speakers according to the 1970 census.

religious affiliations were major factors in the voting. An attempt has been made to assess their relative strength through a statistical analysis. (See Table 10.2.)

These figures show that the religious factor was the most important determinant of the separatist votes: 76.6 percent of the variance of the affirmative votes among the individual election districts is explained by the percentage of Roman Catholics in these districts. Although it is also significant at the 0.001 level of confidence, the linguistic factor adds only 2.2 percent to the variance. Together, the combination of religious and linguistic factors explain 78.8 percent of the variance of the affirmative votes.[*]

The establishment of the new canton was assured by affirmative majority in the Jura as a whole, but the negative votes cast in the three southern, French-speaking districts and in German-speaking Laufen made it unlikely that that the new canton would include the entire Jura region. The RJ finally gave up on Laufen, which confirmed in another plebiscite that it wanted to stay with Berne at least provisionally. After the separation of the new canton Jura from Berne, Laufen became an enclave at a considerable distance from Berne. The constitutional amendments of 1970, anticipating this situation, had provided that Laufen be given a free choice of remaining with Berne permanently or of joining one of three other cantons: Solothurn, Basel-Land, or Basel-Stadt. This involves several further plebiscites and, at the time of this writing, the selection process is still underway.

Although it easily abandoned Laufen and therefore its claims to the historic boundaries of the ancient bishopric, the aim of the RJ has always been that the new canton must include all six of the French-speaking districts. Accordingly, the separatists waged a strong battle to prevent the three southern districts from staying with Berne. Since the negative majorities in the districts of Courtelary and La Neuveville were heavy, having 76 percent and 66 percent of the votes respectively, it could not really hope for success there. The battle therefore concentrated on the district of Moutier, where the negative majority of 57 percent was less lopsided. The religious boundary of the region bisects this district. In 1970, 38 percent of the Swiss citizens residing there were Roman

---

[*]It is interesting to compare these results with an earlier regression analysis on the basis of the 1959 referendum and the 1960 census (Mayer, *The Population of Switzerland*, p. 737). At that time, only male Swiss citizens were used in the calculations because women did not have the vote in 1959. In 1959, the religious factor explained 67 percent of the variation, while the linguistic factor added 5.5 percent. The increasing salience of the religious factor was probably caused by the hardening of the conflict between the two dates. Whether the addition of women to the electorate also contributed to the religious polarization remains an intriguing, albeit unanswerable, question.

Catholics, and a number of communities along its northern border had Catholic majorities. In the town of Moutier, the capital of the district, where 55 percent of the Swiss citizens were Protestants in 1970 and 44 percent were Catholics, the balloting in 1974 had been extremely close: 2,194 voters or 50.8 percent had opted for Berne, while 2,124 voters or 49.2 percent had voted for the new canton. Tensions rose very high in this town as both sides struggled to prevail. Frequent fights between the separatist and antiseparatist youth groups resulted in considerable property damage and some injuries. The entire social and cultural life of the district became divided. Shops and restaurants were patronized exclusively by one side or the other, and even some families split on the issue, causing members on opposite sides to stop speaking to each other.

However, the RJ did not prevail at the ballot box. The second plebiscite, on March 15, 1975, confirmed the results of the first. All three southern districts voted to stay with Berne: Courtelary with 10,802 votes to 3,268, La Neuveville with 1,927 to 997, and Moutier with 9,947 to 7,740. In the town of Moutier, with 96 percent of the eligible voters participating, the vote for Berne was 2,524 to 2,238 or 53 percent to 47 percent. In accordance with the 1970 constitutional provisions, 14 communities along the prospective border now demanded the third plebiscite; 13 of these, including the town of Moutier itself, were in the Moutier district, and one was located in the Delemont district. These referenda were held on September 7 and September 14, 1975. Nine communities on the northern border of the Moutier district voted to join the new canton, and five others opted to stay with Berne, including the town of Moutier, where once again the antiseparatists carried the day with 2,540 votes or 54.1 percent to 2,151 or 45.9 percent. When these results became known on the evening of September 7, the frustrated separatists engaged in violent battles with police in the streets of Moutier.

The precise boundaries of the new canton Jura had finally been established. They follow very closely the historic line of the medieval defensive alliances, and they coincide virtually completely with religious boundaries. With the exception of one tiny community with 65 Catholic residents—since it did not adjoin the district boundary, it could not vote in the third plebiscite and thus could not join the new canton—all communities with a Catholic majority joined the new canton, while all communities with a Protestant majority remained with Berne.

The RJ then began to operate on two tracks simultaneously. On the one hand, it accepted the verdict of the first plebiscite of 1974, which assured the creation of the new canton. Its leaders played very active roles in the various preparatory procedures necessary to effect the separation of the new canton Jura from Berne. They participated in these activities in their capacities as individual members of various established political parties rather than in their roles as RJ leaders, for the RJ is strictly nonpartisan. The political parties nominated candidates for the constituent assembly and the provisional government elected in 1976 as well as for the elections to the new parliament and the new cantonal government that took place in the fall of 1978. It was no coincidence that nearly all elected officeholders were RJ members or sympathizers, regardless of party affiliation.

On the other hand, active involvement in the creation and the running of the new canton did not mean that the separatists had now renounced their claims to the entire French-speaking area. The RJ immediately announced that it considered the second and third plebiscites invalid, blaming the refusal of the three southern districts to join the new canton solely on the supposedly negative votes of immigrants from the German parts of the canton. As Beguelin put it, "If one examines the frontiers of the new canton, one finds that with one exception they are determined by the origin of the inhabitants: In the North we find those communities in which the native-born Jurassians predominate, in the South those communities where they have become a minority."[6] Therefore, Beguelin declared, the southern border of the canton Jura was dictated by Bernese immigrants who had settled in a French-speaking area annexed in 1815. He also argued that plebiscites are unjust, artificial devices that only serve to confirm a previous ethnic encroachment. Buguelin insisted that this can only lead to further disputes because the Jurassians will never accept that they should be deprived of part of their fatherland. He said that a canton Jura had been created, but that the Jura problem had not been solved. Accordingly, the RJ keeps reiterating that it will continue the struggle and will not rest until the entire French-speaking territory has been liberated.

Beguelin's argument that native-born Jurassians are now in the minority in the three southern districts is true, but he conveniently omits the fact that a large proportion of those inhabitants who originated from the German-speaking area are now fully assimilated second- or third-generation French-speakers.° The census of 1970 shows that 27,150 persons or 50 percent of Swiss citizens residing in the three southern districts held citizenship in German-speaking communities in the old part of Berne or in other German-speaking cantons. But of these only 7,996 or

---

°Swiss citizenship is communal and hereditary. For instance, a person may have been born and raised in Geneva, living all his life and speak only French, yet be the descendant of a migrant from Zurich and therefore a citizen of Zurich. He might also acquire citizenship in Geneva, for a fee. He would then have dual citizenship in Geneva and in Zurich, unless he specifically requested Zurich to remove him from the role of citizens.

29.5 percent declared German as their mother tongue in the 1970 census. Even if the separatist demand that only "autochthonous" Jurassians be permitted to vote could have been met, the assimilated French-speakers surely could not have been excluded from the plebiscites, regardless of their own or their ancestor's origin. Such a procedure might have changed the voting majority in a few southern communities, such as the town of Moutier where 12.6 percent of Swiss citizens were German-speakers in 1970. However, as has been mentioned, the Swiss constitution does not permit the exclusion of any of the inhabitants of a community from voting on a matter with which they are directly concerned.

Nevertheless, the splitting asunder of the French-speaking area is keenly regretted in the north, which has not given up hope that part or all of the south might someday join the canton Jura. To give expression to this hope, the following article was included in the constitution of the canton Jura. "The canton Jura can accept any territory which was directly affected by the plebiscite of June 23, 1974, if this territory has legally seceded according to both federal law and the law of the affected canton." Despite its fairly inocuous formulation, this article was widely considered an act of aggression against Berne; it was disapproved by the federal parliament, and, therefore, is not legally valid. All other articles of the new constitution were approved. On September 24, 1978, a nationwide plebiscite was held in which 82 percent of the Swiss voters gave their assent to the accession of the new canton Jura to the Swiss Confederation through an amendment in the federal constitution that enumerates all cantons of the Confederation.

STILL A JURA PROBLEM

The Republic and Canton Jura began functioning as a separate canton on January 1, 1979. The transition was smooth, facilitated by a tripartite committee consisting of representatives from the cantons Jura and Berne and from the federal government. This committee will continue to operate until all the manifold administrative and legal details entailed by the separation have been settled.

However, the hopes of the Swiss voters that their friendly acceptance of the new canton would finally solve the Jura conflict were quickly dashed by Beguelin, who acknowledged the overwhelming affirmative vote of September 1978 with the battle cry "The struggle continues!"°

°Just possibly, the conflict might have been resolved if the three southern districts had also separated from Berne to form an independent Canton of their own. The RJ might have accepted such a solution. Although this idea was mentioned by a few people, it was not considered realistic because most of the southern antiseparatists have strong emotional attachments to Berne. They consider themselves genuine Bernese, regardless of their French mother tongue.

Indeed, the RJ and its now independent offspring in the south, called "Unité Jurassienne," peremptorily demanded that the town of Moutier be ceded immediately by Berne and that negotiations be started promptly between the two cantons about an eventual annexation of the three southern districts by the canton Jura. This militant talk raised a veritable storm of indignation all over Switzerland, and the tempers of the equally militant antiseparatists in the south were running high. With some justification, the separatists are complaining that their freedom of expression is being abridged in the south, where they have great difficulty in renting meeting halls, especially in some southern communities where the contracts of teachers known as separatists have not been renewed.° Several violent incidents have again occurred in Moutier and elsewhere in the south, perpetrated in turn by opposing sides.

The official authorities of the new canton Jura are not involved in the continuous agitation in the south. Their relations with other cantons, including Berne, and with the federal government are absolutely correct and polite. It is Beguelin, who has refused a fulltime position in the Jurassian goverment to keep himself free, who continues to keep the pot boiling. For the first time in the existence of the RJ, he has scheduled its annual delegates' meeting in a southern community, deliberately provoking the wrath of the antiseparatist youth group that has vowed to prevent the meeting. According to a sarcastic Beguelin, the purpose of the meeting is to test the freedom of assembly in the south.[7] He is also stirring up the cry for "liberation" in the small community of Vellerat, which wants to join the canton Jura but has not yet been able to do so because it is not located on the cantonal border. Beguelin does so knowing full well that its accession is not contested and that it is merely a matter of time until legal arrangements can be made in an exchange for another German-speaking community that could not vote to stay with Berne.

Beguelin's extremism, however, no longer goes unchallenged. He may have overextended himself in an incident that he created in the spring of 1979, when the new canton Jura planned a festival celebrating its birth. Delegations from all other cantonal governments had been invited and had accepted, as did the federal government. Then, during a debate in the federal parliament about the continuing tensions in the south, a separatist deputy from the southern Jura reiterated the claim that the plebiscites had been invalid and fraudulent. In his answer, the federal minister of Justice, Kurt Furgler, called the deputy a liar. As the federal representative on the previously mentioned tripartite committee, Furgler

---

°In many parts of Switzerland, teachers are selected by the school committee but not appointed by it; they are elected by the voters, generally for a fixed term of years at the end of which they must again be reconfirmed by the voters. Teachers do not have indefinite tenure; the voters' verdict is final.

had been scheduled to head the federal delegation and to present the welcoming address on behalf of the federal government. Beguelin immediately demanded a retraction, and, when Furgler refused, Beguelin declared him persona non grata and announced that the RJ would not participate in the festivities if Furgler were present. The embarassed Jurassian government was forced to cancel the festivities at short notice in order to avoid violent disturbances.

This debacle not only caused great indignation throughout the country, but also led to a rift within the RJ. Roger Schaffter resigned the vice-presidency of the movement, and the head of the Jurassian government, Lachat, and several others resigned their memberships in it. According to Jean Wilhelm, a veteran separatist member of the federal parliament, Beguelin's political hyperbole, his patronizing tutelage, and his quest for personal power have cost the RJ many sympathies in the Jura and thrust it into a profound crisis.[8] It remains to be seen whether cooler heads, such as Schaffter and Wilhelm, will eventually prevail over Beguelin and his hardliners. In the meantime, no final solution of the Jura conflict is in sight.

NOTES

1. Kurt B. Mayer, *The Population of Switzerland* (New York: Columbia University Press, 1952), chap. 8. See also Kenneth D. McRae, *Switzerland: Example of Cultural Coexistence* (Toronto: Canadian Institute of International Affairs, 1964).

2. Paul-Otto Bessire, *Histoire du Jura Bernois et de l'Ancien Evêché de Bâle* (Porrentruy, 1953). See also Kurt B. Mayer, "The Jura Problem: Ethnic Conflict in Switzerland," *Social Research* 35 (Winter 1968): 707–41, and Hans Peter Henecka, *Die Jurassischen Separatisten* (Meisenheim am Glan: Anton Hain, 1972).

3. Albert Comment, Hans Huber, and Hans von Greyerz, *Gutachten über die Vereinigungsurkunde des Jura mit dem Kanton Bern an den Regierungsrat des Kantons Bern* (Bern: Staatskanzlei, 1948).

4. Erich Gruner, "Die Jurafrage als Problem der Minderheit in der Schweizerischen Demokratie," *Civitas* 23 (March 1968): 523–37.

5. Charles Becqeut, *L'ethnie Française d'Europe* (Paris: Nouvelles Editions Latines, 1963); and Guy Heraud, *L'Europe des Ethnies* (Paris: Nouvelles Editions Latines, 1964).

6. Roland Beguelin, "Ein Kanton Jura ohne Losung der Jurafrage," *Neue Zürcher Zeitung*, February 6, 1976.

7. The meeting took place on March 15, 1980 in a restaurant in the Moutier district, accompanied by street battles between the opposing parties in which three participants were injured.

8. "Rassemblement in der Krise?" *Neue Zürcher Zeitung*, March 1, 1980; and "Restposten in der Jurafrage," *Neue Zürcher Zeitung*, March 6, 1980.

11

AGENDA FOR RESEARCH
Charles R. Foster

If, as Peter Katzenstein has recently written, the shape of our political future will resemble the shape of our political past, it behooves us to encourage systematic research into the causes and effects of the revival of ethnic minorities. The agenda for such research is broad.

First, we need to develop a categorization of minorities to go beyond statistical analysis of population, language, economic, and social statistics to an analysis of the historical development of the political culture of the regions. In some cases, as in Brittany, the region is not yet properly defined.

Second, we need to analyze the subjective component of the ethnic regions. The analysis of linguistic, economic, and ethnic differences is an inadequate tool to explain the rise and fall of regional movements. What is needed is thoughtful examination, through the use of survey research, of the feelings of the ethnic minority and its use of the language. In some cases, as in Scotland and Wales, minorities have varying strengths of ethnic loyalty. Multiple loyalties are accepted and respected.

Third, the relationship between the economies and the ethnic groups must be studied more systematically so that the frequent question of whether greater autonomy will lead to a higher standard of living can be answered on the basis of complete and sound economic data.

Fourth, in order to understand the causes of political mobilization in minorities, political scientists must broaden their methodological tools to include the conceptual frameworks used by psychologists and anthropologists. The use of the political culture approach to describe macrolevel concerns by referring to microlevel characteristics should be employed. The strength of this approach is its ability to interrelate political and cultural values with structural variables.

These problem areas are not to be taken as complete or mutually exclusive. They simply illustrate the great group of problems still to be explored. From the standpoint of knowledge, we stand closer to the beginning than to the end of research on mobilization of ethnic minorities.

APPENDIX:

MINORITIES IN WESTERN EUROPE

Austria

   The Slovenes of Carinthia
   The Magyars in Burgenland
   The Croats in Burgenland

Belgium

   Flemings in Flanders
   Walloons in Wallonie
   The Germans in the province of Liege

Britian

   The Gaels of Scotland
   The Lowland Scots
   The Gaels of the Isle of Man
   The Gaels of Northern Ireland
   The Welsh
   The Norman French on the islands of Jersey and Guernsey

Denmark

   The Germans of North Schleswig
   The Faroe Islanders
   The Greenlanders

Finland

   The Swedish Lapps
   The Lapps

France

   The Occitans
   The Catalans of Roussillon
   The northern Basques
   The Corsicans
   The Alsatians

The Flemings of Westhoek
The Bretons

Federal Republic of Germany

The Danes of North Schleswig
The north Frisians

Ireland

The Gaels

Italy

The Piedmontese
The Occitans of Piedmont
The Romagnolis from Emilia-Romagna
The Friulians
The Sauris of Friuli
The Ladins of the Dolomites
The Aostans in the Aosta Valley
The South Tyroleans
The Slovenes of Trieste
The Sards
The Greek Croats and Albanians of the Messogiorno

Luxembourg

The Letzeburgers

The Netherlands

The West Frisians

Norway

Nynorsk
The Lapps
The Finns of northern Norway

Spain

The Catalans
The Basques
The Galicians

Sweden

The Lapps
The Finns in the Torne Valley

Switzerland

The Ticinese
The Jurassians
The Rhaetians

ABOUT THE EDITOR AND CONTRIBUTORS

CHARLES R. FOSTER, a specialist in bilingual education in the US Department of Education, serves concurrently as secretary of the Committee on Atlantic Studies. He has taught at Indiana University and the College of William and Mary and has been published extensively on German politics. His most recent publication is *Comparative Public Policy and Citizen Participation in the U. S. and Germany* (New York: Pergamon Press, 1980).

JACK BRAND was born in Aberdeen, Scotland, and went to the University of Aberdeen and the London School of Economics. He has written on nationalist movements in Britain and Spain and is preparing a book on comparative European nationalism.

ROBERT P. CLARK, professor of Political Science at the George Mason campus of the University of Virginia, is a specialist in Basque affairs. His most recent book is *The Basques: The Franco Years and Beyond* (Reno: Nevada Press, 1980). He is currently working on a political history of the Basque insurgent group, ETA.

DAVID H. FORTIER is an assistant professor in the department of Anthropology at the University of Massachusetts. He is working on a larger study of the Breton movement based on extensive field work.

KURT MAYER is a professor of Sociology and the director of the Institute of Sociology at the University of Berne, Switzerland. From 1950–66 he was a professor of Sociology at Brown University.

JOHN OSMOND is editor of Wales's new fortnightly cultural and current affairs magazine, *Arcade*. Formerly, he was a Welsh Affairs correspondent for the *Western Mail*. He has authored *The Centralist Enemy* (Llandybie: Christopher Davies Press, 1974) and *Creative Conflict: The Politics of Welsh Devolution* (London: Routledge & Kegan Paul, 1978).

RICCARDO PETRELLA is presently working at the Commission of the European Committee in Brussels.

ORIOL PI-SUNYER, a native of Barcelona, studied at the University of London, National University of Mexico, and Harvard University. He is a professor of Anthropology at the University of Massachusetts, Amherst, and the author of several books and articles on the change process in modern complex societies.

FLAVIA PRISTINGER is an associate professor of Economic Sociology in the department of Political Science of the University of Padua. She is completing a book on the political culture of the South Tyrol.

PETER SAVIGEAR is a senior lecturer in Politics and dean of the Faculty of Social Sciences, Leicester University. He has published articles on French history and on Corsica and is completing a political history of Corsica.